Building a Privacy Program
A Practitioner's Guide

Edited by

Kirk M. Herath, CIPP, CIPP/G
Vice President, Associate General Counsel and Chief Privacy Officer
Nationwide Insurance Companies

Contributors

Lori L. Mininger, JD, CIPP, CIPP/G, CIPP/C, CIPP/IT
Director, Chief Privacy Officer
Alliance Data

Rebecca Richards, CIPP, CIPP/G

Dorene Stupski, CIPP, CIPP/C
Director of Information Protection and Privacy
Marriott International

Chris Zoladz, CIPP, CIPP/G, CISSP, CISA, CPA
Founder
Navigate, LLC

An IAPP Publication

Written by Gerry Duffy
Cover design by -ing designs, llc.
Book design and layout by Juanita Reed, Moonlight Graphics

ISBN 978-0-9795901-1-5

Library of Congress Control Number: 2011929473

ADVANCE PRAISE FOR
BUILDING A PRIVACY PROGRAM

There is no more important work for a privacy professional than establishing a strong privacy office with all of the elements of a strong program—people, policy, process and technology—that will sustain and reinforce a culture of privacy throughout an organization. Building a Privacy Program: A Practitioner's Guide *should be required reading for all privacy professionals, wherever they are placed in their organizations. From operationalizing privacy to finding friends in all the right places, this book provides practical and valuable guidance. A strong privacy office is a force multiplier for effective data protection.*

~ Nuala O'Connor Kelly, CIPP, CIPP/G, Senior Counsel, Information Governance & Chief Privacy Leader, General Electric Company

Thanks to this extraordinary work, corporate privacy officers will now have at their fingertips a best-in-class educational and professional resource. This comprehensive yet easy-to-use volume is not only substantive but also aspirational—guiding privacy officers to the high ground where they and their companies earn consumer trust and confidence.

~ Robert R. Belair, Partner, Arnall Golden Gregory LLP

Building a Privacy Program: A Practitioner's Guide *belongs on the bookshelf of privacy, security and compliance officers in every corporation, organization and government agency. Herath and team have accomplished what so many have wanted for so long—a comprehensive cookbook for privacy programs. This guidance will go a long way toward reducing the incidents and errors of the past and helping create a culture of privacy.*

~ Richard Purcell, CIPP, CEO, Corporate Privacy Group

EDITOR

Kirk M. Herath, CIPP, CIPP/G
Vice President, Associate General Counsel and Chief Privacy Officer
Nationwide Insurance Companies

Kirk Herath is vice president, associate general counsel and chief privacy officer for Nationwide Insurance Companies and affiliates based in Columbus, Ohio.

Among other things, Kirk heads up a team that has primary responsibility for corporate privacy policy and implementing privacy across all lines of business. He represents Nationwide's interests on many industry and business privacy groups and before legislative and regulatory bodies. He is responsible for all legal issues impacting privacy, information security, technology and information systems, contracts and supply services management, confidentiality and data integrity. Under Kirk's leadership, Nationwide has been selected as one of the Top 10 Most Trusted Companies for Privacy (number one in the insurance sector) five times by the Ponemon Institute.

Kirk is past president of the International Association of Privacy Professionals and is still very active within the association serving on several committees. He also served on the U.S. Department of Homeland Security's Data Privacy and Integrity Advisory Committee from 2005 to 2011. He speaks regularly on a broad array of issues.

Kirk received undergraduate degrees in political science and history from the University of Cincinnati and has a master's degree in international affairs from the American University in Washington, D.C. Kirk holds a law degree from Capital University Law School in Columbus, Ohio, and is admitted to the Ohio Bar. Kirk is also a Certified Information Privacy Professional (CIPP) and a Certified Information Privacy Professional/Government (CIPP/G).

CONTRIBUTORS

Lori L. Mininger, JD, CIPP, CIPP/G, CIPP/C, CIPP/IT
Director, Chief Privacy Officer
Alliance Data

Lori Mininger has more than six years of working experience in data privacy law and practice. Lori is the chief privacy officer of Alliance Data, heading a team of compliance professionals who focus specifically on privacy and business support. Lori has responsibility for Alliance Data's privacy compliance program, which includes privacy strategy, training and awareness, policy development and implementation, monitoring, management and board reporting.

Prior to joining Alliance Data, Lori held the position of privacy manager at Accenture and provided legal counsel to the business on U.S. data privacy and security issues. Lori also spent four years at Nationwide Mutual Insurance Company, providing legal counsel to its various businesses on data privacy and security issues.

Lori is licensed to practice law in the state of Ohio and is an IAPP-certified privacy professional holding CIPP/C/G/IT designations. Lori holds a bachelor of science degree from the University of Toledo and a law degree from the University of Toledo College of Law.

Rebecca Richards, CIPP, CIPP/G

Becky Richards joined the Department of Homeland Security as director of privacy compliance in 2004. In this capacity, Becky is responsible for the privacy compliance process at DHS. The Privacy Compliance process includes: Privacy Threshold Analysis, Privacy Impact Assessment and Privacy Act System of Records Notice requirements. She educates employees and leaders on best practices and performs audits of privacy compliance (required by some international agreements). Becky was a 2008 Federal 100 award recipient from *Federal Computer Week* magazine, which recognized the top executives from government, industry and academia who had the greatest impact on the government information systems community in 2007.

Prior to working at the Department of Homeland Security, Becky was director of policy and compliance at TRUSTe, the independent nonprofit privacy seal program. Prior to working at TRUSTe, Becky worked at the U.S. Department of Commerce as an international trade specialist working on the landmark U.S.-EU safe harbor accord.

Becky received her BA from the University of Massachusetts, Amherst, a master's degree in international trade and investment policy and an MBA from George Washington University.

Dorene Stupski, CIPP, CIPP/C
Director of Information Protection and Privacy
Marriott International

Dorene Stupski has more than 10 years of experience in the privacy and compliance practice. Dorene is the director of information protection and privacy at Marriott International, heading a global team of privacy professionals responsible for privacy strategy, training and awareness, management reporting and privacy policy development.

Prior to joining Marriott International, Dorene was chief privacy officer for Alliance Data and compliance manager for Primary Payment Systems. Dorene has a master of business administration degree from Capital University School of Management and a law degree from Capital University Law School.

Dorene is a Certified Information Privacy Professional (CIPP) and a Certified Information Privacy Professional/Canada (CIPP/C). She co-chaired the IAPP KnowledgeNet Columbus, Ohio chapter.

Chris Zoladz, CIPP, CIPP/G, CISSP, CISA, CPA
Founder
Navigate, LLC

Chris Zoladz is the founder of Navigate LLC, a consulting company focused on providing comprehensive strategic and tactical information protection and privacy consulting services. Prior to founding Navigate in April 2009, Chris was the vice president of information protection and privacy at Marriott International, Inc., a function he created in 1999. Chris joined Marriott after a 13 year career at Ernst & Young, where he last served as the mid-atlantic area office director of IT auditing and security services.

Chris is a past president and a founding board member of the International Association of Privacy Professionals (IAPP) and recipient of the 2006 IAPP Vanguard Award as the chief privacy officer of the year. He was named one of the best privacy advisors in 2010 by *Computerworld.*

ABOUT THE IAPP

The International Association of Privacy Professionals (IAPP) is the world's largest association of privacy professionals, representing more than 8,000 members from businesses, governments and academic institutions across 68 countries.

The IAPP was founded in 2000 with a mission to define, support and improve the privacy profession globally through networking, education and certification. We are committed to providing a forum for privacy professionals to share best practices, track trends, advance privacy management issues, standardize the designations for privacy professionals and provide education and guidance on opportunities in the field of information privacy.

The IAPP is responsible for developing and launching the first broad-based credentialing program in information privacy, the Certified Information Privacy Professional (CIPP). The CIPP remains the leading privacy certification for professionals who serve the data protection, information auditing, information security, legal compliance and/or risk management needs of their organizations. The program has since grown to include the CIPP/G, CIPP/C and CIPP/IT. Today, many thousands of professionals worldwide hold an IAPP privacy certification.

In addition, the IAPP offers a full suite of educational and professional development services and holds annual conferences that are recognized internationally as the leading forums for the discussion and debate of issues related to privacy policy and practice.

PREFACE

This book would not have been possible without a lot of people putting a lot of time into it. Heartfelt thanks go out to the core editorial and content team for the innumerable hours spent scoping, writing and editing each chapter. Simply put, this book would never have been without the extremely hard work of the following core team members:

Lori L. Mininger – CIPP, CIPP/G, CIPP/C, CIPP/IT, Director, Chief Privacy Officer, Alliance Data

Rebecca Richards – CIPP, CIPP/G

Dorene Stupski – CIPP, CIPP/C, Director of Information Protection and Privacy, Marriott International

Chris Zoladz – CIPP, CIPP/G, CISSP, CISA, CPA, Founder, Navigate, LLC

I cannot speak more highly of these four individuals, their work ethic and their sense of duty to the privacy profession.

One of our initial core team members was unable to be with us throughout the entire process. However, Renard Francois, CIPP, regulatory and compliance attorney for Caterpillar Financial Services Corporation, helped us in the early phases as we scoped the book and designed the initial outline.

Once the manuscript was "done," several people graciously spent a great deal of time reviewing it and providing the core team with their feedback and suggestions for improvement. Their time and effort helped improve the final product a great deal. Thus, special thanks go out to:

Joanne McNabb – CIPP, CIPP/G, Chief, Office of Privacy Protection, State of California

Gail Obrycki, CIPP, President, GO 2 Consulting, LLC

Naoina Gartee, Esq., Contracts Representative, NRECA

One of the things we set out to do in this book was provide a great deal of useful information and templates—charts, checklists, forms—that a privacy professional could use immediately. We owe several individuals and their organizations a special debt of gratitude for their contributions in this regard.

For the Selected Privacy Program Organizational Design and Six Sigma Operational Templates, we thank:

James Koenig – CIPP, Leader, Privacy Practice, PricewaterhouseCoopers

Emmanuelle Galland – CIPP, Manager, Privacy Practice, PricewaterhouseCoopers

And for significant contributions to the appendix, we thank:

Meaghan K. McCluskey—LL.B, CIPP, Senior Privacy Research Lawyer, Nymity Inc.

Finally, every book needs someone to tie it together. Gerald Duffy was able to take all of our disparate ideas, thoughts and ramblings and meld them together into a coherent format. He is a fantastic writer. Dave Cohen, knowledge manager at the IAPP, served as our project manager and doer of all things large and small. He kept us on track and prodded us along when we went astray. This book would never have become a reality without Gerry and Dave's capable assistance.

Finally, this book is a snapshot in time. Laws and practices will continue to change and evolve, and we the professionals will need to change the way we address them. Frankly, this fact is what makes our profession so interesting and keeps us engaged in our work. Therefore, this book, too, will change over time. We intend to update it periodically in the coming years. I take pleasure in sharing what we got right with the entire team, and accept for myself any oversights, omissions and factual errors. I look forward to your feedback in the months and years to come.

– Kirk Herath

TABLE OF CONTENTS

CHAPTER 4: PRIVACY PROGRAM GOVERNANCE **131**

CHAPTER 1

Introducing Privacy –
Fasten Your Seatbelts

Privacy has become a central theme of our times and we, as individual citizens, all have a common interest in it. The heart of the matter is that we want the information we share about ourselves—private information that personally identifies us—to remain in good hands. That goal has never been more challenging.

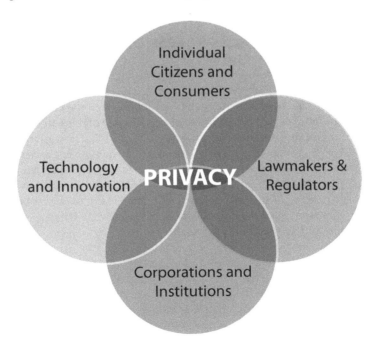

Every time we submit personal information to an online entity—a web storefront, a bank, an institution, a new form of social media—we increase our exposure and the potential risk that information about us will be abused or even more seriously, criminally exploited. Lawmakers at all levels—national, state, international—are striving to create and amend legislation to establish and protect basic privacy-related rights. Self-regulatory bodies—professional and industry-based associations—have created standards so that organizations can implement best practices for processes that in one way or another involve the use of personally identifiable information.

Privacy is a moving target. No sooner are new laws and standards enacted than new game-changing technologies and innovations throw more balls in the air. For example, as this book goes to press, there is spirited debate about the role of the phenomenon of "behavioral advertising," whereby marketers track your online activity and tailor ads just for you, based on what you searched for, where you went and where you lingered. Marketers argue that you, the consumer, no longer have to waste your time and clutter your Web browser with ads you would never read. On the other hand, consumers want to know more about the code and scripts that work behind the scenes to provide the necessary data. Some are calling for more transparency and the freedom to opt in or out.

THE WORLD OF THE PRIVACY PROFESSIONAL

As a professional, you may have found your way to privacy management from any number of routes. If you're new to the profession, welcome. We'd like to say from the outset that we believe privacy management to be more than complying with the law, though that is a crucial aspect of the job. But step back a moment and—as one of our early reviewers said—you can legitimately see the profession as a calling. You'll find that later in the book, we talk about "evangelizing." To evangelize you need a gospel to preach. As our reviewer pointed out, the privacy gospel is more than legal compliance, more than meeting a business need for customer trust. It's also about protecting individual rights and enabling societal values essential to the functioning of a democracy, which is why, at least in part, we have privacy laws. Placing your mission in such a context will help you through the ups and downs, inspire team members and draw in key stakeholders.

There's no doubt that privacy management is now part of our social, corporate and institutional fabric, and our profession has come a long way over the past decade. What began as almost an oddity (Privacy? Really?) is now one of the most talked-about public policy and legal issues of our day. While privacy-related issues may not be the main subject of most laws or regulations, it's likely that they appear somewhere in the details.

And we privacy professionals find ourselves being tossed around by not only changing legislation, but also by the prevailing political winds. Depending on whose political star is ascendant, privacy-related public policy issues rise in importance, but then fall away again. The cycle is endless. Anyone who has been in the profession for a few years has already witnessed a number of different federal proposals, under both Republican and Democratic majorities, for a uniform breach notification standard. During every legislative cycle, interested lawmakers have proposed various kinds of increased or enhanced security controls, either through legislative or regulatory fiat. But then the proposals fade away again, unenacted.

We are also witnessing the transformation of privacy management from being solely a means of complying with the relevant laws and regulations to a broader concept that includes seeing the privacy policy as something of value, something that can actually produce a return on investment. After all, organizations can now attract and engage customers by demonstrating that they are vigilant stewards of personally identifiable information and offering consumers a choice about how data about them is used. Privacy as a valuable commodity has now entered the sphere of marketers and is a potential contributor to the bottom line.

Privacy professionals are, of course, consumers themselves and understand the common concerns and easily grasp the implications of developments such as the behavioral advertising we mentioned earlier. From a business standpoint, it's useful to have analytic data to target consumers and deliver tailored advertising for products and services. But could some of this information be used for elicit purposes? Certainly; in the hands of unscrupulous players, such information could be diverted in a way the consumer would not approve. But marketers may legitimately ask whether arcane and burdensome regulation is the answer. They may ask: Who has been harmed and to what extent? Shouldn't we be more concerned about the speedy evolution of government surveillance at all levels—local, state and federal? You will of course hear compelling counterarguments from consumers and their advocacy groups. Be prepared to be part of the action as this topic, and others like it, play themselves out during the coming years. Your life as a privacy professional will never be boring.

SOME HELP TO NAVIGATE THE TERRITORY

No wonder then that you—a privacy professional new to the field or already practicing in it—have picked up this book. As privacy professionals, we need to go about our business with in-depth knowledge of an ever-more complex field. We need reliable, up-to-date resources, we need qualified and talented colleagues and we need guidance—and confidence—to navigate the waters. This book was compiled from contributions by some of the country's best minds and experienced professionals in the business. Think of it as a compass to take along on the journey.

The publisher of this book—the International Association of Privacy Professionals (IAPP)—

began as a small group of privacy officers who wanted to collaborate, develop best practices and develop new ideas for the profession. What began as a small group has now blossomed into a truly international association of thousands of individuals, including privacy officers, privacy specialists, lawyers and compliance professionals.

This book is written in the original spirit of the IAPP: to provide new privacy professionals— either new to an existing privacy organization or, more likely, someone who has been tasked to build a new privacy organization from scratch—with a framework of best practices. While this book contains a lot of information, it is not intended to be the definitive source for the topics discussed. However, it is a very good starting point for anyone interested in the topic who wants to be successful at building a privacy office in an organization—private sector, public or nonprofit. The book sets out to cover the basics and point you to the resources that you will need to address the privacy management needs of your particular organization.

We have organized this book in a manner that leads the novice or intermediate professional through the ins and outs of privacy—from the laws that govern your processes day in and day out to the many aspects of organizing a privacy operation. We have tried to strike a balance between the general and specific. We didn't want to inundate you with too much detailed information, but we also didn't want to gloss over topics in a way too general to be useful. The contributors—with their cumulative decades of experience in the field—have worked hard to provide material that is both pragmatic and inspirational. We hope we have succeeded and that you will use this book as a tool, a resource and a starting point for your own efforts in creating or maintaining and running a privacy operation.

THE PRIVACY OFFICE'S FIRST DUTY: COMPLYING WITH THE LAW

A privacy program's first step is to identify those privacy-related laws and regulations that apply to the organization and determine how best to comply with them. Some sectors— healthcare and finance, for example—have specific and substantial legal mandates with which they must comply. Organizations with overseas operations must also be careful to meet the requirement of country-specific and international regulations. Even if the framework of laws and regulations were static, managing compliance would be an enormous challenge. What makes the area far more complicated is that the ground is always shifting. For example, as we worked on this book, the U.S. Congress passed the Dodd-Frank Wall Street Reform and Consumer Protection Act in July 2010. We already know that these new laws will have a great impact on which agencies regulate and enforce different aspects of existing privacy-related laws. But the details about actual roles and responsibilities are still being hashed out by legislators and agencies. You'll find references to this new legislation in Chapter 2, which covers the legal framework for privacy management. Where possible, we've tried to indicate the direction the planned changes are taking. The point to remember, however, is that the goal posts are constantly moving.

Chapter 2 provides an overview of the patchwork quilt of state and federal laws and international frameworks that a U.S. privacy officer will likely need to understand and work with to be successful. The chapter is not intended to be a definitive treatise on privacy laws or even to be comprehensive. It's also important to understand that the book is not intended to provide legal advice. This guide is, however, a good place to begin, and it provides the reader with a framework and resources needed to analyze, understand and comply with laws that pertain to your organization. We have included some primers on terminology and suggestions for how to begin gathering information on how your organization collects and uses data. In addition, there are many references and Web addresses that will lead you to key resources for all you will need to know. Beyond the covers of this book, there are many good sources available, including other IAPP resources that go into much greater depth about these laws and frameworks.

The chapter also discusses the evolution of privacy from Brandeis and Warren's famous right-to-privacy article up through the present, as well as insights into different global approaches to privacy. (Please note that, while the book does discuss and explain international laws, it is primarily directed at a U.S. audience.)

Because analyzing laws and how they impact your organization is a key activity every privacy professional must understand, we've included information about the following major pieces of legislation, regulations and rules:

- Gramm-Leach-Bliley Act
- Health Insurance Portability and Accountability Act (HIPAA)
- Children's Online Privacy Protection Act
- Fair Credit Reporting Act
- Controlling the Assault of Non-Solicited Pornography and Marketing Act (CAN-SPAM)
- Telemarketing Sales Rule
- Junk Fax Prevention Act
- Driver's Privacy Protection Act
- Electronic Communications Privacy Act
- Privacy and anti-discrimination laws
- Privacy and the U.S. Constitution, state constitutions and international directives

In presenting the various laws, we spent a great deal of time trying to determine the best framework for understanding the scope and implications of each law. We recognized that, while some privacy professionals are lawyers and paralegals, many are not. So, we tried to come up with the most logical and obvious lens through which any law should be viewed. For each piece of legislation, law, regulation or private code of conduct, we applied the same series of questions to help address the key aspects:

- Why does the law exist?
- Who is covered by this law?
- What types of information (or what applications of information) are covered?
- What is required or prohibited?
- Who enforces the law?
- What is the risk if our organization doesn't comply?

Understanding why a law exists is important, because that tells you—literally—what sort of practices and behavior legislators or regulators or courts wanted to limit or eliminate. Understanding who is covered by a law helps you to quickly determine whether the law even applies to your organization. If not, you need go no further. In the same manner, if you know the types of information or processes covered by a law, you can quickly determine whether your organization's operations fall within the law's scope. Finally, knowing who administers and enforces a law—and understanding the risks and potential costs of noncompliance— enables your organization to make decisions by weighing risks and benefits.

In addition to introducing the most substantive laws, we spend time discussing the important role played by the Federal Trade Commission (FTC) in data privacy and security regulation. This includes the FTC's function under the Federal Fair Trade Act and its historic role in defining Fair Information Practices. We also help the reader understand the role played by other federal and state regulatory agencies, state attorneys general, private codes of conduct and the paramount importance of contracts in governing a third-party data. Finally, while this book is aimed primarily at privacy concerns and management in the United States, we recommend that every U.S.—based privacy professional—regardless of whether their organization currently has overseas operations—at least survey the most important international laws and standards.

DEVELOPING THE PRIVACY OFFICE

Like navigating your way through the plethora of privacy-related laws and regulations, creating or further developing a privacy program is no simple thing. Many people in your organization will not have encountered the concept of a privacy program before. Some may be curious, others dubious. So it's not unusual for the work of a privacy program team to include extensive outreach, education and even beyond that, evangelism. An effective and successful privacy program is built not just on knowledge of the relevant laws and how to comply with them but also on proactive strategies, persuasion, political savvy, adaptability and a passion to get an exciting new organizational function up and running. It's a tall order.

Chapter 3 gets down to the nuts and bolts of creating a privacy program from scratch—or further developing an existing program. It provides the new privacy professional with a "how to" cookbook of ideas on such things as the importance of documenting everything from objectives to policies and procedures. It also lays out potential strategies for getting started and how to manage your privacy compliance program in the long term.

The chapter follows a logical flow and takes you through the series of steps needed to build a privacy program. The steps include explanations of how to

- define and create the organization's mission statement, objectives and strategies;
- assemble and organize a team capable of running the program and interacting with key internal and external constituencies;
- build a policy framework that explains your organization and manages its information lifecycle;
- train employees and contractors and communicate with key audiences;
- operate the privacy program, including all of the typical tasks as well as how to perform a privacy impact analysis, and
- test and improve the privacy program and determine whom you can ask and enlist to assist you.

Building Relationships: Partnering for Success

Chapter 3 also deals with a topic that is seldom explained and stressed enough but is central to the success of a privacy program. As a privacy professional, you will likely have to work with diverse groups and business units across your organization. And you'll need to know how to collaborate with your colleagues and bring them on board as partners to your efforts. At the heart of these efforts are good working relationships. Chapter 3 describes some of the typical functional areas—legal, marketing, HR, for example—you will need to work with as you develop and run your privacy program. The chapter outlines what is needed to create internal strategic relationships across your organization. Your program will rise or fall depending on you or your team's ability to work with an astute understanding of internal politics. Behind every successful privacy program stand solid working relationships and trust.

For your program to be successful, you'll need support at all levels of your organization, from the boots on the ground—the frontline employees, for example, who handle customers' personally identifiable information every day—to the executive offices and board of directors. We introduce you to the importance of acquiring executive sponsorship at the top. (This topic is so crucial that we go into even greater depth in Chapter 4.)

We show how the most vital relationship for you and your program is with your organization's information security program. Information security is the technical foundation for privacy protection. Your organization's information security department and, more specifically, the chief information security officer (CISO) or equivalent, drives technical solutions and controls that are essential to maintain privacy and essential to your program's success. You have shared interests and, as a result, are common allies. Fostering a sound working relationship with your CISO will be high on your priority list.

Your organization's internal auditing group is another important ally. Depending on your company's culture and organization, the internal auditors have the potential to become your quality assurance program, helping you test the privacy controls that you have put into place. Even if your program contains control assurance elements—for example, some sort of monitoring and assessment procedures—the internal auditors should be on your short list of contacts when you find a problem that no one else is willing to fix. Why? Because, unlike the vast majority of privacy programs, the internal auditing group generally has a direct line to the board of directors and executive suites. Develop good relations with them and they can become your enforcement arm. Use their clout to help make your program succeed.

Other players and potential allies you will need to cultivate include the office of general counsel staff, business unit heads and the managers of other staff offices, such as human resources. It's quite possible that the office of general counsel may be where your program resides—the majority of companies, particularly heavily regulated financial services companies—place their privacy program here. Nevertheless, your colleagues representing the other areas across your organization can help you scale your advice. Make sure they understand your policies and objectives. Make sure, too, that you befriend the heads of business units, especially those whose activities have the most privacy-related exposure and therefore pose the greatest risk. Marketing and sales departments fall into this category because they not only tend to collect vast amounts of personally identifiable information, but also they are interested in leveraging the information to help meet their business goals. Other areas worthy of special attention are departments that handle sensitive financial or health information. Finally, your human resources (HR) department, which usually has an overall responsibility to govern corporate policies, can become a key enforcer for your program.

The book's contributors have drawn on their diverse and varied experience in starting and then running privacy programs. But we recognize, of course, that there can never be a one-size-fits-all approach to privacy management. As a result, some of these suggestions, ideas, tactics and strategies may work well for your privacy program and the current lay of the land. Some of them you will likely set aside, perhaps for some time in the future. How you proceed will naturally depend on the culture and structure of your specific organization. The book will offer you options. And while there is no single way to run a privacy program, the ideas and activities discussed should be considered, because in our collective experience… they work. That said, by remaining open-minded and being willing to experiment, you may well end up developing a hybrid privacy program of your own. The field is new enough for plenty of new approaches. If your approach succeeds, don't forget to share it with your profession. That's part of the ethos of privacy professionals which will help the field grow to meet the challenges of the future.

RUNNING THE SHOW DAY TO DAY

Anyone who has built something from the ground up knows that there comes a time when the headiness of the initial creative process has to give way to a more administrative mindset. It doesn't mean you abandon the search for new solutions and better performance; it just means there's a store to run now. Chapter 4 provides you information and suggestions for handling the day-to-day operation of your privacy program. It'll be immediately obvious that your program is not a static thing. An organization is a living, breathing entity; its reality is fluid.

For example, your marketing and sales functions will float new initiatives that may challenge your existing privacy policies. New technologies will present new business opportunities as well as pose new risks to privacy. Reorganizations and mergers and acquisitions will stir the pot, with new executives and philosophies shaking up the old reporting structures and departmental alliances. New laws, regulations and industry standards will require fast adaptation of policies and procedures. A rare, accidental or criminal breach of privacy information may occur that suddenly thrusts your organization into a public relations crisis and your program into the limelight. In such an environment then, it's no wonder that your privacy program will constantly be working on two jobs in particular:

- Defining—from a privacy management perspective—the contributing roles of everyone in the enterprise
- Figuring out how to scale your operation

Chapter 4 provides you with strategies for handling both constant tasks.

Because of the constraints of the limited budgets and resources you are likely to work with, scaling your operation is always an exercise in puzzle-solving and canny management. Privacy management touches every aspect of an organization, because, in the end, it's all about the data which your enterprise gathers, uses and stores. But the ubiquitous nature of data, including sensitive personally identifiable information, can work to your advantage. You can be a Tom Sawyer and develop strategies to get others to help you accomplish your goals. So, you will ask yourself, how can we get that fence painted without having to do all the work ourselves?

Keeping Friends in High Places and on the Front Lines

If you needed executive sponsorship and guardian angels at the outset of your program, be prepared to see maintaining these invaluable relationships as ongoing work. If the high-level support you needed to get started was forthcoming, well done! However, if you fail to get support for your nascent program up front, you risk never having enough resources or political clout to really get the job done. Chapter 4 provides you with the ingredients for getting buy-in from the top, aligning privacy to business objectives and obtaining high-level accountability from the business operations. You must become, and be seen to be, part of the business's solution, not part of its problems.

Chapter 4 reminds you that communicating well and regularly across the organization is essential. We will show you how to target your communications to a wide variety of constituencies—the board, senior executives, mid-level managers and rank-and-file employees—all of whom are important to your success. Our advice also includes ways to communicate your program to your organization's customers who, after all, are the actual beneficiaries of your program and whose trust you need to stay in business.

We take a relatively deep dive into how to work with the many interests across an organization. You do not necessarily work with constituent groups in the same way; each has its own different interests and objectives. For example, you will find by working with sales and marketing colleagues, who are consumers of information for marketing purposes, that they have much different objectives than your organization's human resources managers. HR colleagues are often most interested in making sure that confidential data is never shared, except on a very limited need-to-know basis, and kept secure.

Walking the Halls, Spreading the Word

To help to deal with the diverse challenges you will face, we describe some ideas for working closely with the following typical constituencies:

- **Sales, marketing, and customer relations**—This is probably the trickiest relationship to cultivate, since these groups may initially see your program as a potential impediment to their own success.
- **Product development**—You can show them how you can help solve their problems.
- **Human resources**—You will acknowledge HR's interest in safeguarding its data, but also recognize that when HR enforces corporate rules, their procedures may intrude on employee privacy.
- **Legal and compliance**—Your program, itself, may likely be housed in this area, but that does not mean that there will be no turf wars or overlapping areas of influence that need to be worked out.
- **IT and IT security**—These groups can be your biggest allies in the fight to

appropriately govern data and determine who can access it and how it is used. Your best friend in the organization should be the chief information security officer.

- **Public and media relations**—These colleagues can help you evangelize privacy across the organization and showcase your program to the public, helping to build stronger bonds of trust with customers.
- **Internal auditing**—Depending on your resources, your organization's internal auditing group is another good ally and can provide you with that basic level of assurance that your program is effective and gaining ground.
- **Third parties** (vendors, contractors, supply chain networks)—With respect to the many third parties your organization may contract with, do you know where your data is? More and more processes, applications and systems, and their respective data, are being outsourced to third parties. Do you govern them appropriately through contracts? Do you assess third parties and make them aware of their responsibilities and duties around your data?

Chapter 4 makes it clear that how you work with other areas within your organization often depends on where your program is located in the organizational structure. We provide some ideas about alternate reporting lines for a successful privacy program. Again, there is no single way to organize your reporting structure; for example, some structures tend to succeed better in highly regulated industries such as financial services.

Data governance is the latest buzzterm to describe information management. It is a cradle-to-grave approach to managing your most important asset—data. Everyone in an organization has an interest in effective data governance. You can even see data governance as almost a microcosm of the management of privacy and security. The relationship between data governance and privacy management is extremely strong. At its core, data governance is about how data is created, collected, processed, manipulated, stored, made available for us and retired. An ever-increasing number of companies are undergoing reviews and transformation of their data governance processes—often through an IT or marketing directive. When these discussions take place, the privacy program needs to have a seat and a strong presence at this table. We will explain why this is important and provide you with tactics for getting that seat.

Additionally, this chapter contains many other successful methods for consideration, each of which will make you more likely to succeed. We provide these by explaining the following:

- How to manage customer preferences (important for companies with opt-out regimes and those that conduct telephone and e-mail sales and marketing campaigns)
- How to keep your privacy program current (a program needs to constantly evolve with the times or risk dying on the vine)
- Methods for keeping you and your team members current on laws, regulations and other areas of knowledge that you will use in your daily activities

- Measuring your program's effectiveness through risk assessments, self-assessments and third-party assessments
- Methods for demonstrating success through metrics and key performance indicators (at the end of the day, you have to produce metrics that tell a positive story)

THE ROAD AHEAD: THE FUTURE OF PRIVACY

Where in the world is privacy headed? Obviously, no one can say for certain. However, it's in the interest of every privacy professional to keep a weather eye on the future. As new technologies appear on the horizon, as legislators start to shape new laws, as business continues to innovate and push the privacy envelope and as consumers express new concerns about their rights—all of this evolving picture falls within the purview of a privacy professional.

Taking cues from knowledge we already have and the views of various industry experts and leaders, Chapter 5 looks into the crystal ball and examines some of the significant drivers and trends in the information economy. The chapter talks about the continuing and formidable momentum behind privacy issues in society. A decade or so ago, privacy began mostly as a Fortune 500 phenomenon, developing as a profession predominantly in the most highly regulated industries such as financial services, insurance and healthcare. However, the picture has been changing rapidly over the past few years and we are now at the point where organizations of all sizes and shapes are employing one or more specialists who are formally responsible for privacy-related programs and management. You, and many others like you, are probably reading this book as a result of this development. And we shouldn't expect this momentum to slow any time soon; on the contrary, the speed of change will likely increase further and the scope of the field will widen.

Compliance with all applicable privacy-related laws, regulations and standards will continue to be a mainstay of a privacy program's work. Regarding enforcement, we will need to understand new regulatory structures, such as the Consumer Financial Protection Bureau (CFPB) and how it will integrate and change existing regulatory authority in both state and federal government.

But while compliance has been the central role of privacy programs to this point, things are changing. Chapter 5 explores the changing role of the privacy professional and how the field has migrated from a strictly compliance-driven focus to a much broader—and perhaps more compelling—role that is responsible for data governance. In addition, corporations are beginning to understand that by taking privacy-related issues seriously—and managing them with innovation and creativity—an effective privacy program can reflect positively on the bottom line. It's perfectly reasonable these days for corporate managers to look for a return on investment when it comes to supporting their privacy functions. Privacy professionals will find themselves not only helping ensure organizations' regulatory compliance but also aligning their efforts to contribute to, and align with, business goals.

Of course, since the profession of privacy is still relatively new, the role of the privacy professional is constantly changing. Within organizations, privacy pros are beginning to find their footing and build the programs and procedures described in this book. Inevitably, this means that privacy professionals and the programs they manage will evolve as the field evolves. Put another way, the skills and knowledge necessary for a successful privacy pro today will not be the skills and knowledge necessary for a successful privacy pro in the future. Chapter 5 looks at what is changing for privacy pros, how the profession is maturing and how the programs we manage are evolving. Topics include the diversification of the field not only within organizations, but across geographical regions, as well as the migration of the privacy function across organizational structures. One cannot discuss how the role of the privacy professional has evolved without discussing the great privacy program migration that has taken place in the past few years.

Where a privacy program should sit in an organization is a much debated subject. Clearly, one truism is that the more highly regulated an industry, the more likely that the privacy office and privacy professionals will sit in their organization's legal area. The compliance group is the privacy program's most likely home. But information technology, finance, security and marketing are other areas where you will find privacy professionals. Probably least likely is a direct report to the CEO. Many organizations have moved their privacy program around—some many times—over the past decade in response to ever complex rules and growing legal risk. Chapter 5 discusses some of the many permutations of how the privacy program can or might be organized in the coming years and what that may mean to you.

Another current trend points to the stabilization of daily privacy tasks and the maturity of established procedures and processes. However, the daily tasks of the privacy professional are not on the verge of becoming stale. Most organizations today are in constant flux, with changing products, business and employees. Governing this will continue to necessitate the updating of policies and procedures and the monitoring of legacy programs. Chapter 5 taps some of the industry's leaders for their sense of how privacy is steadily becoming a recognized and essential function in organizations of all kinds.

So, we can expect that change will be a constant in the field of privacy. Technological advances, new business models and shifting societal expectations all result in a complex—and some would say unstable—environment. Perhaps more than any other skill, privacy professionals today and in the future will require agility. Understanding emerging trends, digging into the latest gadgets and technologies and closely watching the legislative environment are critical functions of any privacy professional's job. Chapter 5 takes a look at what we might expect in areas such as employee privacy; radio frequency identification (RFID), the smart grid and smart meters; information security laws, breach notifications, emerging markets and data protection laws, global harmonization, Privacy by Design and accountability. We will also look at the impact of the Internet, particularly social media and behavioral advertising, and forecast its impact on privacy and the privacy professional in the future.

The future will demand a key quality in privacy professionals: agility. How do you start to prepare for this? Chapter 5 examines some strategies you can use, including redefining the privacy role, rotating through departments and business units, developing multicultural literacy, understanding legal and technical disciplines and instilling direction and leadership. Start thinking about and working on some or all of these strategies now and you will be preparing yourself for privacy-related challenges during the coming years.

MORE DETAILS, TOOLS, TEMPLATES AND RESOURCES

A book of this length and scope can only take you so far. We have tried to provide you with ideas, describe typical situations you are likely to meet, and outline proven best practices. We've pointed you to resources where you'll find the source texts for the laws and regulations of the legal framework you'll work within. Finally, we offer you an appendix with additional information. Some items expand on specific topics—such as data governance—referred to earlier in the chapters. Other resources include checklists and templates. For example, you'll find a sample checklist for self-assessments and making sure your organization is in compliance with the law. You'll also find sample job descriptions for key positions, such as that of a chief privacy officer.

We considered that topics such as details of the compliance requirements of the Payment Card Industry Data Security Standard (PCI DSS) belonged best in the appendix. For example, you can find a table presenting the levels that PCI DSS ascribes to its different levels of transactional volume and the validation requirements that apply to each level. Other resources include a sample organizational charter, alternative structures for building a privacy program, a sample communications plan and a risk assessment model from the University of Arizona. If your organization operates overseas, there's a page devoted to resources where you can gain an understanding of the privacy-related initiatives at work in other countries.

Finally, we wish you success in your work as a privacy professional. The contributors to this book know from direct experience the kinds of daily battles you will face, the victories, the setbacks, and, ultimately, the satisfaction of successfully making privacy management an effective reality in an organization. We hope this book proves useful to you. We'll judge its success when we hear that you, too, have been successful.

CHAPTER 2

Privacy's Legal Framework

This chapter provides an overview of the patchwork of privacy-related laws and regulations that most U.S. organizations face today. The aim of the chapter is not to provide legal advice but simply to present the concepts and main features of numerous major pieces of privacy protection legislation that may apply to organizations based in the United States. You'll also find links to resources that include the more detailed information you will need to analyze, understand and comply with the various laws and their requirements. While this chapter describes the legal framework in which your privacy program will operate, you should always consult with experienced legal counsel when assessing legal compliance requirements and strategies.

Future Impact of the Dodd-Frank Wall Street Reform and Consumer Protection Act of 2010

It's important to note here that the recent Dodd-Frank Wall Street Reform and Consumer Protection Act, passed by Congress in July 2010, will have a great impact on which agencies regulate and enforce different aspects of privacy-related laws. The actual roles and responsibilities are still being determined. You'll find references to this new legislation throughout this chapter. Where possible, we've tried to indicate the direction the planned changes are taking.

For details of the law, see:

http://banking.senate.gov/public/_files/TheRestoringAmericanFinancialStabilityActo-f2010AYO10732_xml0.pdf

---

DEVELOPMENT OF LEGAL MANDATES

The stewardship of privacy is driven fundamentally by laws. The concept of legal protection against violations of privacy has a long history. In the United States, Samuel Warren and Louis Brandeis, writing in an 1890 article called "The Right to Privacy," first advocated the protection of privacy in response to the threats posed by the print technologies that enabled newspapers and photographs. Fast-forward to 1974. Following the recognition that new computer technology used by federal agencies was capable of collecting, storing and maintaining vast amounts of personally identifiable information, the U.S. Congress passed the Privacy Act. Legislators wanted to establish a code of fair information practice for government agencies. For example, The Privacy Act specified that personal information could not be shared without the individual's written consent, except in limited situations; individuals had the right to access and amend their records.

Early Privacy Regulation Milestones	
1890	"The Right to Privacy" by Louis Brandeis and Samuel Warren
1947	Article 12 of the Universal Declaration of Human Rights
1960	"Privacy" by William Prosser
1966	U.S. Freedom of Information Act
1967	*Privacy and Freedom* by Alan Westin
1970	U.S. Fair Credit Reporting Act
1973	Fair Information Practice Principles defined by the U.S. Health, Education and Welfare Privacy Commission
1974	U.S. Privacy Act
1978	France Data Protection Act
1978	First International Conference of Data Protection and Privacy Commissioners
1980	Organization for Economic Cooperation and Development (OECD) "Guidelines Governing the Protection of Privacy and Transborder Data Flows of Personal Data"
1981	Council of Europe Convention on the Protection of Personal Data

In the last two decades, the need for privacy protection has accelerated. Advanced computer technology, the emergence of the Internet (especially the proliferation of online commerce), and easy access by large corporations to vast amounts of data have all contributed to the increasing pressure to protect personally identifiable information. Consumers now face entirely new and sophisticated threats to their privacy, such as identity theft and unauthorized use of their personal data. As a consequence, they demand that their personally identifiable information be legally safeguarded. The result is a complex, continually evolving web of federal, state and country-specific privacy laws.

It's certain that privacy programs will always face fresh challenges as companies harness new technologies. For example, each new generation of the code that developers use to create Web pages will open up more opportunities to track information about consumers. Individuals will be forced to wonder who is looking over their shoulders—and who is gathering what data and for what purpose. Protecting privacy will continue to be a concern.

Different Approaches to Privacy Laws Around the Globe

Individual nations differ in their approach to privacy protection. In the United States, for example, legislators recognizing the potential harm and risk to individuals of breaches and the misuse of data have identified key sectors of civic life in which privacy protection is of special importance. For example, in the realm of healthcare, patients are made aware that medical information about them will not be disclosed, used or shared without their knowledge and/or consent. In the arena of financial transactions, laws now require consumer reporting agencies—the main source of credit ratings—to disclose the personal information they hold that influences an individual's chance to successfully apply for credit. These laws also strictly govern how companies may share information with third parties and affiliates. In addition, website operators are restricted in soliciting and collecting information from children under the age of 13. They must include in their online privacy statements the details of when and how children have to seek parental or guardian permission to disclose certain information. They must also obtain verifiable parental consent.

Differing from the United States in its approach to privacy, the European Union (EU) has enacted broader, more comprehensive laws. The EU has established a uniform standard that is designed to ensure individual privacy protection and facilitate the free movement of personal data between member countries. The following table illustrates how the two philosophies differ as they relate to the protection of data about employees:

Country	Approach to Employee Privacy Protection Legislation
United States	Emphasizes **employer duties** with the following features: • Security concerns predominate • Continuous, multi-dimensional employee monitoring is acceptable • Intrusive background checks are acceptable with consent, and increasingly required • Employee expectations of privacy are very limited
European Union member states	Emphasizes **employee rights** with the following features: • Privacy concerns predominate • Monitoring only permitted with specific legal justification • Limited background checks • Employees have broad privacy expectations and rights

Other countries—such as Japan, Canada, Australia and, more recently, Mexico and South Africa—have enacted laws to protect the personally identifiable information of citizens. The focus of this chapter is on U.S. privacy-related laws. If your organization operates overseas or conducts business offshore, international laws that regulate personally identifiable information will be discussed briefly, and pointers to additional information will be provided.

Legislative Lay of the Land for U.S. Organizations

If your company or institution is based in the United States, your operations will be subject to a variety of privacy laws at both the federal and state level. The sources for these laws can be broken down into four categories: statutes, regulations, case law and common law. Your organization may also be subject to various sector-based standards, which result from voluntary self-regulation. For more information about state and federal privacy laws, see appendix, pp. 210-230.

Source of Law	Basis for Law
Statutes	Laws enacted by passage of local, state and federal legislation
Regulations	Rules promulgated as a result of laws administered by a regulatory agency, such as the Federal Trade Commission
Case law	Court decisions that interpret the obligations under a law or regulation
Common law	Customs and general principles that may be embodied in court decisions; common law serves as precedent or is applied to situations not covered by statute

Agencies Administering U.S. Privacy Laws

The main U.S. state and federal agencies and offices that administer privacy protection laws in the United States include the following:

- Federal Trade Commission (FTC)
- Consumer Financial Protection Bureau (CFPB)
- Federal Communications Commission (FCC)
- Federal financial institution regulators, including the Office of the Comptroller of the Currency (OCC) and Federal Reserve
- Department of Health and Human Services (HHS)
- Office for Civil Rights (OCR)
- Center for Medicare and Medicaid Services (CMS)
- Department of Transportation (DOT)
- State attorneys general (SAGs)
- State departments of insurance (DOIs)

The following diagram shows how these various agencies currently interact:

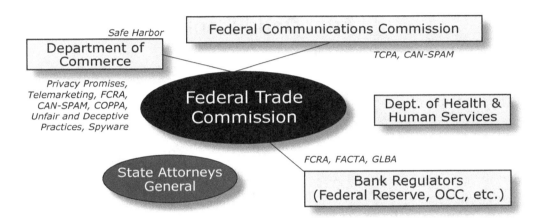

Before Dodd-Frank

In addition to these regulators, other government agencies play a role in securing private information, including:

- Federal and state departments of labor
- Equal Employment Opportunity Commission (EEOC)
- National and state labor relations boards

Changes to the Current Regulatory Regime Expected Soon
The near future will bring changes to the overall scheme of how the various regulatory
bodies work together. The Dodd-Frank Wall Street Reform and Consumer Protection Act,
passed in July 2010, represents sweeping change in the regulation of the financial industry.
As the structure of enforcement roles and responsibilities gradually emerges in the coming
months, privacy professionals will need to closely monitor developments. The future picture
may well look something like this:

After Dodd-Frank

Sources of Privacy Law for U.S. Organizations

The tables below include the primary privacy laws that affect U.S. corporations. Organizations that transact business overseas must also meet the requirements of any international and country-specific laws that apply.

Federal Laws Governing Privacy

The following table includes the primary privacy-related laws enacted and enforced by the federal government:

U.S. Federal Legislation	Agency Responsible
Gramm-Leach-Bliley Act of 1999 (GLBA)	CFPB, state departments of insurance and attorneys general (see next table for more details)
Health Insurance Portability and Accountability Act (HIPAA) of 1996	DHHS Office for Civil Liberties and SAGs
Controlling the Assault of Non-Solicited Pornography and Marketing Act (CAN-SPAM) of 2003	FTC
Children's Online Privacy Protection Act of 1998 (COPPA)	FTC
Fair and Accurate Credit Transactions Act of 2003 (FACTA)	FTC and CFPB
Fair Credit Reporting Act (FCRA) of 1970	FTC and CFPB
Telemarketing Sales Rule (TSR)	FTC and SAGs
National Do Not Call Registry	FTC
Telephone Consumer Protection Act (TCPA) of 1991	FTC, FCC and states
Driver's Privacy Protection Act (DPPA) of 1994	Private right of action (trial bar)
Electronic Communications Privacy Act (ECPA) of 1986	Law enforcement
Federal Trade Commission Act (Section 5: Privacy and Security) of 1914	FTC

State Laws Governing Privacy

States have passed laws that attempt to fill in real or perceived gaps in the federal privacy laws. For example, although the U.S. Constitution does not explicitly provide a right to privacy, some state constitutions grant a right of privacy for individuals. For example, the California Constitution (Article 1, Section 1) specifies that: "All people are by nature free and independent and have inalienable rights. Among these are enjoying and defending life and liberty, acquiring, possessing, and protecting property, and pursuing and obtaining safety, happiness, and privacy."

U.S. State Legislation	Examples of Coverage
State constitutional right to privacy	Some states apply right of privacy to: Employees of state government To employers (for example, California)
General: state-specific statutes	Some state statutes: • Regulate unfair competition • Prohibit unfair and deceptive acts or practices • similar to those prohibited by FTC privacy • regulations • Require breach notification—the majority of states require companies to notify affected individuals if the security of their confidential personal information is breached • Regulate use and display of social security numbers • Regulate appropriate access to medical and health data • Require proper disposal of sensitive personally • identifiable information • Require appropriate safeguard measures to protect sensitive personally identifiable information • Prohibit "marital status" discrimination • Place limits on drug testing and use of polygraphs
Specific: California SB1	In the financial sector, the scope of this California law exceeds that of the Gramm-Leach-Bliley Act (GLBA) with respect to limiting what financial institutions can do with personal data
Common tort laws	These laws cover the invasion of privacy (disclosure of private information), intentional infliction of emotional distress, appropriation, public disclosure and "false light"

See appendix, pp. 210-230, for a list of state and federal security breach notification, Social Security number usage and data destruction laws.

International Privacy Laws

If your organization operates or has transactions with customers overseas, your privacy office will need to familiarize itself with the various international and country-specific laws that apply. Many U.S. organizations have dealings with European countries, so the European Union Data Protection Directive is a key piece of legislation to understand. Other countries, such as Canada, Japan, Argentina, Mexico and Australia, have robust legislation that covers privacy issues.

Foreign Legislation	Agency Responsible
Organization of Economic Cooperation and Development (OECD) legal guidelines for privacy protection and trans-border flow of personal data	Country-specific supervisory authority
EU Data Protection Directive	Country-specific supervisory authority
Australia–Privacy Act	Office of the Privacy Commissioner
Japan–Personal Information Protection Law (Act)	Public Management Ministry
Canada–Personal Information Protection and Electronic Documents Act (PIPEDA) of 2000	Office of the Privacy Commissioner of Canada (Note: Canadian provinces have their own, often stricter, laws)
Asia-Pacific Economic Cooperation (APEC) privacy framework	Voluntary compliance with guidelines

The Organization for Economic Cooperation and Development (OECD) Guidelines on the Protection of Privacy and Transborder Flows of Personal Data form the basis of all other subsequent privacy laws, including the FTC's Fair Information Practice Principles (FIPPs). The OECD guidelines lay out the principles on which their privacy initiative is based. OECD recognizes that

- although national laws and policies may differ, member countries have a common interest in protecting privacy and individual liberties, and in reconciling fundamental but competing values such as privacy and the free flow of information;
- automatic processing and transborder flows of personal data create new forms of relationships among countries and require the development of compatible rules and practices;
- transborder flows of personal data contribute to economic and social development;
- domestic legislation concerning privacy protection and transborder flows of personal data may hinder such transborder flows.

For more detailed information about international and country-specific privacy laws, see appendix, *Resources for Understanding Privacy Initiatives in Other Countries*, p. 182, and *Privacy Legislation Worldwide*, p. 205.

Self-Regulation: Industry Standards and Codes of Conduct

In addition to law-based regulation, there are also many U.S. voluntary and contractual initiatives—some sector-specific, others comprehensive—that have established standards and codes of conduct for the communities of interest they serve. The following table includes some of the more notable efforts.

Self-Regulation (Voluntary)	Sectors Affected
Payment Card Industry Data Security Standard (PCI DSS)	All organizations (worldwide) that collect, process, store or transmit cardholder information from any card branded with the logo of one of the credit card brands
Direct Marketing Association (DMA) Privacy Promise	Businesses interested in interactive and database marketing
VeriSign and TRUSTe	E-commerce entities wishing to meet recognized industry privacy requirements
Children's Advertising Review Unit (CARU) guidelines	Media advertising to children below the age of 12
Network Advertising Initiative (NAI) guidelines	Online advertising, particularly targeting or behavioral, that potentially harms individuals

General Legal Terms in Privacy Laws

Legislation generally uses legal terms to describe key elements of privacy protection. Below you'll find a list of frequently used terms with which you and your team will need to become familiar. If you have any doubts, consult your legal counsel.

Term	Sample Definition
Person	Any entity with legal rights, including an individual (a "natural person") or a corporation (a "legal person").
Jurisdiction	The authority of a court to hear a particular case. A court must have jurisdiction over both the type of dispute ("subject matter jurisdiction") and the parties ("personal jurisdiction"). Government agencies have jurisdictional limits also.
Preemption	A conflict of law doctrine—preemption exists when a superior government's laws supersede those of an inferior government.

Notice	A description of an organization's information management practices.
	• Notices have two purposes
	o Consumer education
	o Corporate accountability
	• The typical notice tells the individual
	o What information is collected
	o How the information is used and disclosed
	o How to exercise any choices about uses or disclosures
	o Whether the individual can access or update the information
	• Many laws have additional requirements
	• Need to distinguish between an internal "policy" and a "notice"
Choice	The ability of a person to specify whether personal information will be collected and/or how it will be used or disclosed.
	• "Opt in" means an affirmative indication of choice based on an express act of the person giving the consent. Generally used where sensitive information—such as healthcare or credit-related data—is going to be used
	• "Opt out" means choice implied by the failure of the person to object to the use or disclosure
	Choice is not always appropriate. But if it is offered, it should be meaningful—based on a real understanding of the implications of the decision. U.S. laws often require choice for marketing communications, particularly where sensitive health and financial information may be shared for non-transactional purposes.
Access	The ability to view personal information held by an organization. This ability may be complemented by an ability to update or correct the information. Some U.S. laws provide for access and correction when the information is used for any type of substantive decision making—such as the use of credit data for investigative purposes or insurance underwriting under state law. Also applies to who can appropriately view, change or use data stored in a database or computer.

UNDERSTANDING YOUR ORGANIZATION'S LEGAL REQUIREMENTS

Understanding and complying with the privacy-related laws, rules and regulations that affect your organization's operations will be the most important challenge facing your privacy office. The domestic and international legal landscapes are always changing. Regulatory bodies and different levels of governments continuously implement new laws; existing laws are constantly amended and are subject to interpretation. If your organization operates around the globe, the legal requirements for how you handle personally identifiable information (PII) can be substantial and complex. For these reasons, it's critical from the outset to think about the particular legal framework within which your organization must operate. The remainder of this chapter provides you with an overview of the following:

- Various key U.S. laws that include privacy-related mandates
- Significant international frameworks that may affect U.S.–based organizations
- Some key country-specific laws

Gathering Information in Your Organization

Start by asking basic questions. As you begin the process of familiarizing yourself with the legislative landscape affecting the personally identifiable information that your organization collects, you should determine the who, what, where, when, how and why that relate to the information.

Query	Example
Who?	Your HR and marketing departments collect, use and maintain personally identifiable information relating to customers and employees.
What?	The personally identifiable information includes credit card payment data, Social Security numbers, driver's license numbers and dates of birth.
Where?	Your HR and marketing department collects personally identifiable information from customers and associates around the world, including the United States, the European Union and the Asia-Pacific region.
When?	Customer information is collected during sales transactions; employee data is collected during the hiring process and updated as necessary.
How?	Your organization collects information via its sales channels, including websites, call-centers and paper-based orders.
Why?	By acquiring this information, you will able to identify the laws that affect your organization and estimate, justify and muster the resources you need to implement domestic and, if relevant, global compliance processes.

Analyzing the Laws

Whenever you want to analyze and understand a piece of legislation that may have an impact on your organization's operations, you can start by asking the following key questions:

Key Questions for Analyzing and Understanding a Privacy-Related Law

For each piece of privacy-related legislation, you can ask the following questions to gain a good understanding. This understanding will form the basis of your organization's own privacy program.

- Why does the law exist?
- Who is covered by this law?
- What types of information (or what applications of information) are covered?
- What exactly is required or prohibited?
- Who enforces the law?
- What is the risk if our organization doesn't comply?

The following sections use these key questions as a template to present the major privacy-related laws.

GRAMM-LEACH-BLILEY ACT

The Gramm-Leach-Bliley Act (GLBA) of 1999, also called the Financial Services Modernization Act, established the first requirements to protect consumers' financial information. GLBA is a comprehensive, federal law affecting financial institutions. The law requires financial institutions to develop, implement and maintain administrative, technical and physical safeguards to protect the security, integrity and confidentiality of customer information. GLBA gives authority to several federal agencies to administer and enforce GLBA's Financial Privacy Rule and the Safeguards Rule. The law also encouraged a state-specific privacy regulatory framework for the insurance industry. This framework has developed over the past decade.

Why Does the Law Exist?

Congress was poised to enact revamped regulation of the banking, securities and insurance industries. At the same time, banks were making news for sharing account information with telemarketers, raising concerns about privacy violations in the financial sector. As a result, the legislators included Title V of the new law to address those concerns.

Who Is Covered by this Law?

- Domestic financial institutions, defined as "any entity that is significantly engaged in financial activities" and including banks, securities firms, mortgage companies, insurers, agents, brokers and dealers
- Many types of entities that are not traditional financial institutions, such as
  - Auto dealers;
  - Financial data processors;
  - Entities that educate or place financial professionals.

What Types of Information Are Covered?

The law covers personally identifiable information that includes information

- provided by a consumer to a financial institution in order to obtain a financial product or service;
- resulting from a transaction involving a financial product or service between a financial institution and a consumer;
- that the financial institution otherwise obtains in connection with providing a financial product or service to a consumer.

Interaction of GLBA and State Laws

Some state laws overlap or complement the requirements of GLBA. Among them are those covering

- Social Security number protection;
- data disposal;
- breach notification;
- medical or health information protection;
- marketing/do not call.

What Is Required or Prohibited?

- Financial institutions must provide customers with notices about privacy and security practices.
- Though financial institutions may share virtually any information with affiliated companies and/or service providers, other laws do place some restrictions on sharing for marketing purposes.
- Financial institutions may also share information with joint marketing partners–other financial institutions with whom it jointly offers a financial product.
- Other than for defined exceptions, financial institutions may share data with non-affiliated companies as long as the consumers have not opted out of such use–they must give consumers a reasonable opportunity (30 days) to opt out prior to sharing.

- Most state fraud laws include an exception that permits the sharing of information for anti-fraud and law enforcement purposes
- The FTC and regulators of financial institutions must promulgate privacy and safeguard rules (Congress recently created the Consumer Financial Protection Bureau, which now has jurisdiction over enforcing GLBA)
- GLBA does not preempt state laws—it serves as the baseline (for example, California law goes much further than GLBA on these matters)

The GLBA Privacy Rule

To establish standards for privacy notices, the FTC and federal financial regulators created the privacy rule, which covers nine categories of information and stipulates that financial institutions

- must give initial and annual privacy notices to customers;
- process opt-outs within 30 days;
- can share information with other third parties for their own use only if no exceptions exist or no opt-out is received;
- must ensure that service providers do not use the data for other purposes.

The GLBA Safeguards Rule

The GLBA Safeguards Rule requires financial institutions to develop an information security program designed to protect customer information. This program comprises administrative, technical and physical safeguards used by a financial institution to access, collect, distribute, process, protect, store, use, transmit, dispose of or otherwise handle customer information. The objectives of the Safeguards Rule are to provide

- administrative security in the form of
  - program definition and administration;
  - risk assessments;
  - management of workforce risks, employee training;
  - vendor due diligence and oversight.
- technical security in the form of
  - computer system, network and applications security;
  - access controls;
  - encryption;
- physical security in the form of
  - facilities controls;
  - disaster recovery;
  - business continuity.

Who Enforces the Law?

GLBA was originally enforced by the FTC and financial institution regulators, as well as state attorneys general. However, in 2010, the U.S. Congress created the Consumer Financial Protection Bureau (CFPB), which now has primary jurisdiction over GLBA regulations and enforcement. As this first edition goes to press, it is not yet clear how the CFPB will interact with federal banking regulators over enforcement.

GLBA does not allow for private rights of action, but failure to comply with a privacy notice is a deceptive trade practice actionable by state and federal authorities. Some states also have private rights of action for unfair and deceptive trade practice violations. However, the FTC still has authority under Section 5 of the FTC Act to regulate corporate privacy and security operations and prevent unfair and deceptive trade practices.

Prior to the recent financial services reform legislation, the following agencies have been responsible for enforcing GLBA regulations. The new law gives primary regulatory and enforcement jurisdiction to the CFPB. As the new law takes effect, it will become clear after 2011 how GLBA will be enforced.

The GLBA laws are administered by eight different agencies, which cover following various entities in the financial industry.

This agency . . .	. . . covers these financial institutions . . .	. . . and provides information here
Board of Governors of the Federal Reserve System	Bank holding companies and member banks of the Federal Reserve System	www.federalreserve.gov
U.S. Commodity Futures Trading Commission (CFTC)	Commodities brokers	www.cftc.gov
Department of the Treasury, Office of the Comptroller of the Currency (OCC)	National banks and federal branches of foreign banks	www.occ.treas.gov
Department of the Treasury, Office of Thrift Supervision (OTS)	Savings associations insured by the FDIC	www.ots.treas.gov
Federal Deposit Insurance Corporation (FDIC)	Banks they insure, not including Federal Reserve System members	www.fdic.gov
U.S. Securities and Exchange Commission (SEC)	Securities brokers and dealers, as well as investment companies	www.sec.gov

National Credit Union Administration (NCUA)	Federally insured credit unions	www.ncua.gov
Federal Trade Commission (FTC)	Institutions not covered by the other agencies	www.ftc.gov

In the past, if an organization was not in compliance with GLBA regulations, these agencies enforced them by levying fines, administering penalties and taking corrective actions.

Going forward, it appears that the CFPB will have this responsibility. However, it is also possible that the CFPB will scale itself through the financial services agencies' exam processes.

What Happens If Our Organization Doesn't Comply?

The consequences of noncompliance include enforcement actions and possible private lawsuits. This includes reputational damages and loss of trust within the marketplace.

Key GLBA Resources from the Federal Trade Commission (FTC)

FTC Privacy Initiatives
www.ftc.gov/privacy
This site is the entry point to the FTC's comprehensive information about privacy and its role in the consumer protection mission.

The Financial Privacy Rule
www.ftc.gov/privacy/privacyinitiatives/financial_rule.html
One key piece of privacy-related legislation is the GLBA Financial Privacy Rule. The FTC provides detailed information about these laws.

The Safeguards Rule
www.ftc.gov/privacy/privacyinitiatives/safeguards.html
Another key piece of privacy-related legislation is the GLBA Safeguards Rule. The FTC provides extensive information about this legislation.

HEALTH INSURANCE PORTABILITY AND ACCOUNTABILITY ACT

Congress enacted the Health Insurance Portability and Accountability Act (HIPAA) in 1996 to improve the efficiency of healthcare service delivery in the United States. HIPAA required the Department of Health and Human Services (HHS) to adopt national standards for electronic healthcare information transactions. Congress recognized, however, that the movement to electronic data exchange in the healthcare sector posed a possible threat to privacy. There was concern that the privacy of protected health information (PHI) of individuals could be compromised. Accordingly, HIPAA mandated that HHS promulgate regulations to protect the privacy and security of electronically transmitted healthcare information.

The Health Information Technology for Economic and Clinical Health (HITECH) Act, enacted as part of the American Recovery and Reinvestment Act of 2009, was signed into law on February 17, 2009, to promote the adoption and meaningful use of health information technology. Among its provisions, the legislation requires that all third-party companies, including "business associates," be held accountable to HIPAA requirements.

HIPAA Definition of "Business Associates"

The term "business associate" has the meaning given such term in section 160.103 of title 45, Code of Federal Regulations.

1. Except as provided in paragraph (2) of this definition, business associate means, with respect to a covered entity, a person who:
    i. On behalf of such covered entity or of an organized health care arrangement (as defined in 164.501 of this subchapter) in which the covered entity participates, but other than in the capacity of a member of the workforce of such covered entity or arrangement, performs, or assists in the performance of:
        A. A function or activity involving the use or disclosure of individually identifiable health information, including claims processing or administration, data analysis, processing or administration, utilization review, quality assurance, billing, benefit management, practice management and re-pricing; or
        B. Any other function or activity regulated by this subchapter; or
    ii. Provides, other than in the capacity of a member of the workforce of such covered entity, legal, actuarial, accounting, consulting, data aggregation (as defined in 164.501 of this subchapter), management, administrative, accreditation, or financial services to or for such covered entity, or to or for an organized healthcare arrangement in which the covered entity participates, where the provision of the service involves the disclosure of individually identifiable health information from such covered entity or arrangement, or from another business associate of such covered entity or arrangement, to the person.
2. A covered entity participating in an organized healthcare arrangement that performs a function or activity as described by paragraph (1)(i) of this definition for or on behalf of such organized healthcare arrangement, or that provides a service as described in paragraph (1)(ii) of this definition to or for such organized healthcare arrangement, does not, simply through the performance of such function or activity or the provision of such service, become a business associate of other covered entities participating in such organized healthcare arrangement.
3. A covered entity may be a business associate of another covered entity.

Why Does the Law Exist?

HIPAA was enacted to establish standards for electronic healthcare transactions and to improve the efficiency of the U.S. healthcare system by encouraging the use of electronic data interchange. Congress understood that acceptance of electronic medical information exchange depended on ensuring the privacy and security of health information.

Note: HIPAA does not preempt stronger state laws; HIPAA merely sets the floor for medical privacy.

Who Is Covered by this Law?

HIPAA applies to three types of "covered entities": health plans, healthcare clearinghouses and covered healthcare providers, as well as their business associates. Note that HIPAA now covers all health-related information. For example, insurers use a lot of health information to pay claims and to underwrite insurance products. However, with the exception of disability and long-term care insurance, all information collected by property and casualty and life insurers is exempted from HIPAA. Additionally, the HITECH Act now effectively treats all business associates as covered entities, and HHS and state attorneys general have direct enforcement power over them.

Entity	Definition
Health plan	Any individual or group plan that pays the cost of medical care. This includes most third-party payers, such as HMOs, Medicare, Medicaid, health insurers, and group health plans.
Healthcare clearinghouse	An entity that receives protected health information (PHI) from one entity and processes the information from a non-standard format into a standard format, or vice versa, for the receiving entity.
Covered healthcare provider	Any provider who transmits health information in electronic form in connection with certain administrative and financial transactions related to healthcare.
Business associate	See box above for a detailed definition.

If an entity that receives or maintains health information is not one of the types listed above, it is not directly regulated by the HIPAA privacy regulations.

What Types of Information Are Covered?

HIPAA covers protected health information that is transmitted or maintained in any form. This includes any information about past, current or future health status, provision of healthcare, or payment for healthcare that can be linked to a specific individual. This is interpreted rather broadly and includes any part of a patient's medical record or payment history. Personal health information that is based on the following list of 18 identifiers must be treated with special care according to HIPAA:

- Names
- All geographical subdivisions smaller than a state, including street address, city, county, precinct, zip code, and their equivalent geocodes, except for the initial three digits of a zip code, if according to the current publicly available data from the Bureau of the Census: (1) The geographic unit formed by combining all zip codes with the same three initial digits contains more than 20,000 people; and (2) The initial three digits of a zip code for all such geographic units containing 20,000 or fewer people is changed to 000
- Dates (other than year) for dates directly related to an individual, including birth date, admission date, discharge date and date of death
- All ages over 89 and all elements of dates (including year) indicative of such age, except that such ages and elements may be aggregated into a single category of age 90 or older
- Phone numbers
- Fax numbers
- Electronic mail addresses
- Social Security numbers
- Medical record numbers
- Health plan beneficiary numbers
- Account numbers
- Certificate/license numbers
- Vehicle identifiers and serial numbers, including license plate numbers
- Device identifiers and serial numbers
- Web Universal Resource Locators (URLs) and Internet Protocol (IP) address numbers
- Biometric identifiers, including finger, retinal and voice prints
- Full face photographic images and any comparable images
- Any other unique identifying number, characteristic or code (note this does not mean the unique code assigned by the investigator to code the data)

What Is Required or Prohibited?

Healthcare organizations and their business associates may not use or disclose personal health information, except as permitted or required by HIPAA privacy and security regulations.

Permitted HIPAA Uses and Disclosures

HIPAA permits healthcare organizations to use or disclose personal health information in the following cases:

- For treatment, payment and healthcare operations (TPO)
- With informed consent, when use/disclosure is in the best interest of the individual

- For public health purposes and research
- Incidental uses/disclosures
- With the written authorization of the individual

Required Uses and Disclosures

HIPAA requires that organizations disclose the use of personal health information:

- To an individual (or his or her representative) upon request
- To the Department of Health and Human Services, for compliance purposes
- As required by law (for example: for subpoenas and law enforcement)

HIPAA Privacy Rule Fundamentals

The act stipulates that healthcare entities:

- Appoint a privacy official
- Limit use and disclosure to the "minimum necessary" data
- Prepare and deliver privacy notices with mandated content
- Maintain records of disclosures
- Respect individual requests regarding disclosures of PHI and confidential communications
- Establish a process for handling complaints
- Ensure appropriate security
- Develop and utilize special rules for psychotherapy notes

HIPAA Security Rule Fundamentals

HIPAA includes a number of provisions for ensuring the security of personal health information. The HIPAA Security Rule applies to personal health in electronic format (EPHI). It requires:

- Reasonable security, given the particular risks and size of the organization
- Comprehensive security with detailed "implementation specifications" that are either required or addressable
- Assessment of the need for addressable specifications—if an entity chooses not to implement them, it must document the reasons as well as the ways the risks will be managed (for example, via an alternative control)

Regarding the coverage of business associates, please note that the HIPAA Security Rule is still under development and is currently still a proposal. However, it seems likely that all its requirements will apply to business associates that are now subject to the HIPAA laws. Business associates are currently regulated by HHS.

American Recovery & Reinvestment Act of 2009 (Stimulus Bill)

Title XIII: Health Information Technology for Economic and Clinical Health (HITECH) Act amends HIPAA as follows:

- Regulates personal health records (PHRs)
- Requires covered entities and public health record vendors to provide notice of security breaches to consumers, HHS and FTC
- Regulates business associates directly under the jurisdiction of HIPAA
- Stipulates that business associates have direct liability under the Security Rule
- Provides new rules for accountings including disclosure, minimum necessary, marketing and fundraising
- Increases penalties

Note: If your organization qualifies as a business associate, be aware that there are different breach notification requirements for HHS and FTC. Consult the appropriate legislation for details.

Who Enforces the Law?

Enforcement for HIPAA falls to the U.S. Department of Health and Human Services (HHS) through the following organizations:

- Office for Civil Rights (OCR)—HIPAA Privacy Rule
- Centers for Medicare and Medicaid Services (CMS)—HIPAA Security Rule
- State attorneys general

What Happens If Our Organization Doesn't Comply?

While a person can still receive criminal sentences of up to 10 years, HITECH amends HIPAA's existing civil penalties into a tiered structure. Amounts now range from $25,000 to $1.5 million, depending on the intent of the unauthorized access or disclosure.

CHILDREN'S ONLINE PRIVACY PROTECTION ACT

The Children's Online Privacy Protection Act (COPPA) of 2000 applies to the online collection of personal information by people and organizations under U.S. jurisdiction from children under 13 years of age. It details what a website operator must include in a privacy policy, when and how to seek verifiable consent from a parent or guardian and what responsibilities an operator has to protect children's privacy and safety online including restrictions on the marketing to those under 13. While children under 13 can legally give out personal information with their parents' permission, many websites altogether disallow underage children from using their services due to the amount of recordkeeping involved.

Why Does the Law Exist?

COPPA legislation was a direct response to the collection and, in some cases, misuse of the personal information of young children by websites.

Who Is Covered by this Law?

The law covers all commercial website operators.

What Types of Information Are Covered?

COPPA covers the collection and use of personal information from children under the age of 13 years via a commercial website.

What Is Required or Prohibited?

With a few exceptions, website operators must obtain verifiable parental consent before they can collect personal information from children online.

Who Enforces the Law?

The law is enforced by the Federal Trade Commission and state attorneys general.

What Happens If Our Organization Doesn't Comply?

An organization that fails to comply can be sued for damages, up to $10,000 per violation.

FEDERAL TRADE COMMISSION'S ROLE IN PRIVACY

Established in 1914 by the Federal Trade Commission Act to prevent practices like anti-competitive business practices and coercive monopolies, the commission now oversees a wide array of legislation designed, in one way or another, to protect the privacy of individuals' personal information. Of all the regulatory agencies in the United States that enforce privacy protection laws of some kind, the Federal Trade Commission (FTC) has traditionally done a lot of heavy lifting under Section 5 of its laws. Section 5 prohibits the use of unfair and deceptive practices. The FTC's initiatives include laws that apply to the following areas:

- Financial privacy safeguards and rules for some non-financial organizations
- Unfairness and deception for non-financial organizations
- Credit reporting for non-financial organizations (via the Fair and Accurate Credit Transactions Act and Fair Credit Reporting Act legislation)
- Children's privacy
- "Pretexting" (using pretense to fraudulently obtain personal information)
- Telemarketing
- Non-solicited pornography and marketing [see p. 47 for more information about the

Controlling the Assault of Non-Solicited Pornography and Marketing (CAN-SPAM) Act of 2003]

FTC Privacy Mission

As quoted in a 2010 paper on information privacy, the FTC previously included a section on its website stating,[1,2]

> *"Privacy is a central element of the FTC's consumer protection mission. In recent years, advances in computer technology have made it possible for detailed information about people to be compiled and shared more easily and cheaply than ever. That has produced many benefits for society as a whole, and individual consumers. For example, it is easier for law enforcement to track down criminals, for banks to prevent fraud, and for consumers to learn about new products and services, allowing them to make better-informed purchasing decisions. At the same time, as personal information becomes more accessible, each of us—companies, associations, government agencies, and consumers—must take precautions to protect against the misuse of our information."*

1. http://business.ftc..gov/privacy-and-security and 2. http://www.navigatellc.net/downloads/Information%20Protection%20and%20Privacy%20The%20New%20High%20Stakes%20Game.pdf

Deceptive and Unfair Acts

The basic consumer protection statute enforced by the commission is Section 5 of the FTC Act, which defines deceptive and unfair acts as follows:

- A **deceptive act** or practice misrepresents or omits a material fact and is likely to mislead consumers acting reasonably under the circumstances
- An **unfair act** or practice causes injury that is:
  - Substantial
  - Without offsetting benefits
  - Cannot reasonably be avoided

Enforcement

The FTC has brought many actions challenging organizations' data security practices. The unfair or deceptive data security practices prosecuted by the FTC include cases where organizations have:

- Made misleading or false promises regarding privacy or security policies
- Failed to implement appropriate privacy and data security policies or otherwise failed to assess risks to customer information
- Failed to encrypt consumer information when stored on computers or in transmission
- Failed to implement reasonable policies and procedures to securely dispose of personal information

In addition to the legislation it enforces, the FTC has also drafted a set of principles to encourage organizations to follow best practices. The following sections describe the Fair Information Practice Principles and highlight the most important of the remaining laws administered by the FTC.

FTC'S FAIR INFORMATION PRACTICE PRINCIPLES

Over the past quarter century, government agencies in the United States, Canada and Europe have studied the information practices of organizations and institutions—how they collect and use personally identifiable information. These agencies have also studied the safeguards that assure those practices are fair and provide adequate privacy protection. In the EU, the study of privacy-related issues has led to the implementation of the comprehensive European Union Privacy Directive. In the United States, the result has been a series of reports, guidelines and model codes, embodied now in the FTC's recommended Fair Information Practice Principles. Please note that the EU bloc still does not consider the U.S. laws adequate for protecting the privacy of EU citizens. The FTC's recommendations—not enforceable by law—represent widely accepted principles concerning fair information practices. The five core principles of privacy protection are as follows:

Core Principle	Requirements

Notice and awareness	• Give consumers notice before any personal information is collected
	• Include key information for consumers, such as:
	  ◦ Identity of whoever is collecting data
	  ◦ Description of planned uses of data
	  ◦ Identity of potential recipients of data
	  ◦ Nature of data collected and means by which it is collected if not obvious (for example: passive electronic monitoring or active request to consumer)
	  ◦ Whether provision of requested data is voluntary or required, and consequences of refusal to provide it
	  ◦ Steps taken by data collector to ensure confidentiality, integrity and data quality
	• Disclose practices:
	  ◦ Clearly and conspicuously
	  ◦ In prominent, unavoidable location
	  ◦ With easy access from both website's homepage and pages where data is collected

Choice and consent	Consumers should have options regarding the use of personal information collected from them. Choice relates to secondary uses of information:

- Beyond those needed to complete transaction
- That is used:
  - Internally, such as placing the consumer on marketing mailing lists
  - Externally, such as transferring data to third parties

Approaches to choice and consent are:

- **Opt-in** scenario requiring consumer to proactively agree to the collection and use of information
- **Opt-out** scenario requiring consumer to reject collection and use of such information
- **Yes/no** option, including ability of consumer to:
  - Tailor information they reveal and its uses
  - Choose separately whether company can include data on internal mailing list or sell it to third parties
  - Have simple and easily accessible way to make choice

Access and participation	Focuses on accuracy and completeness of data. It refers to an individual's ability both to access personal data—for example, to view data in an entity's files—and to contest data's accuracy and completeness. Access must encompass:

- Timely and inexpensive access to data
- Simple means for contesting inaccurate or incomplete data
- Mechanism by which data collector can verify information
- Means to add corrections and objections to data file and have updates sent to all data recipients

Integrity and security	Ensures data is kept accurate and secure. The following guidelines apply:

- Collectors must take reasonable steps to provide consumers with access to data, and destroy untimely data or convert it to anonymous form
- Security involves both managerial and technical measures to protect against loss and the unauthorized access, destruction, use or disclosure of the data, such as:
  - Managerial measures including steps to limit data access and ensure that individuals with access do not use data for unauthorized purposes
  - Technical security measures preventing unauthorized access and including encryption in data transmission and storage, password-imposed limits on access and data storage on secure servers

Enforcement and redress

Some kind of enforcement is a must, otherwise the Fair Information Practice Principles are merely suggestions and don't ensure compliance. Alternative approaches to enforcement include:

- Industry self-regulation
- Legislation to create private remedies for consumers
- Regulatory schemes enforceable through civil and criminal sanctions

Appropriate means of individual redress include, at a minimum, institutional mechanisms so consumers can express concerns

- Self-regulatory system for investigating complaints
- Ensuring consumers know how to access such a system

If the self-regulatory code has been breached, consumers should have a remedy, including:

- Righting the wrong and compensation for harm suffered
- Monetary sanctions serving not only as compensation for victim but also as incentive for industry compliance
- Industry codes providing alternative dispute resolution compensation mechanisms

Note: A recent report about online privacy by the Internet Policy Task Force of the Department of Commerce—*Commercial Data Privacy and Innovation in the Internet Economy: A Dynamic Policy Framework*—indicates possible future modifications to the FTC's Fair Information Practice Principles. See the FTC's website to follow developments in this area.

FAIR CREDIT REPORTING ACT

The FTC's Fair Credit Report Act (FCRA), first passed in 1970, regulates the collection, dissemination and use of consumer information, including consumer credit information. Along with the Fair Debt Collection Practices Act (FDCPA), it forms the basis of consumer credit rights in the United States. FCRA was amended in 1996 with provisions for non-consumer-initiated transactions and standards for consumer assistance, and again in 2003 with provisions related to identity theft—via the Fair and Accurate Credit Transactions Act (FACTA) of 2003. Among other things, FACTA created a new legal framework for how companies must protect against identity theft (see "Red Flags Rule" below); how companies can legally share consumer report information (the definition of which was broadened) between affiliates for marketing purposes, and new legal duties for furnishers of consumer report information.

Why Does the Law Exist?

In the 1940s, merchants began sharing information in order to facilitate credit for consumer durables. By the 1960s, consumer credit was critical—but individuals could be harmed by inaccurate information that they could neither view nor correct.

Who Is Covered by this Law?

FCRA covers consumers, credit reporting agencies (CRAs) and any individual or organization that either furnishes or uses information to or requests a credit report from a CRA. The law views a "consumer reporting agency" as any organization that assembles or evaluates consumer information for the purpose of regular furnishing of consumer reports to third parties in exchange for a fee.

The law also applies to all companies that use consumer report information (CRI) for marketing purposes. FCRA covers almost any entity that offers credit. The law also includes some exceptions, for example, for companies that work in fraud prevention.

Note: This area of privacy law may prove contentious in the future, since the FTC wants to include anyone who defers payment of any kind—including a paper boy—to a creditor. Court challenges are likely down the road. The recent 2010 federal financial services reform legislation has charged the newly formed CFPB with regulating how financial services companies use credit-related information. It is not yet clear where the line of demarcation is "officially" drawn between regulating the use of credit data by non-financial firms, ostensibly regulated by the FTC, and the use by financial services firms, now regulated by the CFPB.

What Types of Information Are Covered?

FCRA covers any information that pertains to credit worthiness, credit standing, credit capacity, character, general reputation, personal characteristics or mode of living when that information is used—wholly or partly—to help establish a consumer's eligibility for credit, insurance, employment or other business purpose. These criteria are referred to as the "seven factors." Other types of information covered include, for example, a driving history obtained from an information aggregator.

What Is Required or Prohibited?

FCRA requires that:

- Third-party data used for substantive decision-making must be appropriately accurate, current and complete
- Consumers must receive notice when information in a consumer report is used to make an adverse decision, including:
  - Notice to applicant with a copy of consumer report **before** taking adverse action, **and**
  - FCRA-mandated adverse action notice **after** taking the adverse action
- Consumer reports may only be used for permissible purposes
- Consumers must have access to their consumer reports and have an opportunity to

dispute and correct errors

- Covered entities must comply with all other requirements on users and furnishers of consumer information
- Users of third-party data comply with other provisions (such as giving adverse action notices)
- Companies must provide consumers with notice and an opportunity to opt out of affiliate sharing of consumer report information for marketing purposes
- All creditors institute the Red Flags Rule (see details below)

In addition, the FCRA:

- Permits an entity—as long as it meets certain protections—to obtain an "investigative consumer report" that contains information sourced from interviews with third parties, such as neighbors and friends of the applicant
- Prohibits the use of third-party data for purposes covered by FCRA unless the data is appropriately accurate and current

Red Flags Rule

The Red Flags Rule requires many businesses and organizations to implement a written Identity Theft Prevention Program designed to detect the warning signs—or "red flags"—of identity theft in their day-to-day operations. If this rule applies to your business or organization:

- Get practical tips on spotting the red flags of identity theft, taking steps to prevent the crime, and mitigating the damage it inflicts
- Learn how to put in place your written Identity Theft Prevention Program

Identifying a red flag in advance can help you spot a suspicious pattern when it occurs and gives you the chance to prevent a costly episode of identity theft. Enforcement of the Red Flags Rule by the FTC went into effect on January 1, 2011.

Key Resources for Understanding the FTC's Fair Credit Reporting Act

Fair Credit Report Act (FCRA) – Legislative Details
www.ftc.gov/os/statutes/fcradoc.pdf
This site presents the entire text of the act.

- FCRA's Red Flags Rule
- www.ftc.gov/os/statutes/fcrajump.shtm

This FTC website provides a comprehensive guide to the FCRA's Red Flags Rule for minimizing the risk of identity theft.

Who Enforces the Law?

FCRA is enforced by:

- Federal Trade Commission
- Consumer Financial Protection Bureau
- State attorneys general
- Private litigants (right of action exists)

What Happens If Our Organization Doesn't Comply?

If an organization fails to comply with FCRA regulations, civil and criminal penalties apply. In addition to actual damages, violators are subject to statutory damages of $1,000 per violation and $2,500 for willful violations. In addition, there are private rights of action by which consumers can act as "mini-attorneys general" and, in conjunction with the trial bar, enforce FCRA laws through private lawsuits and class actions.

LAWS REGULATING MARKETING COMMUNICATIONS

Anyone who has received unsolicited marketing calls at home at dinnertime or unwanted catalogs in the mail appreciates the laws that seek to regulate the communication from marketers. The cluster of laws that specifically protect consumers from unsolicited communications from marketers includes:

- Controlling the Assault of Non-Solicited Pornography and Marketing (CAN-SPAM) Act of 2003
- Telemarketing Sales Rule of 2009
- National Do Not Call Registry of 2004
- Junk Fax Prevention Act (JFPA) of 2005

The following laws and rules afford additional protection for personal information:

- Telephone Consumer Protection Act (TCPA) of 1991
- U.S. Postal Code (includes, for example, the enforcement of a decency code where if a mail recipient finds material offensive, the sending organization must add them to its do-not-mail list)
- USPS Move Update Rules (these rules state, for example, that if your organization does direct mailing, at least 70 percent of your mailing-list addresses must be accurate to avoid fines)

Opting In and Opting Out

Many companies that collect personal information still require consumers to actively opt out of receiving further marketing communications, usually via an online check box or automated telephone response. In some rare cases, companies still require customers to send in forms (the State of California requires all companies to include a model opt-out form in all privacy statements for state residents). U.S. rules generally stipulate that consumers must have an opt-out choice with respect to marketing communications, such as:

- Telemarketing calls using a live operator
- Faxing to existing customers
- Traditional e-mail
- Third-party sharing for marketing purposes (GLBA)
- Affiliate sharing for marketing purposes (FACTA/FCRA)

In other cases, the law requires companies to assume that consumers don't want to receive marketing material and those that do have the choice of opting in. These requirements can pertain to:

- E-mail and SMS (text messaging) to wireless devices
- Pre-recorded telemarketing messages
- Faxes to consumers with whom a business relationship doesn't exist

---

Key Resources for Learning About Privacy and Marketing

Direct Marketing Association (DMA)
www.the-dma.org
The DMA is a global trade association of businesses and nonprofit organizations using and supporting multichannel direct marketing tools and techniques. DMA advocates industry standards for responsible marketing—both online and offline, promotes relevance as the key to reaching consumers with desirable offers and provides research, education and networking opportunities to improve results throughout the end-to-end direct marketing process. In addition, DMA offers consumers the DMAChoice mail preference service—a way to control the types and volume of direct marketing material that arrives in the mailbox.

Network Advertising Initiative (NAI)
www.networkadvertising.org
The NAI provides voluntary self-regulatory principles for advertisers and tools for consumers to manage their privacy online with regards to marketing messages.

Interactive Advertising Bureau (IAB)
www.iab.net
The IAB comprises more than 460 media and technology companies that are responsible for selling online advertising in the United States. Working with its member companies, the IAB evaluates and recommends standards and practices and fields research on interactive advertising.

American Association of Advertising Agencies (4As)
www.aaaa.org
4As is the national trade association representing the advertising agency business in the United States. See specifically their information about "online behavioral advertising" and the latest industry efforts to create an online icon to educate online consumers about the marketing and advertising techniques being used by retailers and their options to opt out.

California's "Shine the Light" Laws

The state of California has responded to consumer sentiment with some strong privacy-related legislation. Research had shown that, given the choice, 87 percent of consumers asked a company to remove their name and address from marketing lists and 65 percent of consumers online decided not to register at a website because they deemed the privacy policy too complicated or unclear. The state's subsequent "Shine the Light" law requires companies to notify California customers of their right to request that a business disclose how it shares personally identifiable information with other businesses for direct marketing purposes. In addition the California Online Privacy Protection Act requires operators of commercial websites—or online services that collect personally identifiable information on consumers residing in California—to conspicuously post a privacy policy statement containing specified information on its website, and comply with the terms of that policy.

The Advent of Behavioral Advertising

Behavioral advertising is emerging rapidly as an online privacy issue. By using various behind-the-scene tools that track an individual's activity while they browse the Web—such as "scripts" embedded in a Web page's coding—advertisers are able to customize and personalize ads based on the information gleaned. Marketers find this precise pinpointing of potential customers very helpful and point out that consumers receive ads that relate to their specific interests. Consumers, on the other hand, are wary about being "observed" without an opportunity to fully understand the extent of the data being collected or an opportunity to opt out.

Scenario: Analyzing Privacy Impact of a New Marketing Campaign

Here's an example of how privacy-related laws can affect a new marketing campaign.

A financial institution's marketing manager decides to run a co-marketing e-mail campaign with a third party. The manager generates a customer list (including names and both postal and e-mail addresses) and shares it with the third party so that the two companies can combine their data and develop an optimal list. The marketing manager must consider:

CAN-SPAM laws (see the following section for details) mandate that:

- The marketing manager cannot share the e-mail address with a third party unless customers have consented to the sharing of this information with a third party
- Both companies must "scrub" their list and remove the information of customers who have opted out

GLBA laws mandate that:

- Customers who have opted out of sharing their information must be excluded from the lists
- The financial institution must comply with its own privacy statement and only use and share the information as explained in its privacy statement

---

The following sections provide more details about the primary protections against unsolicited marketing communications.

CAN-SPAM

The U.S. Congress passed the Controlling the Assault of Non-Solicited Pornography and Marketing Act (CAN-SPAM) in 2003 to address the rapid growth in unwanted commercial electronic mail messages. The law requires senders of marketing e-mails to comply with certain requirements by allowing recipients to opt out of receiving future e-mail marketing messages. It also encourages businesses that may unwittingly assist senders of spam (for example, Internet service providers) to assist the FTC in identifying such spammers.

Why Does the Law Exist?
CAN-SPAM was federal legislators' response to the privacy violations caused by unsolicited e-mail advertising. With the ever-increasing use of e-mail communications by marketers, consumers experienced a dramatic rise in the number of unwanted messages ("spam") they received. Not only are spam e-mails inconvenient, annoying and time-consuming to deal with, but they also affect the performance of computer systems and pose security threats. In addition, because spam consumes electronic storage space on their systems, recipients and Internet service providers experience a financial impact.

Who Is Covered by this Law?
CAN-SPAM legislation applies to any individual or organization that advertises products or services via electronic mail whether to or from the United States.

What Types of Information Are Covered?
Transmission of "commercial electronic mail messages," defined as e-mail messages whose primary purpose is advertising or promoting a product or service.

What Is Required or Prohibited?
The CAN-SPAM legislation prohibits

- False or deceptive messages or headers
- E-mail recipients from suing spammers or filing class-action lawsuits

The law requires that marketers:

- Include a working return e-mail address
- Include a physical address
- Identify messages as commercial in nature
- Offer a clear and conspicuous opt-out mechanism

- Process opt-outs within 10 days
- Follow additional FTC rules
- Follow special FCC rules for messages to wireless devices

Spam to Cell Phones and Wireless Devices

The Federal Communications Commission (FCC) maintains a directory of domains associated with cell phones and wireless devices—opt-in consent required to send commercial messages to addresses in these domains. The consent form must include statements that the individual:

- Agrees to receive mobile service commercial messages (MSCMs) sent to the wireless device from an identified sender
- May be charged by the wireless provider in connection with receiving such messages
- May revoke authorization at any time

The sender cannot charge any fees in connection with the consent or revocation process and must comply with other process and format rules.

Who Enforces the Law?

CAN-SPAM is enforced by the FTC, state attorneys general, Internet service providers (ISPs) and other federal agencies for special categories of spammers (such as banks). An individual running a mail server might be able to sue as an ISP, but this would likely be cost-prohibitive and would not necessarily hold up in court. Individuals can also sue using state laws dealing with fraud, such as the Commonwealth of Virginia law that gives standing based on actual damages, in effect limiting enforcement to ISPs.

What Happens If Our Organization Doesn't Comply?

The FTC aggressively enforces CAN-SPAM and has so far levied fines and penalties on violators to the following extent:

- More than $3 million in fines and civil penalties for improperly labeled sexually explicit content
- More than $5 million for misleading e-mail content
- More than $1 million for misleading headers (in "From" and "Subject" lines)
- Almost $1 million for failure to offer or honor a consumer's opt-out choice—even with no deception at all

---

Key Resources for Understanding CAN-SPAM

Full Text of CAN-SPAM Legislation
www.ftc.gov/os/caselist/0723041/canspam.pdf

FCC Information About CAN-SPAM
www.fcc.gov/cgb/policy/canspam.html

TELEMARKETING SALES RULE (TSR)

The Telemarketing Sales Rule (TSR), first issued by the FTC in 1995, gives effect to the Telemarketing and Consumer Fraud and Abuse Prevention Act. The U.S. Congress enacted the law to help protect consumers from telemarketing deception and abuse. The law directs the FTC to prescribe rules that prohibit deceptive telemarketing acts or practices. TSR also includes provisions that require many organizations to subscribe to the National Do Not Call Registry. Managed by the FTC and created in 2003, the National Do Not Call Registry is a list of phone numbers submitted by consumers who wish to limit the number of unsolicited and intrusive telemarketing calls they receive.

Key Resources for Understanding the Telemarketing Sales Rule

FTC – Business Compliance with the Telemarketing Sales Rule
www.ftc.gov/bcp/edu/pubs/business/marketing/bus27.shtm

FTC – Details of the Rule
www.ftc.gov/bcp/rulemaking/tsr/tsrrulemaking/index.shtm

Why Does the Law Exist?

Supported by new electronic call technology such as auto-dialing, the practice of telemarketing has increased rapidly during the last several decades. Consumers have frequently reported the use of deceptive or abusive tactics by telemarketers. This legislation gives consumers added privacy protections and defenses against unscrupulous telemarketers and help consumers tell the difference between fraudulent and legitimate telemarketing.

The FTC's decision to create the National Do Not Call Registry was the culmination of a comprehensive, three-year review of the Telemarketing Sales Rule, as well as the FTC's extensive experience enforcing the rule in the previous seven years. The FTC also held numerous workshops, meetings and briefings to solicit feedback from interested parties and considered more than 64,000 public comments, most of which favored creating the registry.

Who Is Covered by this Law?

TSR requires sellers and telemarketers, whether making outbound calls to or receiving inbound calls from consumers, to provide certain material information before the consumer pays for the goods or services that are the subject of the sales offer. Organizations, businesses or individuals that conduct phone solicitations or hire third-party companies to do the job must comply with the rule. There are exemptions and partial exemptions for certain organizations. For example, a nonprofit organization or charity may make calls on its own behalf and a company may contact consumers with whom it has existing business relationships and who have not opted out. However, these organizations must also honor individual requests not to receive future calls and must have a written process in place (including training of personnel) to ensure compliance.

Key Resources for Managing Do-Not-Call Registries and Lists

National registry
If your organization telemarkets products or services to consumers via unsolicited phone calls, federal law requires that you subscribe to the national registry. If your organization is exempt (for example, it is a charitable institution or nonprofit), then you do not have to subscribe, but you can nevertheless, if you wish, use the registry, follow good practice and "scrub" your call lists.

For complete details of this government initiative and details of the rule, see:

- www.telemarketing.donotcall.gov
- www.ftc.gov/bcp/rulemaking/tsr/tsrrulemaking/index.shtm
- www.fcc.gov/cgb/donotcall (fact sheet)

State lists
In the wake of the federal legislation, many states have instituted their own do-not-call laws. Identify the states in which your organization operates and check their requirements.

For state-specific information, see:
www.the-dma.org/government/donotcalllists.shtml

Corporate
Your organization will be best served if it centrally manages its own DNC list so that all business units draw from and contribute to the same database. However, outsourcing is also a possibility; there are several third-party companies that offer centralized DNC management services and help you meet your own DNC obligations.

What Types of Information Are Covered?

The rule covers information that would likely affect a person's choice of goods or services or the person's decision to make a charitable contribution. More simply, it is information a consumer needs to make an informed decision about whether to purchase goods or services or make a donation.

The do-not-call (DNC) provisions of the rule cover any plan, program or campaign to sell goods or services through interstate phone calls. This includes calls by telemarketers who solicit consumers, often on behalf of third-party sellers. It also includes sellers who are paid to provide, offer to provide or arrange to provide goods or services to consumers. The National

Do Not Call Registry also covers intrastate telemarketing calls under the FCC's rules.

Some types of calls are not covered by the National Do Not Call Registry. TSR exemptions include:

- Nonprofits, political organizations, public opinion pollers and charities calling on their own behalf (however, if a third-party telemarketer calls on behalf of a charity, a consumer may ask not to receive any more calls)
- Calling lists of consumers with existing business relationships (for example: it's acceptable to call existing customers who have bought from you within the past 18 months as well as prospects within 90 days of an inquiry, unless they tell you not to call)
- Inbound calls, providing you don't affirmatively upsell without the customer's oral consent (their consent allows you to proceed even if they are on your organization's do-not-call list)
- Most business-to-business calls
- Companies not subject to FTC jurisdiction (but FCC and state attorneys general have jurisdiction over these)

What Is Required or Prohibited?

TSR requires sellers and telemarketers to provide certain information either orally or in writing. This information includes the following:

Basic TSR Requirements for Outbound Sales Calls	Explanation
Provide identity of seller	The seller is the entity that provides goods or services to the consumer in exchange for payment. The identity of the telemarketer, or person making the call, need not be disclosed if it is different from the identity of the seller. If the seller commonly uses a trade name that is registered with appropriate state authorities, it is fine to use that name instead of the seller's legal name.
Explain purpose is to sell goods or services	TSR requires that the purpose of the call be disclosed truthfully and promptly to consumers. How you describe or explain the purpose of the call is up to you, as long as your description is not likely to mislead consumers. For example, it would be untruthful to state that a call is a "courtesy call," if it's a sales call.
Describe nature of goods or services offered	This is a brief description of items you are offering for sale.
Explain prize promotion rules, if applicable	If the consumer asks, you must disclose—without delay—instructions on how to enter the prize promotion without paying any money or purchasing any goods or services.

Additional stipulations of the Telemarketing Sales Rule require the seller to:

- Screen names against the National Do Not Call Registry (see below for more details)
- Display caller-ID information
- Comply with special rules for automated dialers
- Limit abandonment of calls
- Confine predictive dialing to the required short time window
- Manage requests by anyone (including from existing customers) to opt out of any future marketing and sales call (data in the corporate do-not-call list)
- Call only between the hours of 8 a.m. and 9 p.m.
- Respect requests not to be called back
- Retain records for 24 months

You must also overlay federal standards with any state laws that apply to your operations. If you are a national company, it is always best (unless your organization can easily manage several different standards concurrently) to set the bar high by using the strictest applicable law as your standard. This may well be a specific state law.

State Telemarketing Rules—Not Preempted by TSR

The majority of U.S. states have telemarketing rules. For example:

- Telemarketers must register and often post bond
- Process rules may differ from TSR (for example: AR, CT, IN, KY, LA, MA, MN, MS, NM, FL, SD, TX and UT have more limited calling times)
- Callers must respect state do-not-call lists (or DMA-TPS) in AK, CO, CT, FL, ID, IN, KY, LA, MA, MN, MS, MO, OK, PA, TN, TX, VT, WI and WY
- Indiana: No exceptions for existing business relationship
- Several states, including IN, exempt licensed sales professionals

Enforcement is via private rights of action and statutory damages.

Who Enforces the Law?

TSR gives the FTC and state attorneys general law enforcement tools to combat telemarketing fraud. The FTC actively enforces this legislation, including the rules of the National Do Not Call Registry, as do many state attorneys general. In addition, the FCC enforces this legislation under a similar regulation for financial services firms.

What Happens If Our Organization Doesn't Comply?

Telemarketing laws are strictly enforced; there is no defense for infractions. Failure to provide any of the required information truthfully and in a clear and conspicuous manner before the consumer pays for the goods or services offered is a deceptive telemarketing act or practice that violates TSR. The violation subjects a seller or telemarketer (including third parties that call on behalf of a charity but continue to call in spite of a request not to) to a civil penalty of $16,000 for each violation. Between 2003 and 2008, the FTC levied fines, penalties and redress amounts totaling $228,607,742. The violations included:

- Ignoring do-not-call requests
- Prerecorded messages
- Use of predictive dialers
- Failure to honor opt outs based on state, federal or corporate lists
- Misleading claims

During that same period, the FCC levied $3,150,000 in fines for TSR violations.

National Do Not Call Registry at a Glance

If your organization is required by law to comply with the National Do Not Call Registry, you must subscribe. The law's provisions require you to:

- Create a profile the first time you access the registry and provide certain limited identifying information, such as:
  - Company name and address
  - Contact person
  - Contact person's telephone number and e-mail address
  - Identify that seller-client on whose behalf you are accessing the registry
- Pay an annual subscription fee (the annual fee is $55 per area code of data (after five) up to a maximum annual fee of $15,058)
- Synchronize your lists with an updated version of the registry at least every 31 days
- Incorporate and manage corporate do-not-call requests into your monthly process for ensuring that all opt-out requests are recorded and honored

It's against the law to call any:

- Number on the registry (unless the seller has an established business relationship with the consumer whose number is being called or the consumer has given written agreement to be called)
- Person whose number is within a given area code unless the seller has first subscribed to and accessed the portion of the registry that includes numbers within that area code and paid the annual fee, if required (telemarketers must make sure that their seller-clients have paid for access to the registry before placing any telemarketing calls on their behalf)
- Person who has requested to be placed on your corporate do-not-call list

---

JUNK FAX PREVENTION ACT

Unsolicited fax communications with marketing messages are strictly regulated by federal legislation and individual states have different opt-in/opt-out requirements. Infractions of the federal law incur liability and are met with potentially hefty fines. Sending unsolicited marketing material via postal mail is not regulated, but it behooves your organization to follow best practices and respect the wishes of consumers who do not wish to receive these types of communications.

The U.S. Congress first addressed the issue of junk faxes in the Telephone Consumer Protection Act of 1991. Although this legislation dealt broadly with larger issues of nuisance telemarketing tactics, it included provisions making it illegal for any person to send an unsolicited advertisement to a fax machine.

Why Does the Law Exist?
Many consumers complained about the nuisance value and costs associated with receiving unsolicited marketing messages via their fax machines. As the problem grew in volume and scope, U.S. legislators acted to prevent or at least minimize such practices.

Who Is Covered by this Law?
The law covers any organization or individual who sends unsolicited marketing material to consumers' fax machines. There are no exceptions to the rule.

What Types of Information Are Covered?
Electronic communications transmitted to consumers' fax machines or computers in the case of computer-to-computer faxes. Only in the case of unsolicited messages via fax and mobile phones are you required by law to offer consumers the chance to opt in. However, offering consumers and customers the opportunity to opt in and actively choose to receive marketing communications is always good practice. This includes text messages and social media. For one thing, you quickly find out which consumers are particularly open to hearing your marketing messages—vital information for running successful campaigns. Additionally, you have impressed those consumers who don't want to hear from you via particular media. By respecting their privacy, you've likely increased the chances of winning their business via other channels.

What Is Required or Prohibited?
The regulations prohibit the sending of unsolicited commercial faxes. The law permits organizations to send faxes to consumers who have:

- Provided consent
- An existing business relationship, as long as the sender provides an opt-out option and obtains consent

Several states—including California, Michigan, Montana, Tennessee and Texas—require opt-in for faxes, though the Telephone Consumers Protection Act **does** preempt state laws.

Who Enforces the Law?

The FCC and state attorneys general enforce JFPA legislation. There is also a private right of action available to consumers.

What Happens If Our Organization Doesn't Comply?

The law authorizes the recipient of a fax sent in violation of the statute (or a regulation promulgated under the statute) to sue the sender in state court to enjoin further violation, recover for actual monetary losses from such a violation—$500 in statutory damages for each violation (whichever is greater)—or both.

The FCC enforces aggressively, and private lawsuits are frequent and expensive for violators. During the first quarter of 2008, fines totaling $3.16 million were levied against violating companies.

Key Resources for Understanding the Junk Fax Prevention Act

FCC – Details of Act, Including Background and Provisions
http://fjallfoss.fcc.gov/edocs_public/attachmatch/FCC-06-42A1.pdf

---

DRIVER'S PRIVACY PROTECTION ACT

The Driver's Privacy Protection Act (DPPA) was originally enacted in 1994 to protect the privacy of personal information assembled by State Departments of Motor Vehicles (DMVs).

Why Does the Law Exist?

The DPPA was passed in reaction to a series of abuses of drivers' personal information held by the government. The 1989 death of actress Rebecca Schaeffer was a prominent example of such abuse. In that case, a private investigator hired by an obsessed fan was able to obtain Rebecca Schaeffer's address through her California motor vehicle record. The fan used her address information to stalk and kill her. Other incidents cited by congress included a ring of Iowa home robbers who targeted victims by writing down the license plates of expensive cars and obtaining home address information from the state's department of motor vehicles.

Who Is Covered by this Law?

The DPPA covers the Department of Motor Vehicles in every U.S. state.

What Types of Information Are Covered?

The law restricts how personal information is released. The DPPA defines personal information as information that identifies a person. Personal information includes:

- Photograph
- Social Security number
- Driver identification number
- Name
- Address (but not the 5-digit ZIP code)
- Telephone number
- Medical information
- Disability information

Personal information **does not** include information about traffic accidents, traffic violations or the status of a driver license.

What Is Required or Prohibited?

The DPPA prohibits any state DMV (or any officer, employee or contractor) from releasing or using personal information about an individual obtained by the department in connection with a motor vehicle record.

The legislation requires state DMVs to:

- Protect privacy of personal information contained in an individual's motor vehicle record
- Get permission from individuals before their personal motor vehicle record may be sold or released to third-party marketers

The act has a number of exceptions. For example, federal, state and local agencies can obtain information from a state DMV in order to carry out their functions, such as proceedings where a motor vehicle was involved.

Who Enforces the Law?

The law is enforced by the U.S. Department of Justice and Office of the Attorney General. State attorneys general also have jurisdiction, and a private right of action exists. Federal civil cause of action is provided for persons whose personal information is obtained, disclosed or used for a purpose not permitted under the DPPA (see 18 U.S.C. Section 2723-24).

What Happens If Our Organization Doesn't Comply?

The act establishes criminal fines for noncompliance and establishes a civil cause of action for drivers against those who unlawfully obtain their information. There are also civil liabilities for violations of the DPPA.

ELECTRONIC COMMUNICATIONS PRIVACY ACT

The U.S. Congress enacted the Electronic Communications Privacy Act (ECPA) in 1986 to extend government restrictions on wiretaps from telephone calls to include transmissions of electronic data by computer.

Why Does the Law Exist?
The development of new computer technologies and the increase in electronic communication—the "wireless revolution"—required legislation to protect personal privacy and stipulate conditions in which access by government agencies is lawful.

Who Is Covered by this Law?
The law covers all government agencies and private organizations that collect personal data through wire, oral or electronic means for the purposes of surveillance or investigation.

What Types of Information Are Covered?
For the purpose of this legislation, **electronic communication** refers to any transfer of signs, signals, writing, images, sounds, data or intelligence of any nature transmitted in whole or in part by a wire, radio, electromagnetic, photoelectronic or photooptical system that affects interstate or foreign commerce. It **does not** include:

- Any electronic or oral communication
- Any communication made through a tone-only paging device
- Any communication from a tracking device
- Electronic funds transfer information stored by a financial institution in a communications system used for the electronic storage and transfer of funds

What Is Required or Prohibited?
The provisions of ECPA specify the circumstances in which it's lawful for government agencies and employers to access private information through electronic surveillance. The legislation's statutes:

- Protect the privacy of the contents of files stored by service providers and of records held about the subscriber by service providers, such as subscriber name, billing records or IP addresses
- Require government entities to obtain a warrant before collecting real-time information, such as dialing, routing and addressing information related to communications (real-time collection of this information is usually done using a pen register or trap and trace device)

**Key Resources for Understanding the
Electronic Communications Privacy Act (ECPA)**

U.S. Department of Justice, Office of Justice Programs—Privacy and Civil Liberties
http://it.ojp.gov/default.aspx?area=privacy&page=1285
This site provides information about ECPA laws, including its titles and amendments. Title
II is referred to as the Stored Communications Act (SCA).

Who Enforces the Law?

There is civil and criminal liability, and either the aggrieved individual or the federal regulators can take action.

What Happens If Our Organization Doesn't Comply?

The law provides a private right of action and authorizes equitable relief, payment of damages (including punitive damages) and attorney's fees and costs. There are statutory damages of $100 for each day of violation or $10,000, whichever is greater.

U.S. LAWS COMPELLING DISCLOSURE

Some U.S. legislation includes provisions that can compel the disclosure of personal information. These include:

- Bank Secrecy Act
- Unifying and Strengthening America by Providing Appropriate Tools Required to Intercept and Obstruct Terrorism Act of 2001 (USA PATRIOT Act)
- Communications Assistance to Law Enforcement Act (CALEA)
- Regulatory reporting requirements (for agencies such as HHS, Federal Food and Drug Administration, and Occupational Safety and Health Administration)
- Civil and criminal subpoenas
- Court rules for e-discovery

Passage of the USA PATRIOT Act legislation resulted in amendments to both the Bank Secrecy Act and the Electronic Communication Privacy Act.

U.S. FEDERAL DISCRIMINATION LAWS IMPACTING PRIVACY

Some U.S. laws that prohibit discrimination also restrict the information that can be collected by employers. These laws include:

U.S. Anti-Discrimination Legislation	What It Does
Equal Pay Act of 1963	Prohibits gender-based wage discrimination
The Civil Rights Act of 1964	Prohibits discrimination due to race, color, religion, sex and national origin
Pregnancy Discrimination Act	Protects women regarding pregnancy and childbirth
Age Discrimination Act of 1967	Protects individuals over 40 years of age
Americans with Disabilities Act (ADA) of 1990	Prohibits discrimination against qualified individuals with disabilities
Genetic Information Nondiscrimination Act (GINA) of 2008	Prohibits discrimination in the area of employment and healthcare benefits, based on genetic information

U.S. PRIVACY LAWS GOVERNING EMPLOYEE RELATIONS

Many pieces of U.S. legislation—not just the laws specifically designed to protect privacy—include provisions for protecting the rights of employees on the job or those seeking a job. These federal and state laws include many that regulate employment and the management of human resources data. In fact, almost every U.S. labor law mandates some form of data collection or data management practice.

Laws that regulate employee benefits management often mandate the collection of medical and other information. Other laws have privacy implications and requirements for data collection and recordkeeping.

U.S. Legislation Affecting Privacy	What It Does
HIPAA Privacy and Security Rules	Regulates use and disclosure of "protected health information" (PHI) by health plans and by an employee's health services
Consolidated Omnibus Budget Reconciliation Act (COBRA)	Requires qualified health plans to provide continued coverage after termination to certain beneficiaries
Employee Retirement Income Security Act (ERISA)	Ensures that employee benefits programs are administered properly
Family and Medical Leave Act (FMLA)	Entitles employees to leave in the event of childbirth or illness

Fair Credit Reporting Act (FCRA)	Regulates the use of consumer reports in the background checks of employees
Fair Labor Standards Act (FLSA)	Establishes a minimum wage and sets standards for fair pay overall
Occupational Safety and Health Act (OSHA)	Regulates workplace safety and record-keeping practices
Immigration Reform and Control Act (IRCA)	Allows for voluntary means for organizations to verify employment eligibility with U.S. Citizenship and Immigration Services and the Social Security Administration
Genetic Information Nondiscrimination Act (GINA) of 2008	Prohibits discrimination in the area of employment and healthcare benefits, based on genetic information

Employers frequently want to know about the background of their employees, existing and prospective. An employer may, for example, want to be sure that an employee qualifies for promotion or advancement. However, FCRA laws provide individuals with certain protections against inappropriate use of their personal information. For example, to use third-party data for screening purposes, an employer must:

- Provide written notice to the applicant that it is obtaining a consumer report
- Obtain written consent from the applicant
- Obtain data from a consumer reporting agency (CRA)—an entity that has taken steps to assure the accuracy and currency of the data
- Certify to the CRA that it has a permissible purpose and has obtained consent

Pertaining to another controversial area of human resources practices, employers should weigh the risks of using search engines or social networking websites to screen prospective employees. In some cases, using these sources may fall under the auspices of the FCRA, particularly if you are using a third party to formally investigate. Additionally, one should never attempt to engineer access to protected content by, for example, deceptively "friending" an individual.

Anti-Discrimination Laws

The anti-discrimination laws strictly restrict the types of information that can be collected during the interview process. For example, an employer cannot ask any questions about an applicant's race, religion, national origin or marital status and must also avoid questions about spouses and relatives, including whether the applicant even has or has had a spouse, children or other dependents. An employer may not require applicants to list all organizations to which they belong.

Restricted Inquiries

During a job interview, employers should avoid asking certain questions, such as those addressed in the table below. If in doubt, always seek your own counsel's opinion.

Area of Inquiry	Examples of Restrictions
Physical characteristics and pregnancy	You can ask questions about an applicant's height and weight only if you can show that all or substantially all employees who fail to meet a height or weight requirement would be unable to perform the job with reasonable safety and efficiency. On the other hand, you may not be able to ask any questions about pregnancy status.
Medical condition and disabilities	While you may be permitted to ask whether and applicant is able to perform the essential functions of the job, with or without reasonable accommodation, you can't ask, for example, about the nature, severity, extent of or treatment of a disability or illness, including mental illness, legal drug use or past addiction to any drug or alcohol.
Citizenship status	You need to clearly state in your application the requirements for a position, including citizenship. You may be able to ask about an applicant's ability to read, write and speak foreign languages, where this relates to job requirements, but you are not allowed to ask whether the applicant is a U.S. citizen, nor can you require the applicant to present a birth certificate or naturalization documents until after hiring, when you complete the Employment Eligibility Verification form (I-9 Form).
Arrest and convictions	You may be able to ask about convictions within the last 10 years for crimes involving behavior that would adversely affect job performance. However, some states prohibit asking about arrests that were not followed by convictions (NY, CT, and WI). Other states' rules vary depending on the type of job.

PRIVACY AND THIRD-PARTY CONTRACTS

An organization cannot contract away its privacy-related liability to the third parties it deals with; in fact, federal regulations such as HIPAA and the GLBA require specific contract provisions when the organization discloses certain personal information to a third party. At best, as part of the contract process you may be able to negotiate favorable indemnification provisions. Generally, it's difficult to make your vendor your insurer.

GLBA Contract Components

Under GLBA requirements, a contract with third parties requires:

- Use of contract language to protect customer information
- Outline of duties of service providers
- Establishment of oversight procedures

In addition, contracts must specify that service providers:

- Have appropriate administrative, technical and physical safeguards
- Are obliged to maintain the security of customer information
- Take appropriate action (including notifying the organization) to address incidents of unauthorized access
- Do not use information for any reason other than providing the contracted service
- Implement appropriate measures designed to protect against unauthorized access to or use of customer information that could result in substantial harm or inconvenience to any customer
- Implement proper disposal guidelines

For more detailed information about GLBA requirements, please see "Gramm-Leach-Bliley Act", p. 27.

HIPAA Contract Components

The HIPAA Privacy Rule regulates covered entities, including what it defines as business associates. Among the provisions of the recent Health Information Technology for Economic and Clinical Health (HITECH) legislation, all third-party companies (including business associates) are accountable to HIPAA requirements.

The confidentiality and protection of protected health information should be part of all general contract terms, but there are additional requirements for business associates. The Privacy Rule requires covered entities to include specific provisions in agreements with their business associates. Contracts must include provisions to:

- Safeguard protected health information that is shared with a third party
- Address how covered entities may share this information with business associates
- Specify that the business associate must amend protected health information in such records (or copies) when requested by the covered entity
- Require business associate to provide an accounting of disclosures upon request from individuals

Organizations should also consider including contract provisions to handle breaches. For example, an organization can require a third party to:

- Notify the organization immediately when a breach is identified
- Provide notice and credit monitoring services for all affected individuals
- Manage the breach
- Comply with all applicable laws

SELF-REGULATION BY THE PAYMENT CARD INDUSTRY

The Payment Card Industry Data Security Standard (PCI DSS) is a worldwide information security standard defined and maintained by the Payment Card Industry Security Standards Council. The council was created by five major credit card brands—Visa, MasterCard, American Express, Discover and JCB. The standard

- was created to help all entities involved in the credit and debit card issuance, acceptance and processing stream prevent credit card loss, theft and resulting fraud through increased controls around data and its exposure to compromise;
- applies to all organizations that collect, process, store or transmit cardholder information from any credit card branded with the logo of one of the card brands, and
- is a contractual standard.

Annual Validation of Compliance

Organizations can validate compliance either internally or externally, depending on the volume of card transactions the organization is handling. Regardless of the size of the organization, it must assess compliance annually. Organizations handling large volumes of transactions must have their compliance assessed by an independent assessor known as a Qualified Security Assessor (QSA), while companies handling smaller volumes have the option of self-certification via a Self-Assessment Questionnaire (SAQ). In some regions, these SAQs still require signoff by a QSA for submission.

Enforcement of PCI DSS

Enforcement of compliance is done by the bodies holding relationships with the in-scope organizations. "In-scope" refers to the level of transaction volume that an organization processes. The volume an organization transacts determines the compliance requirements of the PCI. (For a summary of requirements by level, see appendix, *PCI Compliance Requirements by Level of Transaction Volume*, p. 180.)

For organizations processing Visa or MasterCard transactions, compliance is enforced by the organization's acquirer. (The acquirer is also referred to as the "merchant bank" and is the intermediary that facilitates the charging of the credit card and payment to the merchant.) Organizations accepting American Express cards deal directly with American Express or its compliance service provider. In the case of third-party suppliers, such as hosting companies that have business relationships with in-scope organizations, enforcement of compliance falls to the in-scope company, as neither the acquirers nor the card brands will have contractual relationships in place to mandate compliance. Noncompliant companies that maintain a relationship with one or more of the card brands, either directly or through an acquirer, risk losing their ability to process credit card payments and being audited and/or fined.

Level/ Tier	Merchant Criteria	Validation Requirements
1	Merchants processing over 6 million Visa transactions annually (all channels) or global merchants identified as Level 1 by any Visa region	• Annual Report on Compliance (ROC) by Qualified Security Assessor (QSA) • Quarterly network scan by Approved Scan Vendor (ASV) • Attestation of Compliance Form
2	Merchants processing 1 million to 6 million Visa transactions annually (all channels)	• Annual Self-Assessment Questionnaire (SAQ) • Quarterly network scan by ASV • Attestation of Compliance Form
3	Merchants processing 20,000 to 1 million Visa e-commerce transactions annually	• Annual SAQ • Quarterly network scan by ASV • Attestation of Compliance Form

For more detailed information about PCI requirements, see appendix, *PCI Compliance Requirements by Level of Transaction Volume,* p. 180.

U.S. STATE PRIVACY LEGISLATION

State Constitutions
Although the federal constitution does not explicitly provide a right of privacy, some states have incorporated an individual right of privacy into their own constitutions. For example, as already mentioned, California provides for a right of privacy in its state constitution.

State Laws
Some states have laws designed to regulate

- unfair competition and prohibit unfair and deceptive acts or practices similar to those prohibited by FTC privacy regulations;
- breach notification—44 states have laws requiring a company to provide notice if the confidentiality and security of personal information is breached.

Some states build on the GLBA's principles of privacy rights, particularly in the insurance sector with regard to rules for

- notice;
- sharing;
- security, and
- disposal.

The corresponding state laws are very similar to the GLBA laws in these areas, but with two additions. Several states 1) provide consumer access and correction rights to their information and 2) cover health-related information.

For a list of security breach laws by state, see appendix, *United States Information Security Laws ~ map*, p. 210, and *U.S. Information Security Laws*, p. 230.

INTERNATIONAL COUNTRY-SPECIFIC PRIVACY LAWS

A large percentage of organizations based in the United States carry out some kind of transactions with customers and partners overseas. Therefore, it's important that your privacy office understands the legal framework of any applicable countries and blocs of nations. The following sections take a closer look at two major privacy laws and frameworks—the EU Data Protection Directive and Canada's Personal Information Protection and Electronic Documents Act (PIPEDA)

For more information about specific resources for understanding privacy abroad, please see appendix, *Key Resources for Understanding Privacy Initiatives in Other Countries*, p. 182, and *Privacy Legislation Worldwide*, p. 205.

EUROPEAN UNION DATA PROTECTION DIRECTIVE

In 1998, the European Union (EU) enacted the EU Data Protection Directive to establish the ". . . protection of individuals with regard to the processing of personal data and on the free movement of such data." (Note that "personal data" is referred to in the United States as "personally identifiable information," the term used throughout this book.) The legislation in the directive applies to all 27 EU member states located primarily in Europe. The member states are Austria, Belgium, Bulgaria, Cyprus, Czech Republic, Denmark, Estonia, Finland, France, Germany, Greece, Hungary, Ireland, Italy, Latvia, Lithuania, Luxembourg, Malta, Netherlands, Poland, Portugal, Romania, Slovakia, Slovenia, Spain, Sweden and the United Kingdom. Being an EU member state places a country under binding laws in exchange for representation in the EU's lawmaking and judicial bodies.

Why Does the Directive Exist?
The EU Data Protection Directive has two primary goals:

- A uniform level of protection for the personal data of EU citizens
- More liberal flow of data between the member states

The directive ensures the harmonization of the data protection laws of the member states, and uniform application and enforcement throughout the EU.

Who Is Covered by this Directive?

The directive covers any operation that processes in any way personally identifiable information. The following definitions apply:

- An identifiable person is someone who can be identified directly, based on the data received or collected, or who can be indirectly identified by compiling and matching the data in particular by reference to an identification number or to one or more factors specific to their physical, physiological, mental, economic and cultural or social identity.
- Processing refers to any operation that affects personal data such as collecting, recording, organizing, storing, adapting, retrieving, consulting, indexing, combining, blocking, disseminating and deleting. Processing can be performed by automated means, but manually processed data is also included.

The directive distinguishes between those who control personally identifiable information and those who process it: data controllers and data processors respectively. (Note that pharmaceutical companies that conduct clinical trials may use a hybrid of these two roles.)

Operator Type	Definition
Data controller	• Individual, public authority, agency or other body that determines purposes and means of processing personal data. The data controller is 　○ Legally responsible for ensuring the rights of data subject are protected in accordance with the Directive 　○ Subject to several Directive-imposed duties 　○ Responsible for purposes for which data is collected and ensuring it is processed in a specific, legitimate way and not further processed in a way incompatible with those purpose A data controller has specific duties 　○ Notifying the individual 　○ Providing access to the information if requested by the individual 　○ Correcting any inaccurate information 　○ Notifying the national supervisory authority of the controller's processing activities (referred to as a "registration")

Data processor	An individual, public authority, agency or other body that processes personal data on behalf of a data controller. Personal data may be processed only if the data subject has given his or her unambiguous consent and the processing is necessary for • performance of a contract; • compliance with a legal obligation; • protection of vital interests of the data subject; • performance of a task carried out in the public interest; • purposes of legitimate interests pursued by controller, except where such interests are overridden by interests in the fundamental rights and freedoms of the data subject.

What Types of Information Are Covered?

The directive grants all individuals certain rights regarding the protection of their personal data. Laws regulate all personal data (even name and work address) with additional rules for "sensitive information." The directive also covers employee data covered by national data protection and labor laws.

What Is Required or Prohibited?

EU Data Protection Directive	Details
Requires that ...	• Personal data is ◦ processed fairly and lawfully; ◦ collected for a specific purpose, which is determined before the data is collected; ◦ adequate and relevant to the purpose of the processing, without being excessive; ◦ accurate, and ◦ kept only as long as necessary • An entity implement both technical and procedural security measures to protect personal data from the risk of accidental or unlawful destruction or accidental loss, alteration and unauthorized disclosure or access • Data subjects are able to ◦ access their personal information and make objections; ◦ request and obtain rectification, erasure or blocking of data, the processing of which does not comply with the provisions of the directive.

Explicitly prohibits . . .	• Processing of sensitive information (defined as data revealing racial or ethnic origin, political opinions, religious beliefs, philosophical beliefs, trade union membership, health and sexual orientation) • Transfer of personal data to countries that do not provide adequate levels of protection for personal data

Transferring Personal Data Outside the EU and Switzerland

There are three ways to transfer personal data outside of the European Economic Area:

- Safe Harbor frameworks (applying to both the EU and Switzerland) under which U.S. organizations may voluntarily adhere to a set of data protection principles recognized by the European Commission and the Federal Data Protection and Information Commission of Switzerland as providing adequate protection for personal data. The Safe Harbor frameworks
  - establish a legal basis for transfer of personal data from the EU to the United States;
  - enforce compliance via the Federal Trade Commission or the Department of Transportation (with respect to airlines)
- Binding corporate rules
- Model contracts approved by the EU

Note: The EU–United States and United States–Switzerland Safe Harbors do not apply to financial services companies. For more information about Safe Harbor, see below.

Exemptions to the prohibition of international transfers include situations where

- there is unambiguous consent of the data subject;
- transfer is necessary for the performance of a contract between the data subject and the data controller, and
- transfer is necessary or legally required on important public interest grounds or for the establishment, exercise or defense of legal claims.

Who Enforces the Directive?

Enforcement of the EU Data Protection Directive is the responsibility of country-specific supervisory and legislative authorities. The directive requires that the governments of member states implement new, or strengthen existing, policies and laws to back up the directive's legislative requirements.

What Happens If Our Organization Doesn't Comply?

Fines and penalties are levied according the corresponding legislation in force in the individual EU nations. In addition, you may be prohibited from transferring personally identifiable information outside the EU.

United States – European Union Safe Harbor

U.S. organizations are assured of Safe Harbor benefits from the date that they self-certify adherence to the principles with the U.S. Department of Commerce (DoC). These principles reflect the FTC's Fair Information Practice Principles. For more details, please see "FTC's Fair Information Practice Principles," p. 39.

Key Resources for United States—EU and Swiss Safe Harbor Frameworks

U.S. Federal Government guide for exporters
www.export.gov/safeharbor
This website includes comprehensive information about the Safe Harbor, its principles and how to join it. Resources include an overview, documents, workbook and helpful hints before self-certification.

EUR-Lex: Access to European Union Law
http://eur-lex.europa.eu
This Web site is the official source for EU law. To see the official EU Directive, use the site's simple search function and enter the directive's Celex document number: 32000D0520.

On an annual basis, organizations must send the DoC—via a letter, e-mail or online form and signed by a corporate officer on behalf of the organization—the following information:

- Name of organization, mailing address, e-mail address and telephone and fax numbers
- Description of organization's activities with respect to personal information received from the EU
- Description of organization's privacy policy, including:
  - Public location of policy
  - Effective date
  - Contact office for complaints, access and other issues
  - Specific statutory body with jurisdiction
  - Name of any privacy programs with whom membership exists
  - Method of verification (for example: in-house, third party)
  - Independent recourse mechanism available to investigate unresolved complaints

Verifying and Certifying a Privacy Policy

The organization must ensure that a verification mechanism is in place. A self-assessment verification process must

- indicate organization's published privacy policy regarding personal data received from the EU is accurate, comprehensive, prominently displayed, completely implemented and accessible;
- have procedures for training employees in its implementation and disciplining them

for failure to follow it;

- have internal procedures for periodically conducting objective reviews of compliance, and
- state that the verification self-assessment should be signed by a corporate officer or other authorized representative at least once a year and made available upon request by individuals or in the context of an investigation or a complaint about noncompliance.

An organization must self-certify that its privacy policy adheres to Safe Harbor principles and make sure that

- the statement is available to the public;
- an accurate Web link is included in the Safe Harbor self-certification form

---

Example of Safe Harbor Self-Certification Statement

"An officer of the organization has reviewed this document and believes that compliance with attestations and assertions made about the Safe Harbor privacy practices are true, and privacy practices have been implemented as represented and in accordance with Safe Harbor Principles."

An organization must have in place a dispute resolution mechanism that

- clearly states how consumers who feel that their privacy may have been violated based on the Safe Harbor privacy principles should contact the organization;
- clearly states how the organization will resolve issues and make the dispute resolution mechanism readily available;
- ensures that third-party dispute resolution mechanisms meet basic criteria, including the following elements
  - ready availability of an affordable independent review by which complaints and disputes are investigated and resolved according to the principles
  - damages awarded via applicable law or private-sector initiatives
  - obligations to remedy problems arising out of failure to comply with the principles
  - sufficiently rigorous sanctions to ensure compliance
  - notifications of persistent failures of Safe Harbor organizations to comply with rulings to governmental body with applicable jurisdiction or to the courts as appropriate

CANADA – PERSONAL INFORMATION PROTECTION AND ELECTRONIC DOCUMENTS ACT

Canada's Personal Information Protection and Electronic Documents Act (PIPEDA) of 2000 relates to data privacy. It seeks to protect the privacy of personally identifiable information (PII) and requires organizations to be accountable for how they process personal data.

Why Does the Law Exist?

The legislation supports and promotes consumer trust and electronic commerce by protecting personal information that is collected, used or disclosed in certain circumstances by providing for the use of electronic means to communicate or record information or transactions.

Who Is Covered by this Law?

PIPEDA governs how private-sector organizations collect, use and disclose personal information in the course of commercial business.

What Types of Information Are Covered?

Personal information refers to data about an identifiable individual but does not include the name, title, business address or telephone number of an employee of an organization.

What Is Required or Prohibited?

The law provides individuals with a number of rights and requires organizations to comply with its provisions.

PIPEDA Constituents	Rights and Requirements
Individuals have the right to . . .	• Know why the organization collects, uses or discloses their personal information • Expect the organization to collect, use or disclose personal information reasonably and appropriately and not use it for any purpose other than that to which they have consented • Know who in the organization is responsible for protecting their personal information • Expect the organization to protect information by taking appropriate security measures • Expect personal information an organization holds to be accurate, complete and up-to-date • Obtain access to their personal information and ask for corrections if necessary • Complain about how an organization handles their personal information if they feel their privacy rights have not been respected
Organizations are required to . . .	• Obtain consent when they collect, use or disclose personal information • Supply individuals with a product or service even if they refuse consent for collection, use or disclosure of personal information—unless that information is essential to the transaction • Collect information by fair and lawful means • Have personal information policies that are clear, understandable and readily available

Though the act requires that affected organizations comply with the Canadian Standards Association's Model Code for the Protection of Personal Information, there are a number of exceptions where information can be collected, used and disclosed without the consent of the individual. Examples include for investigations related to law enforcement or in the event of an emergency. There are also exceptions to the general rule that an individual be given access to his or her personal information. Also, be sure to check provincial laws; they can be stronger than the national standard.

Who Enforces the Law?

PIPEDA does not create an automatic right to sue for violations of the law's obligations. Instead, PIPEDA follows an ombudsman model in which complaints are taken to the Office of the Privacy Commissioner of Canada. The commissioner is required to investigate the complaint and to produce a report at its conclusion. The report is not binding on the parties but is more of a recommendation. The commissioner does not have any powers to order compliance, award damages or levy penalties. The organization complained about does not have to follow the recommendations. The complainant, with the report in hand, can then take the matter to the Federal Court of Canada. The responding organization cannot take the matter to the courts, because the report is not a decision and PIPEDA does not explicitly grant the responding organization the right to do so.

What Happens If Our Organization Doesn't Comply?

PIPEDA provides a complainant the right to apply to the Federal Court of Canada for a hearing with respect to the subject matter of the complaint. The court has the power to order the organization to correct its practices, publicize the steps it will take to correct its practices and award damages.

Key Resources for Understanding the Personal Information Protection and Electronic Documents Act (PIPEDA) of Canada

Full Text (Bilingual) of PIPEDA Legislation
http://laws.justice.gc.ca/PDF/Statute/P/P-8.6.pdf

Resource for Canadians about PIPEDA
www.pipedainfo.com/
This is PIPEDA's own information website. It includes comprehensive resources for understanding the legislation.

IAPP Reference Article by Kris Klein for Canada-Related Privacy Issues
www.privacyassociation.org/store/product/425639fa-29c5-406c-8502-cbbdcf2949cd

---

PRIVACY INITIATIVES OF INTERNATIONAL ECONOMIC BLOCS

There are two major initiatives by economic trading blocs—APEC and OECD—to promulgate principles and practices to protect personally identifiable information while inspiring consumer confidence and promoting commerce.

APEC Privacy Framework

The countries that make up the collective economies of Asia-Pacific Economic Cooperation (APEC), including the United States, have created a framework of guidelines and recommended practices for commercial enterprises in the realm of privacy protection. The FTC has recently alerted participants that it will enforce the APEC framework, presumably under its authority to regulate unfair and deceptive trade practices. The member economies

- recognize the importance of protecting information privacy and maintaining information flows among economies in the Asia Pacific region and among their trading partners;
- acknowledge that the potential of electronic commerce cannot be realized without government and business cooperation to develop and implement technologies and policies, which build trust and confidence in safe, secure and reliable communication, information and delivery systems and which address issues including privacy;
- understand that a lack of consumer trust and confidence in the privacy and security of online transactions and information networks is one element that may prevent member economies from gaining all of the benefits of electronic commerce;
- realize that a key part of efforts to improve consumer confidence and ensure the growth of electronic commerce must be cooperation to balance and promote both effective information privacy protection and the free flow of information in the Asia-Pacific region, and
- endorse the principles-based APEC Privacy Framework as an important tool in encouraging the development of appropriate information privacy protections and ensuring the free flow of information in the Asia-Pacific region.

The APEC Privacy Framework recognizes the importance of

- developing appropriate privacy protections for personal information, particularly from the harmful consequences of unwanted intrusions and the misuse of personal information;
- recognizing the free flow of information as being essential for both developed and developing market economies to sustain economic and social growth;
- enabling global organizations that collect, access, use or process data in APEC member economies to develop and implement uniform approaches within their organizations for global access to and use of personal information;

- enabling enforcement agencies to fulfill their mandate to protect information privacy, and
- advancing international mechanisms to promote and enforce information privacy and to maintain the continuity of information flows among APEC economies and with their trading partners.

OECD Privacy Guidelines

The OECD recommends that member countries

- take into account in their domestic legislation the principles concerning the protection of privacy and individual liberties set forth in the OECD guidelines;
- endeavor to remove or avoid creating, in the name of privacy protection, unjustified obstacles to transborder flows of personal data;
- cooperate in the implementation of the guidelines, and
- agree as soon as possible on specific procedures of consultation and cooperation for the application of the guidelines

---

Key Resources for Privacy Initiatives Among Economic Blocs

APEC Fact Sheet
www.apec.org/en/About-us/About-APEC/Fact-Sheets/~/media/Files/AboutUs/Factsheet/FS_CPEA_020710.ashx
This document about APEC Cross-border Privacy Enforcement Arrangement includes information about the APEC Privacy Framework.

OECD Guidelines on the Protection of Privacy and Transborder Flows of Personal Data
www.oecd.org/document/18/0,2340,en_2649_34255_1815186_1_1_1_1,00.html

---

PRIVACY INITIATIVES IN OTHER NATIONS

Some countries, such as **Argentina, Australia** and **Japan** have already developed national privacy policies and enacted legislation to back them up. As individual economies recognize the importance of promoting commerce while at the same time protecting the personally identifiable information of individual consumers, more legislative initiatives will develop around the globe in the coming years.

Individual cultures may take a very different approach to the protection of personal information, and not every nation shares Western values in this respect. In any case, your privacy office will need to analyze and understand the privacy policies and laws of any country in which your organization operates or carries out transactions. For more information about country-specific approaches, see key online resources listed in the appendix, *Resources for Understanding Privacy Initiatives in Other Countries*, p. 182, and *Privacy Legislation Worldwide*, p. 205.

CHAPTER 3

Developing a Privacy Program

Chapter 2 introduced the various elements of the legal framework that may apply to your organization and within which your privacy office will have to work. This chapter provides you with an understanding of what it takes to get a privacy program off the ground or to review and enhance an existing program. The topics include everything from the initial thinking you'll need to do to the nuts and bolts of operating a privacy program day to day.

STARTING WITH THE BIG PICTURE

The following section will help you think about the first steps:

- Creating a mission statement
- Determining objectives
- Developing privacy strategies

CREATING A MISSION STATEMENT

A privacy mission statement is the compass that helps keep all aspects of your privacy operations on course. In just a few clear sentences, it communicates to stakeholders across all your different lines of business—from legal to human resources to sales and marketing—where the organization stands on privacy. Employees must know how to respond when their daily activities intersect with the privacy realm; how to comply with often complex and changing regulatory requirements, and how the value of privacy can further their organizational responsibilities and goals. Moreover, your customers, partners and the auditors and regulators with whom you deal need to feel confident that they understand how your privacy policies and procedures will affect them; that you are meeting any legal requirements, and that you are protecting their interests.

To that end, the process—with all its discussion, revision and winnowing—of creating a simple-language, pithy, well-crafted mission statement enables you to identify core privacy values, shape policy that aligns with those values, determine key objectives and, finally, detail the strategies that will become the privacy reality for your organization.

Key Questions for Creating a Mission Statement

Who is the audience for your mission statement (the entire organization or just your privacy office)?

What's the life cycle of the information you collect, use, disseminate and retain?

How will you provide reasonable assurance that valuable business and personal information is

- identified and prioritized based on its value;
- adequately safeguarded from misuse and theft, regardless of the technologies used and changes in business models;
- maintained in a manner that satisfies legal requirements, and
- appropriately available to meet business needs?

Eventually, your mission statement will help you create a privacy statement which has an entirely different purpose. Whereas a mission statement is an internal document meant to guide the formation and development of your privacy program, a privacy statement is the formal and detailed public declaration of your organization's promise to steward and protect personally identifiable information. Guidelines for creating a privacy statement appear later in this chapter.

Key Privacy-Related Concepts and Terms You'll Need to Know

Mission statement of Company Code of Conduct

Your mission statement is primarily an internal document. It succinctly describes your organization's philosophy and level of commitment to privacy and the protection of personally identifiable information. By articulating the importance of privacy, the statement provides high-level guidance for your privacy program.

Corporate Privacy Policy

A privacy policy is an internal document that not only embodies the spirit of your mission statement, but also provides operational guidance for your organization. It spells out in detail how you want your employees, procedures and processes to respond when operations intersect with privacy concerns. Employees throughout the entire organization who read your privacy policy should be in no doubt about how to perform their jobs and job-related activities in relation to your philosophy, goals and strategic initiatives.

External Privacy Policy or Notice

A privacy statement is an external document. The statement is the result of enacting your policy and of extensive work on specific privacy procedures and processes, appearing in your public communications and prominently on your corporate website. It explains to your customers how you plan to use and protect their personally identifiable information and when and how they can limit the sharing of that information.

Once you have created a mission statement that describes your operating principles at a high level, you are ready to determine specific objectives. These objectives will help you design and execute a structured, cost-effective process to identify and protect the value of the organization's information. It helps here to think of your privacy operations in the form of a three-step cycle in which you continuously assess the current privacy environment, remediate the gaps you find, monitor, obtain metrics for compliance and audit for verification and process improvements. This cycle is described in detail later in this chapter.

Key Questions for Determining Objectives

- What measures will determine whether an outcome is successful and effective? For example, will you track the number of
  - Technologies or business processes reviewed for privacy compliance;
  - Privacy incidents handled;
  - People trained;
  - Complaints received and handled properly;
  - Internal reviews conducted?
- Have you included all key stakeholders in the development of privacy objectives, policies and procedures?
- Do you have enough information to describe the stakeholders' processes, concerns, issues and pain points regarding privacy?

DETERMINING OBJECTIVES

A clearly defined statement about your privacy mission helps you create the strategies, policies and procedures you need to implement it. The objectives spell out in clear terms how individuals, groups, departments or the organization as a whole must act to fulfill the mission and produce the desired outcomes. It is critical that after you determine the objectives you clearly document, effectively communicate and constantly improve them as actual practice and reality become the teachers.

Documenting Essential Information

Your objectives must be clearly documented. The form this documentation takes will depend very much on the particular requirements of your industry, the nature of your organization and who among the staff is involved in the day-to-day management of privacy operations. The documents themselves may be as simple as a performance plan or more inclusive like a business plan, executive plan or charter. During the documentation process, it's a good idea to involve your colleagues who tend to the business side of your organization. By coupling the regulatory requirements with business needs, you will create practical policies and procedures. As a result, your plan will be achievable and its policies and procedures applicable and relevant to your business and the levels of risk you present. Partnering with your business stakeholders during the drafting stage of certain policies and procedures will give them a sense of ownership, engage them and reduce the likelihood of barriers when you implement policies and procedures. In the final analysis, it's the collaboration with the business that determines the shape of your privacy outcomes. For an example of a "privacy program charter," see appendix, *Privacy Program Charter*, p. 183.

Communicating Confidently and Clearly

Understand your business. The clearest mission statement and the best-thought-out objectives in the world will not succeed without an ongoing effort to communicate essential information to all the players whose roles intersect with the privacy realm. You will need to take every opportunity to initiate, facilitate and promote activities that foster awareness of the organization's privacy mission, its objectives and its day-to-day, nuts-and-bolts procedures. Especially in the beginning of this process, you will need to "walk the halls," to reach out to all affected business units to understand their specific processes and concerns with the area of privacy. In doing so, you will lay the groundwork for a positive relationship and enhance your chances of success in future engagements.

Preparing to Improve Over Time

It's vital for everyone to understand that the topic of privacy is not going away. Right from the start, your organization must commit—on a regular schedule of at least once a year—to revisit, review and refine the framework of objectives and procedures that determine your privacy operations. Objectives may need to be revised over time and procedures must keep in step as the business evolves and laws and regulations change. By measuring hard outcomes against objectives, you'll be able to clarify what needs to improve.

DEVELOPING YOUR PRIVACY STRATEGIES

As you develop the strategies for your privacy program, you will

- create strategic internal partnerships;
- begin developing programs for compliance, monitoring and improvement;
- develop global privacy initiatives, as applicable;
- define metrics for measuring success, and
- prioritize the work based on risk

Creating Strategic Internal Partnerships

A successful privacy office depends on strong partnerships with other departments within the organization, including business units such as human resources, sales, marketing, product development and any other areas where your colleagues collect, use and store personally identifiable information. You will also want to develop internal partnerships with parts of the organization that manage, for example, internal audits, information security, compliance and legal and regulatory issues (in some organizations, compliance and legal issues may be combined).

Best Practice Recommendation: Acquiring Executive Sponsorship

Even before you start the work of creating your privacy program, it is essential that you do the groundwork by securing a clear mandate and strong support from the highest executive levels of your organization. Your privacy operation will need teeth; your executive sponsors can provide them.

By helping to develop relationships that are built on trust, the alignment of shared missions and mutual benefit, you will enable these departments to understand and embrace the organization's focus on privacy operations and the value they bring. Building these partnerships takes hard work, focus and time and should not be shortchanged. Because every organization has its own culture, politics and protocols, you will need to find the best way to work with yours. The effort will be worth it; strong relationships will produce effective results and prove sustainable over time.

The following section looks at some of the key partnerships and the role they play in realizing effective privacy operations. As you work on developing relationships, you may want to create a list and map of stakeholders. For an example of a stakeholder map, see appendix, *Stakeholder Map for Change Management and Communications*, p. 184.

Best Practice Recommendation: Working with Information Security

One goal of your privacy program should be to mesh privacy and information security operations. Through close teamwork and collaboration, your organization will benefit financially and procedurally from the elimination of redundant and duplicated efforts. Work with your CIO and your Chief Security Officer to clarify areas of responsibility. Your colleagues in information security are charged with ensuring that only staff who meet the need-to-know guidelines of your policy can access the data. Security is inherently a technical function; it provides the technology to support your privacy policies. Your job is to ensure that staff follow the privacy policies—from the perspective of legal requirements and compliance. The demarcation line for responsibility between the security and privacy functions will differ between organizations, depending on the allocation of resources to each area.

Information security is probably the most vital area where a strong partnership with your privacy office is needed; a working relationship with this organizational partner is essential.

Information security is the technical foundation for privacy protection. Your organization's information security department drives the technical solutions and controls that are essential to maintain privacy. Because of shared interests, it is also a win-win proposition—a fact that, in itself, will help facilitate the relationship. Your privacy team can expect to collaborate closely and frequently (even daily) with the staff who manage information security.

Internal auditing colleagues are responsible for assessing and reporting compliance with company policy and legal requirements. A partnership with your internal auditors can help you ensure that your organization complies with its privacy mandates. The auditors can also help ensure that other business risks—of which privacy-related concerns are usually one example—are evaluated and understood. If your organization's privacy initiative is relatively new, the internal auditors can elevate the visibility of the privacy aspect of compliance. They can be your "stick;" let them help you.

Office of counsel colleagues may be key partners, too. While in many organizations the privacy function actually resides within the office of counsel, in the cases where the offices are separate, you will need to develop a strong tie with counsel.

Business units such as marketing, human resources, production and e-commerce also play an important role in the overall effort to implement privacy policy and procedures. When working with your colleagues in the business arena, your privacy office will have to skillfully address privacy issues and internal conflicts. You will need to communicate to business colleagues not only the contractual obligations they have with third parties but also the restrictions imposed by your organization's promises to consumers in its privacy statement.

Some business groups may view you as an impediment to success. The key here is to help business colleagues understand that privacy-related considerations don't have to hinder their operations and prevent them from fully achieving their objectives. It's therefore essential that you understand the end goal and help business colleagues meet their objectives in a legally compliant and privacy-sensitive fashion.

For example, a company that administers pension plans promises not to share personally identifiable information. This provision is written into the legally binding contract between the two entities. However, marketing staff decide that it would be useful to cross-market products or services using the valuable personally identifiable information that has been collected. In this case, the organization has a clear legal responsibility to honor its contract, and the marketer's request will have to be declined. It's the job of the privacy office to explain such legal limitations and offer suggestions for how to proceed in light of the contractual limitations—for example, by renegotiating the terms of the contract. By working with a business unit to identify possible solutions to legal and compliance issues, you will certainly foster future relationships with your business partners.

Best Practice Recommendation: Developing Internal Partnerships

As you develop your strategy, consider how you can

> **understand** how business colleagues see the world;
>
> **familiarize** yourself with the concepts and vocabulary nearest and dearest to them;
>
> **present** privacy in as much of a business context as practical;
>
> **demonstrate** that you can help them meet their objectives, manage their privacy risks and offer them solutions (for example, by providing alternative but compliant ways to achieve the same objectives);
>
> **encourage** them—through productive collaboration and mutual respect—to view you as a trusted and value-adding advisor;
>
> **help** them build in privacy requirements during the design phase for new products and services, and
>
> **groom** them as privacy advocates whom you include in key discussions about strategic initiatives and future plans that have privacy implications

---

Once your organization's initial objectives are in place, you can begin to develop the specific strategies and tactics you will need to carry them out. For example, you should plan to

- build flexibility into your strategies and regularly review them (because technology changes and legal and societal norms shift);
- make the accountability of your privacy operation transparent for all to see;
- provide advice, backed up by tangible, measurable results;
- integrate privacy operations into your organization's existing processes;
- leverage existing staff, technology and programs, and
- build a strong foundation of best-in-class policies, procedures and practices that address the access, use, disclosure and disposal of business and personal information consistent with industry standards and federal and state law

Begin Designing Programs to Assess, Monitor and Improve the Verification Process

Not only does your privacy team have to implement comprehensive policies and procedures to meet the privacy-related expectations of customers and employees, but also they have to demonstrate that the results comply with applicable laws, rules and regulations. Monitoring compliance is a vital element in your privacy operations to ensure that policies and procedures are adhered to and that your organization, when required to, is able to show that the privacy program is of sound design and operating effectively. As you begin to develop your own assessment process, monitoring for compliance and auditing procedures, keep in mind the following activities:

Activity	What to do
Documenting your processes	Develop a means to document your compliance, monitoring and review process. This may include a document that you use to review compliance on a regular basis (for example: every 2 to 3 years or when major updates to programs occur). **Notes:** • The American Institute of CPAs (AICPA) offers its member comprehensive resources about privacy, including recommendations for documentation. For more information, see *Key Resources for Generally Accepted Privacy Principles*, p. 127. • If you're starting a new privacy program, compliance and auditing groups in your organization are probably already active in meeting the requirements of legislation such as the Sarbanes-Oxley Act. In this case, you can leverage their ongoing efforts as part of your program. • There are also many governance, risk and compliance (GRC) tools, such as software applications, that will help you manage data and documentation.
Developing self-assessment tools	Consider developing self-assessment tools, independent of internal audit or external reviews. Ideally, for example, set up a quarterly assessment process where internal privacy controls are reviewed for compliance by the privacy department. The privacy department becomes involved in the business and knows how the privacy program is working.
Using the most suitable resource for audits	Verification assessments can be performed by internal audit or the compliance department or by an external party. Regardless of who performs the assessment, it should validate the program's effectiveness, employee and department compliance and opportunities for improvement.

Developing Global Privacy Initiatives

For organizations that operate within domestic borders, managing privacy is a challenge. For multinational organizations whose operations additionally span many countries and cultures, however, the tasks become even more formidable. If your organization works across the globe, you will need to develop a global strategy that covers privacy issues in all relevant markets and geographies. In doing so—as with all international dealings—your privacy team must be aware that cultural norms, as well as legal requirements, vary a great deal. What works with respect to one country or culture may be completely alien, or even illegal in another.

Best Practice Recommendation: Crafting a Global Privacy Initiative

As your privacy team crafts a global privacy policy, keep in the mind the following objectives:

Approach privacy from a global perspective, as consumer expectations and certainly legal requirements are greater in some international markets

Develop and **customize** privacy activities such as policy development, awareness programs and training, while considering international cultures and norms

Secure a budget for the demanding job of developing and maintaining materials in multiple languages and locations

Remain aware of the potential challenges of obtaining reliable translations of statutes, clarifying ambiguities in the requirements and assessing the intensity of enforcement

Implement procedures to keep abreast of the legal requirements in each international market in which your company does business (for example, certain countries require you to register with their relevant agencies)

Defining Metrics for Measuring Success

How are you going to demonstrate to your management and colleagues that your program is successful? It's a truism to say that if you don't measure something, you can't manage it; however, this is especially relevant in the field of privacy management. Much of your work in a privacy office may take the form of "consulting" work for different areas of your organization, with few tangible results to show at the end of it. Though it is sometimes a challenge, establishing metrics to measure the effectiveness of your privacy program is important. In fact, this is more difficult for successful privacy programs because they prevent "bad things" from happening; you can't measure what doesn't happen. For example, security breaches and lawsuits simply may not happen because you are doing your job well. You can point out that, in this case, a lower number, like a golf score, is a positive metric. Although it's a challenge, you should still work actively to produce metrics and key performance indicators that help you justify and promote the privacy operation. Metrics will also help you build a business case for resources and budget and enable you to measure and reward the performance of individual team members; you will certainly need the facts and figures to back up your proposals.

As your privacy program gets underway, you can generate metrics by measuring and tracking a number of events; such as

- awareness communications;
- completion of required training programs;
- number of policy memoranda issued (for example, an internal memo about a specific privacy-related topic, such as the use of CCTV within the organization);

- number of information privacy risk assessments completed;
- general employee awareness of privacy issues and policies (demonstrated by survey results);
- favorable audits;
- number of incidents;
- frequency of incidents;
- business type of incidents, and
- number of complaints

Show your colleagues that you pay attention to their input and take action. For example, you can write and strategically disseminate policy memos that document and enumerate instances where your privacy office has acted on the advice of colleagues in other areas of your organization. And you can get a sense of perceptions of people—customers, partners and so on—who are viewing your privacy policy and procedures from outside the organization. You can learn, for example—via market surveys conducted and evaluated by outside organizations—about the extent of the trust with which others hold you in regard.

Note: For more information about, and examples of, privacy metrics, see Chapter 4, "Metrics and Key Performance Indicators that Demonstrate Success," p. 158.

Prioritizing Work Based on Risk

As you establish and operate a privacy office, you can be certain of one thing—there will always be too much work and never enough people to handle it. The privacy arena is growing constantly and expanding in its scope and complexity; there is no organization or part of an organization that is unaffected by privacy concerns. And this is unlikely to change any time soon. Because your work is cutting-edge—and, as a result, probably not fully appreciated across the organization—you will have to fight for resources, human and monetary. For these reasons, to succeed in this environment, you will initially need to decide on, document and communicate the areas that need the most attention. Use a risk-based approach to inform your decisions. Your focus, priorities and proposed activities should all align with and support your organization's overall goals.

Establishing priorities based on risk also helps you decide how best to spend your own valuable time. That's why it's important to take the time to initially assess your current environment to identify existing controls, if any, and develop a risk-based remediation strategy. It will be very easy to get wrapped up in the endless stream of individual issues flowing over the transom. However, it is wise to set aside time for yourself and your team to think over your activities and strategies. You need time to develop sound policies that will stand a good chance of success.

Of course, priorities are not carved in stone. Your list will shift as your needs and the demands of your organization change and as the emergence of new regulations dictates. For example, you may decide that it would be very beneficial to your efforts and evangelism for your privacy office to demonstrate some quick and highly visible results. Picking "low-hanging fruit" can therefore be an early priority. Examples of these quick wins are effective relationship building, training and education. If you establish good relationship early on, you will be able to engage with individuals and find out if and where they are having issues with the privacy team. This type of feedback is invaluable and gives you the opportunity to address the problem and produce fast, positive changes.

ASSEMBLING YOUR PRIVACY TEAM

To begin the process of creating your privacy program, you will need the right people on board; your privacy program will only be as strong as the combined talents of the people who work in it. It behooves you to assemble the best team you can and structure it in a way that will best serve your organization. During this phase of setting up your program, you will typically

- determine the most effective way to structure your team;
- create the right combination of experts;
- offer career paths to your team;
- obtain professional certification, and
- manage budgets.

Determining the Most Effective Way to Structure Your Team

After your organization determines what kinds of information it collects, think about which privacy team structure would work best. For example, privacy functions can be located in legal, information technology (IT) and human resources (HR) groups, as well as embedded in other operations. In these cases, the privacy program will operate in the background and may not be immediately visible to the organization's senior executives. Depending on the requirements of your organization, this approach may be adequate. On the other hand, you might propose a structure that maximizes the visibility of your program for colleagues across the organization. It's sometimes the case that the privacy program will begin with a simplified approach and then, as it matures, grow and evolve into a more layered structure.

For example, you may find that your organization will best be served by a centralized team of privacy experts. Alternatively, the size and needs of your organization may require the creation of a large cross-functional team to carry out privacy-related work. You could also form a virtual privacy team (VPT) across your organization so that key stakeholders from each affected functional area, division or subsidiary company are represented on the VPT. For different approaches to creating an organizational structure for a privacy program, see appendix, *The Privacy Program's Organizational Structure*, p. 192.

Best Practice Recommendation: Forming VPTs and Steering Committees

The make-up of the VPT and steering committee will vary according to the size of the organization and its culture and politics. However, the VPT members should be

- include at least mid-level managers who represent the geographic areas in which your organization conducts business;
- have a good understanding of the business as it relates to personally identifiable information, and
- come from, where applicable, functional areas such as human resources, sales and marketing and legal.

The steering committee should

- consist of more senior business leaders who represent the appropriate geographic regions and disciplines;
- provide the necessary gravitas to help ensure others in the organization embrace privacy and will be from many of the same disciplines as the VPT members.

These representatives in turn lead the privacy compliance team in their own business unit or staff office. The extent to which privacy issues affect each area will determine the size and scope and its privacy operation. By using this model, you can scale appropriately and centrally manage and coordinate the activities of many employees actively working on your corporate privacy.

Types of privacy team models include the following examples, though, as we mentioned above, what often happens is that the program will evolve from the first to the second model as the program matures and develops:

Type of model	Features
Simplified	Single privacy officer who: Has an all-encompassing role and reports to an executive and has no formal connection to a business product or service area Is required to be the eyes and ears of the organization and relies on others to bring privacy issues forward

Layered	A privacy team that: Reports informally between privacy office and business units Includes individuals assigned by business units to be their "eyes and ears" to act as liaison between business unit and privacy office Is created by a corporate privacy committee or centralized privacy office Is part of a compliance program Is part of the marketing team (note: there's a risk here of lack of independence and objectivity when the role is placed in a business unit such as sales and marketing)

Note: Regardless of the model implemented, the business leaders and their teams are ultimately accountable for the organization's adherence to privacy policies and legal requirements. While accountability for funding or performing the privacy-related project lies with the affected business, the privacy officer can be, and usually is, responsible for helping it become compliant. In practical terms, the privacy office's efforts help support a business unit's accountability by providing the necessary policies, advice and ongoing collaboration.

Creating the Right Combination of Experts

Assembling the right privacy team for your organization is a critical job. The privacy office team is responsible for building an organizational culture that understands privacy issues and their ramifications. It'll be their job to train staff across the organization on the importance of privacy, complying with regulatory requirements and adhering to organizational privacy policies. A key goal of the team is to work with the entire organization to ensure that privacy considerations are addressed upfront when plans are made to update any program, system or initiative. Building this team will require decisions about hiring and bringing on board the types of professionals who will best carry out the challenging tasks of a privacy operation.

Working with key parties such as human resources, information security and business operations, a privacy team is instrumental in fostering awareness and ensuring compliance with legal and regulatory obligations as well as procedures across an organization. In organizations whose needs require a sizable privacy operation, the privacy team may comprise individuals with different backgrounds. In some industries—for example, the technology sector—companies may combine privacy operations and information security in the same reporting structure. Privacy professionals who are also lawyers often find themselves working as counsel to the information technology and information security groups in their organizations, creating the opportunity to further cement relationships. In other organizations, a single individual may have to wear a number of hats.

The following table illustrates examples of the different roles that can contribute to a privacy program. The roles may be bundled into a single group or, depending on the size and nature of the organization, located in various groups to form a wider virtual team. The privacy programs in some organizations—especially those just starting a privacy initiative—may hinge on a single individual who is then supported by colleagues from various other functions. Typically, privacy programs represent a mixture of the different approaches. The last four roles in the following table often reside outside the privacy team itself, but they represent important allies.

Privacy Team Specialists	Role
Privacy analyst	Is typically responsible for managing legal and operational risk related to sensitive information assets across the organizations May continuously assess business unit operations, developing policies, procedures and training, overseeing data use agreements, executing projects and consulting on new business initiatives
Privacy manager	Is responsible for providing oversight, guidance and support across the organization Enhances data privacy and information protection initiatives, promoting strong privacy practices within the organization Ensures compliance with privacy laws and promotes best practices in the areas of client, customer and employee privacy
Chief privacy officer (CPO)	Is the senior privacy leader within the team Handles all aspects of compliance, training, lobbying and policy making concerning laws and standards by interpreting federal and state privacy laws, breach laws and other related laws and regulations Is typically seen as the organization's overall expert on privacy matters
Information security specialist	Offers information security expertise which may be helpful in understanding highly technical legal and regulatory requirements or other standards such as the Payment Card Industry Data Security Standard Helps liaise with the information security team Helps advise how to build technical requirements into design to ensure that privacy requirements are addressed
Line-of-business privacy steward	Works within the business but takes on privacy responsibilities that may include issue-spotting and compliance
Country privacy officer (if applicable)	Works within a subsidiary of an EU country, liaises with the local data protection authority (DPA), handles local privacy issues and reports on a dotted-line basis to the CPO
Privacy attorney	Conducts in-house privacy counsel work with the CPO to advise the business and teams on the most relevant legal issues May be housed in the privacy office, if it is part of the office of general counsel May work in the general counsel's office but be tasked to support the privacy office May be represented by outside counsel

Legal professional	Provide legal and regulatory guidance
	May be a paralegal who assists attorney with legal research and writing
Compliance manager or consultant	Ensure business implements decisions made (taking into account legal and regulatory recommendations)
	Work more in operations than legal function
Communications expert	Draft communications and handle notifications and media issues

For sample job descriptions of key privacy program roles, see appendix, *Privacy Team Specialists–Roles and Sample Job Descriptions*, p. 185.

Offering Career Paths to Your Team

If you want to develop and retain a top-notch team, you will need to offer your privacy professionals a career path and opportunities for enrichment and certification. Obviously, for some specific roles this may be predetermined by your human resources organization's personnel development policies. For example, your organization may already have a career structure in place for attorneys and paralegals. In the case of other roles—such as privacy specialists, privacy consultants or privacy coordinators—this may not be the case. As a result, you may need to create specific job descriptions and design a career track you think will work, then obtain the necessary buy-in of your HR managers.

Obtaining Professional Certification

Privacy professionals can affirm their expertise by obtaining industry-recognized privacy certifications. Knowing whether or not a potential member has been certified for privacy work may help you determine whether he or she has the knowledge base necessary to do the job. Certification is not essential, but it is a good vehicle for ensuring that staff are up to date on recent developments in the privacy area. You can also make the obtaining of certification part of team members' performance objectives and a consideration when promotion is a possibility.

The International Association of Privacy Professionals (IAPP) offers five credentials for privacy professionals, including specialized certification for people working in a government organization, those who work in the IT arena and those who reside in Canada and operate under Canadian regulations. Each designation is designed to demonstrate mastery of a principles-based framework and knowledge base in information privacy in a legal or practical specialization. To achieve any of these credentials, an individual must pass the IAPP's Certification Foundation exam. This exam covers elementary concepts of privacy and data protection from a global perspective. The Certification Foundation is designed to provide the basis for a multifaceted approach to privacy and data protection and to allow for the specific application of IAPP privacy certifications to build upon this foundation with minimal repetition. For more information, see the IAPP's website at www.privacyassociation.org/certification. For details of the five certifications, see appendix, *Certifications Offered by the IAPP*, p. 204.

Managing Budgets

A large part of your budget will go to support the team and its efforts. As you prepare budgets for both internal and external costs, you can start planning for the following items, where relevant:

Type of Budget	Includes Costs Such As . . .
Internal	Payroll and fringe benefits Internal overhead costs Travel expenses Continuing education Attendance at privacy conferences Privacy training sessions Subscriptions to privacy and security publications Subscriptions to legal research websites Membership fees—IAPP and bar associations Registration fees—state legal registration requirements Media—laptops and cell phones Office supplies
External	Hire outside counsel Engage consultants License software for activities such as conducting an information inventory

BUILDING A POLICY FRAMEWORK

You've led the development of your organization's privacy mission statement, you've defined your objectives and you've developed the strategies that will guide your privacy program. The next step is to build or further develop the framework of privacy policies and procedures that make your privacy program a daily reality. The most obvious and visible element in the framework will be the **privacy statement** you hang on your shingle. This statement tells the outside world—and reminds your own colleagues throughout the organization—just exactly how you intend to secure and steward personally identifiable information. It becomes a contract with your employees and customers. Consumers are already well aware of privacy statements; after all, they accompany almost every online transaction and are frequently distributed in printed form during a visit to a healthcare provider or at the bank when you apply for a loan.

As you develop your policy framework and prepare to create a privacy statement, you can use the **information life cycle** to structure your activities. For example, you'll need to

- map personally identifiable information and record an inventory;
- classify the information;
- investigate how different groups in your organization use the information;
- examine how the information flows through your organization;
- determine how the information is stored in your organization, and
- determine what happens when information is no longer needed (when and how it is disposed of).

Mapping Data Across the Organization

Knowing which areas of your organization collect or receive personally identifiable information and the flow of such information requires detective work and can be a significant and resource-intensive challenge. Remember, too, that you're dealing with a moving target; the data your organization holds is constantly in flux and can change quickly, without notice. You can start to map data by using the standard forms various departments use, both online and paper versions, and trace the collected data to where it resides—for example, in an IT system or a filing cabinet. There are also IT and security forensics tools that you can use to map data. Your organization may also receive data from third-party vendors—such as insurance benefits administrators—and via purchase agreements and contracts.

As you map data, record your findings. Depending on your needs and the complexity of the data landscape, you may find that using a tool such as Microsoft Excel or Microsoft Access to create a database or a simple spreadsheet is sufficient. If the scale of your organization or your needs require it, consider using a commercially available tool to inventory the information.

When you start to inventory your organization's data holdings, it's a good idea to use a standard questionnaire. You are less likely to overlook key questions as you talk with your various program managers. This process will help you understand the nature and pedigree of the data you discuss. If your organization operates a data loss prevention program—typically part of your IT or information security program—you can leverage it to track your company's data, regardless of where it resides. Such a program can provide you with not only a comprehensive inventory of the data you collect and store, but also detailed information about where and on which servers or computers the data actually resides, and who is responsible for it. You'll be looking for data

- about employees;
- about customers;
- used by you but owned by clients (especially if you provide services);
- that is co-owned with another entity.

Locating Data About Employees

Typically, your organization will store data about employees—not only its own staff but also its contractors and possibly other organizations' employees and contractors. If you're a multinational organization, keep in mind that certain European countries and other nations have strict laws that govern how to handle personnel data. To avoid noncompliance, you will need to familiarize yourself with the international laws that apply to your organization's overseas operations. Working with your HR business partners will be key in helping you understand the lifecycle of information about employees.

Identifying Customer Data

Of all the kinds of information your organization manages, customer-related data will likely be the easiest to identify. In most cases, this is the master record data you store when individuals or companies purchase your services or products. Outside of sales, other groups in your organization will need to access customer data to complete transactions such as shipping, invoicing and future marketing efforts.

Best Practice Recommendation:
Online Survey to Locate Personnel Data

Personnel data can be the hardest kind of personal data to find; first-line supervisors may maintain shadow files on their employees, making the data more vulnerable to loss or illegal use.

However, you can create a simple template-based survey (online works best) that you send out to business and staff offices or procure commercial information inventorying software. The survey simply asks for the type of information they collect or need to conduct their business operations. Collect the responses and you have a reasonably complete inventory of your organization's personnel data. It's also a good idea to periodically send out the survey to make sure that the scope hasn't changed.

As you identify who has access to the data, determine if the groups with access are creating additional copies of the data, thus increasing risk. Different groups in your organization may also need to outsource personally identifiable information for particular processes. For example, your accounting group may use an outside contractor to process payment collections. Your marketing colleagues may hire external consultants to help identify sales trends. Company affiliates sometimes make it a practice to share data for marketing purposes. On the other hand, because of limiting agreements with producers and customers, some affiliates don't permit sharing for marketing but do allow it for servicing the customer. It's important that you identify and monitor these kinds of activities carefully; that way, your privacy office will be able to help assess risk of a breach and make recommendations accordingly.

Identifying Client-Owned Data

If you're a service provider and maintain data on behalf of a client, you must be familiar with your contractual agreements. You need to know what the client permits you to do—or not do—with their data and their expectations about how you handle it. For example, if the client has audit rights to your program, you should segregate client-owned information logically—even if it's kept on the same server with other customer and client data. One client should not be privy to the data of others. Any agreement about client-owned data should discuss what happens to the data once the relationship is discontinued. You also want to be aware of any legal requirements that may come with client-owned data. Remember too that a company often collects data as part of sales agreements, which may well limit the use of the data to servicing purposes only. Thus, it's important to identify areas where these limitations exist; you don't want to run afoul of contracts and find yourself in breach (and without customers). Your colleagues in the legal group can assist you with this work.

Defining Co-Owned Data

If you work closely with partner organizations, you may find you have joint ownership of some sensitive data. For example, if your company co-sponsors a sweepstakes with a credit card company, both companies may want certain usage rights for the data collected from contestants. In this case, both sides need to clearly define the rights and uses of the data. It's good practice to include audit rights in such an agreement so you can ensure that a partner is not in some way misusing data and potentially impacting your brand.

Establishing Responsibility for Data

As you develop the inventory of personally identifiable information in your organization, begin to think about who controls the data. Is it your company or are you acting on behalf of another company? For example, if you were not the original collector of the data, consider the following questions:

- What exactly is your relationship with the individual's information?
- Will the individuals whose data you're storing expect to hear directly from you?
- Do you need to tag the data with special instructions or classifications?
- Is the data subject to a particular regulatory regime (for example: HIPAA), specific privacy policy or controls?

Classifying the Data

By classifying the data you find, you can easily narrow the scope (and cost) of what you need to protect and how. However, data classification is a simple concept in theory, but often difficult in practice. At a minimum, you need to have three basic classifications:

- Publicly available information, such as marketing material and fact sheets

- Information for use only inside the organization, such as organizational charts and marketing plans
- Confidential information, such as personally identifiable information, intellectual property and trade secrets

Each of these basic classifications comes with its own appropriate use and protection requirements. Obviously, confidential data and documents will require the most protection. Data inventorying and classification can be a challenge, but there are commercial tools on the market that can help you automate and create consistent, sustainable documentation. Your colleagues in data security will likely be part of your efforts in this area.

Managing Data Subject to Special Requirements

Some of the personally identifiable information your organization collects and stores will need to be managed according to line of business or organizational structure. For example, data in some areas of your organization may be subject to the regulatory framework that applies to financial information—such as the Gramm-Leach-Bliley Act. Any healthcare-related data will likely come under the auspices of the Health Insurance Portability and Accountability Act. You'll need to address these special requirements in each business unit's policies and procedures. Document them; they don't exist unless you write them down. And after you've documented the rules in question, you'll need to make sure you can assess compliance and enforce it. For more information about assessments, see "Foundational Work: Assessments", p. 105.

CREATING YOUR PRIVACY STATEMENT OR POLICY

Creating and then managing a privacy statement can take a lot of time and effort. As mentioned earlier, it is the mission statement that helps your organization focus on its privacy goals. The privacy statement, however, is the detailed, public face of your organization's privacy policy. It needs to cover the basics of who, what, where, when, how and why you are collecting personally identifiable information from individuals. The format of the notice—hard copy, online notice at the point of collection, online but a link at the point of collection or over the phone—will dictate how detailed you get.

Keeping the Privacy Statement Current

You need to have ongoing processes for reviewing and updating your privacy statement when necessary. For instance, businesses often begin collecting new types of information, customer contact information changes and data may or may not be shared for marketing purposes as new products or services are developed. Obviously, when circumstances change, an organization needs to notify its customers and provide an opportunity for them to opt out.

Tip: Maintain a list of all locations where your privacy statement resides. When you update the statement, you can then be confident that every copy of the statement remains current. In addition, local country laws may dictate modifications to the privacy statement. The privacy office should keep a copy of all versions (translated into English) as well.

PROVIDING TRAINING AND COMMUNICATIONS

As part of a broad initiative to educate employees in your organization, training and building awareness are an essential part of your privacy operation. As a privacy professional, you already understand that it's the responsibility of an organization—and a regulatory requirement—to ensure that associates know how to protect the privacy and security of all data. You need to educate your staff about what is required and ensure they understand why privacy is relevant and important. Existing staff and new employees must understand the organization's policies and procedures and have the knowledge and skills necessary to comply with privacy-related requirements.

Training should be cyclical and include refresher sessions to keep staff current. Ideally, refresher training occurs at least once a year. However, events such as the enactment of a new law may require training on a more frequent basis. You will need to decide whether training should be mandatory or optional, or some combination of both. And of course, you will want to give thought to role-based training; the needs of different employees or groups may vary greatly. To facilitate the most effective learning, try to design training sessions that are interactive and engage your colleagues. As a result of repeated effective training and awareness building, privacy thinking will eventually become embedded in your organization's culture. When this happens, staff will automatically consider the privacy implications of whatever task is at hand.

To carry out an effective training program, you will typically

- build the case for education and training;
- develop or acquire commercially available training;
- modify or develop the content specific to the business;
- deliver the training;
- extend the training through communications, and
- measure and communicate training results.

Building the Case for Education and Training

The most effective way to ensure the success of your privacy mission is to establish a solid privacy awareness program. The goal of that program is to incorporate the concept of privacy into the mindset of everyone who works for the organization. The key means to that goal is training. An effective training program will make sure that employees in your organization are on the same page, that their actions reflect the company's privacy policy and that they help prevent mishaps. The privacy team should build a compelling case for training and highlight the following elements:

- Principles in the company's privacy policy
- Any applicable regulatory requirements
- Potential penalties for noncompliance
- Common privacy-related and potentially costly mistakes that can be avoided via minimal training
- What a privacy and security breach/incident is and how and when to report it to the privacy office
- Additional training benefits to the organization, such as
  - Lower incident-response costs
  - More efficient ways to do business

This will help you both identify the strategic business objectives for the training and garner the support of an executive-level sponsor.

Developing Training

Once you have the support of an executive sponsor, the privacy team should create or acquire a fundamental and adaptable training program that builds knowledge and skills. It should clearly demonstrate its value through alignment with organizational priorities and the privacy mission statement. By reinforcing the connection of privacy training to the business and organizational success, you will establish a foundation, set expectations, and outline priorities. The privacy team's first task is to create an action plan. In the plan, you will define training and communication paths—for example, training modules, team meetings and newsletters. At a high level, the action plan also

- identifies who will receive the training (target audience);
- describes how and when the training will be delivered;
- establishes the desired outcomes and how to track them, and
- specifies who is responsible for delivering the training.

Key Questions for Creating a Training Program and Action Plan

- Is your schedule for implementing the training realistic?
- Do parts of your organization already require employees to take multiple trainings and potentially have difficulty allotting more time?
- Have you surveyed the various options for training (formal classroom training, self-paced, web-based learning and so on)?
- Do you have buy-in from key stakeholders?
- Have you identified appropriate benchmarks and a method for measuring the success of your privacy and security training?
- How will you conduct training differently for the various roles and businesses within the organization?
- If your organization is multinational, where staff speak different languages, how will the training accommodate language differences?
- Who has to be trained, how often, and how will you track it?
- What is an acceptable completion rate (internal audit usually has guidelines, and there may also be regulatory requirements)?
- Will employees be tested after training, and will there be remediation if needed?
- Do you have an adequate training budget and know who will pay for it?
- Have you have identified the needs of your target audience?
- How will training be rolled out (for example: one-time, annually, part of new hire training or after an incident)?

In addition to formal training, you can also use other tools to educate staff and enhance the privacy culture in your organization. For example, you can

- initiate collaboration with your colleagues throughout the organization;
- specifically reinforce the connection between privacy operations and business goals with business leaders, and
- eliminate an "event" mentality and help develop a solid framework of procedures based on the constant, ongoing importance of privacy issues.

Delivering the Training

Depending on the number of individuals to be trained and the size, structure and physical distribution of your organization, you may need a number of training options. These include:

Training Element	Alternatives
Delivery medium	Classroom training
	Workshop approach
	Remote
	Online
	Documentation (written and online)

Ongoing support	Train-the-trainer strategy
	Power users
Delivery approach	One-time
	As needed
	Self-paced learning
	Occasional refresher
	By specialty area or general audience

Extending Training Through Communications

Your privacy program can accomplish many of its training goals via formal and informal sessions delivered online or in classrooms. However, employees will need continuous prompts and reminders to keep privacy issues and responsibilities on their radar screens. Useful techniques for keeping the topic fresh include:

- Video messaging—pushing pop-ups to employees' desktops
- Voicemail campaigns
- Screen saver messaging
- Posters
- Supplies, pens, "padfolios" and calendars
- Blogs
- Online reference guides
- Games and contests—trivia games on your intranet
- Tip of the week
- FAQs

An excellent tool to manage your communications is a communications plan that helps you to organize the what, who, when and how of your effort. For a sample plan and template, see appendix, *Communications Plan*, p. 195.

Tip: A great day to kick off your first newsletter is on January 28, which is Data Privacy Day.

Measuring and Communicating Training Results

Part of your training initiative will be to measure and communicate success to stakeholders outside the privacy group. Create a set of metrics with which to compare goals to actual results. Ways of measuring results include evaluating:

- Participation rates by, for example:
  - Keeping participation logs based on registration documentation or sign-in sheets (for classroom training)

- ○ Running system reports (for online training)
- ○ Compiling a report from the data
- Success and retry rates (if participants are tested)
- Behavior change by:
  - ○ Analyzing your incident response data for correlation with training or lack of it
  - ○ Tracking and the number of privacy-related queries from associates and determining and reporting whether:
    - Lower numbers reflect improved understanding of privacy
    - More complex questions reflect a deep awareness of privacy issues and a better understanding of the potential risks involved

While measuring results is not always straightforward, the privacy team must develop a process to collect meaningful metrics and report them to management. Reporting can take the form of a one-page dashboard that is easily reviewed and digested and shows progress compared to the defined goals.

Best Practice Recommendation: Teaching the Legal and Regulatory Framework

Your training program must make it clear to employees that privacy is their responsibility and that it is fundamentally driven by legal and regulatory requirements along with the company's policy requirements. After training, employees should have a good understanding of all legal requirements that apply to the organization training. They must also understand that compliance should be built into all transactions with customers and should be part of any message from the organization to the outside world. Key sources of privacy legislation include:

- Health Insurance Portability and Accountability Act of 1996 (HIPAA)
- Gramm-Leach-Bliley Act (GLBA)
- Children's Online Privacy Protection Act (COPPA)
- Fair Credit Reporting Act (FCRA)
- Telephone Consumer Protection Act (TCPA)
- Controlling the Assault of Non-Solicited Pornography and Marketing Act (CAN-SPAM)
- Personal Information Protection and Electronic Documents Act (PIPEDA)—Canada
- EU Data Protection Directive 95/46/EC

For comprehensive descriptions of these laws, see Chapter 2, *Privacy's Legal Framework*, p. 15.

Educating the Enterprise

There are enterprise-wide aspects to a comprehensive privacy program that will complement formal training and help reinforce with employees the critical nature of privacy protection and maintaining confidentiality. One aspect of privacy that concerns every employee in the organization is the use of nondisclosure agreements and confidentiality notices. These notices make it very clear from the outset that employees are stewards of company data and that they need to understand the importance of protecting personally identifiable information and other sensitive data.

Nondisclosure Agreements and Confidentiality Notices Reinforce Privacy Training

Part of your mandate is to ensure that employees keep the organization's private information confidential. Training is one way to set basic norms—dos and don'ts—within an organization, but a nondisclosure agreement (NDA) is also a great means of providing the organization with the ability to enforce these basic norms. An NDA is the usual basis for protecting information assets such as customer data, inventions and trade secrets. The creation of such an agreement brings together the privacy team, colleagues in HR and business partners to discuss and agree on personnel privacy policies right from the beginning. The following are important elements in a nondisclosure agreement:

- Definition of confidential information—this can be defined by state, federal and international laws and regulations (for example: GLBA, HIPAA and the European Data Protection Directive)
- Exclusions from confidential information
- Obligations of receiving party—these can be defined by state, federal and international laws and regulations (for example: GLBA has specific handling requirements for non-affiliated third parties that receive sensitive data)
- Time periods—these include destruction requirements and their timing

Sensitive data and communications typically fall into the following categories:

- Personal confidential information, which is private information about a single individual
- Organizational confidential (proprietary) information, which is private information about a business (for example, trade secrets)
- Confidential governmental and classified military information

Privacy requirements should clearly identify the specific

- data and communications that are sensitive and confidential or trade secrets;
- places where and media through which this communication takes place (for example: over the Internet or outside of a secure data center).

Training for Global Management of Privacy

Because the legal framework of international markets constitutes a vast landscape of country-specific laws, regulations and standards, the subject of global management presents multinational corporations—and any organization that routinely conducts overseas transactions—with a significant training challenge. Employees whose work involves international transactions will typically need

- in-depth subject matter expertise and background;
- understanding of global legal and regulatory requirements;
- knowledge of local language and culture, and
- relationships with country-specific regulators and key contacts.

Key Resources for Privacy Professionals in Multinational Organizations

Asia-Pacific Economic Cooperation (APEC) – www.apec.org

This organization's activities include initiatives such as the "APEC Data Privacy Pathfinder Projects." The goal of these projects is to develop a system in the APEC region that ensures accountable, cross-border flows of personal information for the protection of consumers while facilitating business access to the benefits of electronic commerce. The United States is a member of APEC.

Organization for Economic Cooperation and Development (OECD) – www.oecd.org

Following the U.S. Privacy Act in 1974, the OECD is the main source for most national legal frameworks today. Its primary mission is helping governments to foster prosperity and fight poverty through economic growth and financial stability. The organization helps to ensure that the environmental implications of economic and social development are taken into account. The organization also provides a setting where governments can compare policy experiences, seek answers to common problems, identify good practices and coordinate domestic and international policies. Privacy issues—for example, defining policy to control cross-border electronic spam—are part of this setting. The United States is a member of the OECD.

OPERATING THE PRIVACY PROGRAM

The following section covers the kinds of work you can expect your privacy program to perform, including:

- Making it happen: a three-step cycle
- Typical tasks of a privacy office
- Foundational work: assessments
- Managing the privacy program day to day

MAKING IT HAPPEN: A THREE-STEP CYCLE

Regardless of whether your organization operates in the public or private sector, the work of implementing privacy policies and procedures and constantly refining and improving them never ends. Rather than looking at the establishment of privacy operations in your organization as a one-time effort, it's best to think of the creation, maintenance and continuous improvement of a privacy program as essentially a three-step cyclical process—a process that is continuously monitoring and improving itself. Based on their experiences of recent years, privacy experts know this all too well. The private sector, especially, has been faced with an ever-expanding array of legislative and regulatory requirements around privacy and information security. In addition to dealing with a changing legal landscape, companies have also had to constantly adjust their processes to accommodate new business goals, technologies and procedural changes.

While the overall process of setting up a privacy program involves complexity, the essential process can be seen as a straightforward three-step cycle:

1. Assess the current privacy-related environment
2. Address the gaps that your assessment identifies and improve privacy program
3. Continuously monitor and audit for compliance and effectiveness and improve as necessary

Step #1—Assessing Current Privacy-Related Environment
The goal of this step is to evaluate current processes, procedures, uses of data and so on. The evaluation will depend on an extensive series of individual assessments that include:

- Analysis of legal requirements
- Evaluation of existing privacy standards, practices and philosophies
- Evaluation of information security practices
- Collection of personal information
- Use of personal information
- Access to personal information
- Disclosure of personal information
- Disclosure of personal information with third parties
- Data integrity
- Data retention and destruction

See appendix, *Assessing the Current Privacy-Related Environment*, p. 197 for an expanded list of questions that address each of the above areas.

After you have worked through these various assessments, you will have conducted the legal analysis that will form the basis of moving forward with your privacy program. The virtual privacy team (VPT), in conjunction with a steering committee, will then be in a position to draft an organization-wide privacy policy. The final part of this step will be a sign-off by the steering committee of senior executives or, in some cases, the board of directors.

Step #2—Addressing the Gaps and Improving the Program

The goal of the second step is to use the results gleaned from the assessments in the first step and then identify and address gaps in your processes and procedures. You and the team will be asking how well the results currently fit in with the organization's existing privacy policies. During this step, the VPT you set up—and, if you have the resources, a small number of outside consultants—conducts a gap analysis and compares the results of the different assessments against the legal requirements and organization's existing privacy policy.

Example of Gap Analysis:
Disclosure of Personal Information with Third Parties

VPT members work with the team responsible for executing contracts in different areas of the organization to evaluate assessment results against existing legal requirements and privacy policies. They may discover they cannot locate copies of contracts, or even that written contracts don't exist. The contracts may not include current confidentiality, privacy and information-security language required by law. The teams identify gaps and develop a plan to address them.

The team then creates project plans to address the gaps, prioritized by risk. For example, the results of assessing organizational access to personal information will reveal how personal information flows through one or more units in your organization and where it is stored. For example, you may learn during this process that HR staff use laptops that store unencrypted data about employee compensation and Social Security numbers, as well as budget information. Other kinds of gaps include the collection of information that is unnecessary to the needs of the business or the granting of broader access than is needed. The privacy team then

- documents the tasks necessary to address the identified gaps;
- develops an actionable project plan that assigns specific activities and completion timelines (this is important if the gap presents a major risk) to each task;
- monitors progress, and
- requests an audit, as appropriate.

Step #3—Monitoring and Compliance Auditing for Continued Success

After your team identifies gaps and puts in place the plans to address them, you will need to create a privacy compliance program to audit the implemented privacy processes and procedures. For practical reasons, it's best if you house the monitoring function in the privacy team you created. Because of their evolving experience in the privacy area, the professionals on the team will be the most capable of carrying out these tasks.

The auditing function preferably should be done by the company's internal audit group or by an external party in an effort to keep this as unbiased and independent as possible. The auditor's responsibility should be to verify and determine the adequacy of the policies, procedures and documents in place—as identified in the assessment, or as required by law or regulations. Additional gaps may be identified and process improvement recommendations made.

For more information about auditing, see, "Leveraging Internal Audits in Privacy Governance," p. 123.

TYPICAL TASKS OF A PRIVACY OFFICE

You can expect your privacy office to perform a variety of tasks. These tasks fall roughly into three main categories of work: strategic, foundational and process.

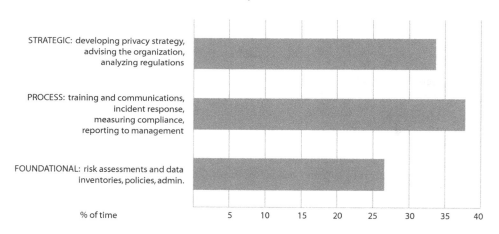

Spectrum of Privacy Professionals Tasks

Earlier in this chapter, we described the kind of **strategic** work your program will perform. You'll remember that this work includes helping to craft a mission statement and objectives, building a presence in your organization, finding executive sponsors, developing relationships with and buy-in from key colleagues, and generally promoting privacy as an important and ongoing consideration in the organization's programs, projects and systems.

Process work refers to managing the day-to-day privacy issues and queries that flow through the office and typically includes reviewing marketing and sales activities (such as e-mail campaigns and websites featuring new products), policy violations (for example, a privacy statement missing from a website), incidents of noncompliance, breaches of data privacy and security and privacy-related complaints. Handling these tasks well—including responding to them efficiently and in a timely manner—will be important, because these frequent interactions with diverse colleagues will contribute to your team's overall reputation throughout the organization. Later in the chapter, we'll cover process work in more detail. The following section introduces the **foundational** work that will form the basis for much of your daily operations.

FOUNDATIONAL WORK: ASSESSMENTS

Much of the work of your privacy program will revolve around your carrying out different types of privacy-related assessments and analyzing the results. The assessments will achieve various ends, including evaluating the impact of your current and planned business processes and systems on the personally identifiable information you obtain and store. The judicious use of well-organized and appropriately scaled assessments is vital to your program's success. Your team will also initiate or contribute to efforts to assess areas such as information security and third-party risk.

Conducting Privacy Risk Assessments
As you strive to identify risk and help chart appropriate courses of action for your organization, assessments will be a key tool. By asking questions in a disciplined, structured and consistent way, you can gather vital information about any area of your organization—IT systems, projects, programs and processes—where privacy issues are a potential concern. You can use assessments to

- proactively evaluate the impact on privacy of a new system or planned update;
- help you review or build a process for reviewing sales and marketing activities in a logical, systematic manner, and
- retroactively examine systems and programs that are already in place.

For an example of an institutional approach (University of Arizona) to risk assessment, see appendix, *Sample Risk Assessment Toolkit from the University of Arizona*, p. 201.

Tip: If your organization is a financial institution, you can find comprehensive resources at the Federal Financial Institutions Examination Council (FFIEC) website: ithandbook.ffiec. gov/it-booklets.aspx. The FFIEC's InfoBase includes a variety of IT Booklets on the subject of risk assessment.

Privacy Impact Assessments

As the privacy field developed, the U.S. federal government mandated that a **privacy impact assessment** (PIA) be performed for programs involving personally identifiable information. Some U.S. states have followed suit. The PIA has also become a de facto standard for commercial companies even if it is executed on a more informal basis than that required in a government agency. PIAs are separate from other processes you use to ensure compliance with regulations and your own data-protection procedures. Many organizations feel that if they complete an information security or compliance audit, then they have completed the equivalent of a PIA. However, while an information security or compliance audit may indeed address some aspects of a PIA, its focus is usually more specific and more limited in scope. Audits may confirm compliance with the law or policy, but they do not look at broader issues. For example, because an audit generally occurs after the fact, its results won't tell you whether a particular program or project address the applicable privacy requirements and have been implemented. By the time an audit is complete and reveals issues, it's already too late to make major privacy-related changes to a program or project.

Deciding When to Conduct PIAs

To operate your privacy program cost-effectively, you'll need to use your resources well. Specifically, you'll need to calibrate the scope of a PIA according to risk and the resources you have at hand. Preliminary analysis helps here. Think of this analysis as a two-step process.

1. List potential PIA candidates, including:
   - new data systems and information-sharing initiatives, and
   - existing systems undergoing modifications or upgrades.
2. Determine whether any candidate system or initiative collects, uses, accesses or disseminates personally identifiable information and for what purpose For example, a system that collects and uses personally identifiable information solely for the purpose of executing a transaction would not justify a PIA, whereas a system that uses personally identifiable information for behavioral marketing would.

In the case of new or planned systems and programs, aim for early involvement; PIAs can have more impact when they contribute to the design and development of a system or project. By conducting a PIA during the design and development phases of a new system or project, your privacy team can help integrate privacy-related thinking while a project is still in development. Not only will you add value to the development process through due diligence and assessments, but also you will educate colleagues and cement partnerships for future projects. If your organization is already operating systems and implementing projects that have not yet undergone an assessment, you should make PIAs a top priority.

Backgrounder: PIAs Originally Developed by Government, Applicable Everywhere

Citizens provide their governments with lots of data—much of it sensitive, such as the personal information U.S. taxpayers send to the Internal Revenue Service every year at tax time.

As government agencies in the United States began to adopt computer technology and amass vast amounts of personally identifiable information, these practices came under scrutiny. As early as the mid-1970s, the U.S. Federal Government recognized the vulnerability of and the need to protect the privacy of citizen data. A commission at the time pointed out that there was no reliable vehicle for asking the question whether "a particular record-keeping policy, practice or system should exist at all" (Privacy Protection Study Commission 1977). During the 1990s, as the collection and use of personally identifiable information proliferated, the privacy impact assessment became the standard methodology for ensuring that private data is collected, used and disseminated in accordance with the Federal Trade Commission's Fair Information Practice Principles. For more information about these principles, please see Chapter 2, *FTC's Fair Information Practice Principles*, p. 39.

The PIA methodology that government agencies use applies just as well to all kinds of non-governmental organizations in both public and private sectors. Complex organizations that share information across a diverse landscape of disparate systems and databases—particularly those whose operational units manage data across different jurisdictions—especially need a structured methodology to assess privacy-related risk. The greater the organizational diversity and spread of disconnected or siloed data, the more the situation requires a standard approach to address privacy and create policies to protect it.

Preliminary Work: The Privacy Threshold Analysis

A preliminary investigation—called a privacy threshold analysis (PTA)—will reveal candidates for privacy impact assessments. You can also use this kind of analysis as you integrate privacy into other organizational processes so that it is quick and easy to identify the new or changed collection of personally identifiable data. U.S. government agencies typically carry out a PTA as the first step in a privacy review. It takes the shape of a relatively short and simple form that collects key data about a system or project. With this data at hand, you can now look more closely at each candidate to determine whether a PIA of some kind is truly indicated. PTA data will typically

- **specify** the personal information your systems and program are—or could be—collecting, generating or retaining and why. IT architects can tell you precisely what kind of personal data their systems could or will collect. Obvious types of information include name, address and Social Security number. Other types of information that can be linked to specific individuals include, for example, IP addresses, data gathered through

social networking sites and information about biometrics, ethnicity, medical information and age.
- **reveal** whether your organization has ever conducted a PIA on a specific information
system. Ideally, a privacy team performs a PIA when a system is either first designed or
later, when it undergoes a significant upgrade. If a PIA didn't occur in either scenario,
then it would be wise to conduct one now.
- **identify** key stakeholders

If you decide to carry out a PIA, you may need to consult with the colleagues who have a
stake in the system or program you're investigating, and they can help you integrate privacy
protection into the project.

Key Resources for Learning about Privacy Threshold Analyses
Below, you'll find links to sample templates used by two different government agencies.

U.S. Department of Justice PTA template –
www.justice.gov/opcl/privacy_threshold_analysis.pdf

U.S. Department of Homeland Security PTA template –
www.dhs.gov/xlibrary/assets/privacy/privacy_pta_template.pdf

The privacy threshold analysis also helps you decide which level of assessment to apply. At
one end of the spectrum, a full-scale PIA will require your team to conduct a more in-depth
analysis by consulting with stakeholders and finding solutions to address concerns and to
mitigate or eliminate identifiable risks, such as vulnerability to privacy breaches. The situation would need to warrant the cost. At the other end of the spectrum, a small-scale PIA
requires less information-gathering and analysis and is a choice you'd typically make when
you decide to focus on only specific aspects of a project.

For example, if your organization decides to overhaul one of its IT systems, your privacy
office might not be involved in the whole project from start to finish, but only in those
stages that impact data collection. Another example: If your business plans a move to a new
building, your involvement need only concern the aspects of the move that involve privacy-
related issues. Another example: If your business decides to consolidate its data-storing
centers to one location in another country, you would definitely want to be involved early on
to provide guidance on any cross-border data transfer issues.

The following section explains how a privacy impact assessment works.

How a Privacy Impact Assessment Works

A privacy impact assessment asks basic questions about the collection and intended use of personally identifiable information. Besides asking about common data—such as the names and addresses of customers—the PIA also probes the use of less obvious private information. This includes employee data that takes the form, for example, of images captured by CCTV monitors or health-related information that is gleaned by a security system designed to capture radioactivity levels sensitive enough to reveal if an individual has undergone chemotherapy. A PIA may also identify the privacy implication of data that an organization collects via social media networks and behavioral targeting techniques. If your organization stores personally identifiable information remotely using "cloud computing" technology, a PIA will highlight that too.

Key Questions Asked in a Privacy Impact Assessment

- What information will be collected (for example: name, address and Social Security number)?
- Why it is being collected?
- What's its intended use?
- With whom will the information be shared?
- What opportunities will individuals have to consent to or decline the collection and use of their personal information (other than for required or authorized uses)?
- How are individuals able to grant consent?
- Can individuals gain access to information and correct as appropriate?
- How will the information be secured?

PIAs can also identify situations where privacy can be threatened when seemingly innocuous pieces of personal information (such as individual website preferences, IP address and proof of age) are combined into a single record.

The privacy impact assessment is a powerful tool. Used effectively, it will

- serve as the first step in identifying the privacy implications and vulnerabilities of an information system;
- create a road map for developing a comprehensive privacy policy to protect personal and confidential information;
- dovetail with the efforts of key associates during early stages of system development and project planning;
- create an iterative process throughout the development life cycle;
- generate discussion and enable decision making on how to address and, if necessary, mitigate identified privacy vulnerabilities;
- call for the implementation of policy controls and ongoing audits (for more information about internal audits, see "Leveraging Internal Audits in Privacy Governance," p. 123.

- support the idea that organizations should first analyze and assess the privacy risks associated with information systems and the data they collect and share—before developing a privacy policy;
- evaluate privacy implications before information systems are created or when existing systems are significantly modified (PIAs can also be conducted for existing IT systems that don't fall into either of these two categories);
- demonstrate how to create a sound policy for your public record, and
- be instrumental in saving your organization unnecessary costs, if applicable.

Key Resources for Learning about Privacy Impact Assessments

E-Government Act – www.gpo.gov/fdsys/pkg/PLAW-107publ347/content-detail.html

Congress passed the E-Government Act in 2002, establishing the role of Federal Chief Information Officer to enhance the management and promotion of electronic government services and processes. The act also established a broad framework of measures that require agencies to use Internet-based information technology to enhance citizen access to government information and services. The act (Section 208) mandates that agencies use privacy impact assessments whenever they develop or procure new technology—or make substantial changes to existing technology—involving the collection, maintenance and dissemination of identifiable information.

Privacy Impact Assessments: Official Guidance – www.justice.gov/opcl/pia.htm

The U.S. Department of Justice Office of Privacy and Civil Liberties (OPCL) provides government agencies with comprehensive resources to help them comply with the requirements of the E-Government Act. The PIA methodology and templates are of use to all organizations that want to assess privacy-related risk and implement best practice policies.

Government of New Zealand: Privacy Commissioner's Office – www.privacy.org.nz/privacy-impact-assessment-handbook

The Government of New Zealand has established itself as a global leader in advocating for privacy protection. This comprehensive handbook includes the why, when and how of PIAs and also describes the contents of a typical PIA report.

The PIA Process

After you decide to conduct a PIA and determine the right degree of depth, you'll kick off the process. A full-scale PIA typically goes through the following stages:

- Reviewing the outcomes and documents from the initial assessment (the privacy threshold analysis)
- Developing the project outline (project motivations, opportunities, business rationale,

scope, design, impact, privacy issues and risks, project plan and key stakeholders)
- Ensuring that the scope and the resources dedicated to the PIA are appropriate
- Holding preliminary discussions with relevant stakeholders
- Conducting an analysis of privacy issues
- Writing the report, which includes the following:
  - Table of contents
  - Introduction and overview
  - Description of the project and information flows
  - Privacy analysis
  - Privacy risk assessment
  - Privacy enhancing and mitigation measures
  - Compliance mechanisms
  - Conclusions
- Distributing report to all stakeholders, if applicable

Early-Stage Projects: Finding the Data You Need

If your privacy team is working with a project in its early stages (an ideal situation), you may find you have insufficient information on which to base decisions. In this case, you can use one or more approaches to dig for more data. For example, you can ask for a project outline, conduct an analysis of stakeholders and scan the environment.

Stage	Recommended Activities
Research and obtain project outline	During the early stages of a project, there may be only limited documentation available. There may also be uncertainty about the scope and intended features. However, you should ask for a copy of all available documents that cover topics such as scope, requirements, project charter and terms of reference. If documents like these are not available, then consult with key stakeholders, project managers and members of the project steering committee.

Consult and analyze	• Undertake a stakeholder analysis
	This analysis involves identifying all groups and business units that have a role or responsibility in the project, as well as anyone who might benefit or be otherwise affected, such as groups that provide technology. Ideally, you'll come out of this exercise with as broad a list of stakeholders as possible, along with a brief analysis of each.
	• Scan the environment
	You can also glean other information from sources peripheral to the project in question. For example, you can look for
	  ◦ information about prior projects of a similar nature
	  ◦ details of prior PIAs on similar projects (if nothing is available, look outside of your own organization)
	  ◦ fact sheets, whitepapers, reports and refereed articles published by industry associations, regulatory bodies and other organizations

Document and report	After you've completed the assessment, document the results in a report. The privacy team typically submits a completed PIA report to the governing or decision-making body associated with the system or project being assessed. The results of the PIA and subsequent insights will guide decision makers in developing the appropriate policies or performing other related tasks. In some organizations, it's also possible for the decision-making to go on during the completion of the PIA report, as the various parties work through the findings. In this case, the final report documents the decisions already made. The community of third parties who have an interest in the outcome of PIAs includes: • Privacy advocates • Records managers • Internal auditors • Risk managers • Legal staff • IT managers • Business managers
Review and assess	As technologies and programs evolve, PIAs need to be kept current. For example, you may find that a program that mitigated all its risks a year ago now has a new program manager and new risks have arisen. If you build in a review-and-assess process from the beginning, all parties will know the maximum amount of time allowed to elapse between PIAs.

Assessing Risks in Using Third Parties

Business increasingly depends on third-party relationships. Third parties include entities such as co-innovation partners, outsourcing service providers and vendors spread across often complex supply chain networks, often with a global scope. Exchanging data with these third parties is an inevitable part of the relationship. And at least some of this data is likely to comprise personally identifiable information and must be protected according to applicable laws and standards, as well as your organization's own policies and procedures.

Managing Privacy with Vendors and Suppliers

The high level of security expected by consumers and customers and a growing global emphasis on legal and regulatory compliance translates into this: An organization must be able to demonstrate that its data governance is up to the task. In addition to getting your own house in order, you also have to evaluate third parties for risk. Effective third-party governance is essential to your privacy program.

Although your privacy office will probably not work directly with third parties, your team can work with procurement and the internal business sponsor for the supplier (for example, HR) and help facilitate the sort of due diligence and care that reflects the responsible stewardship of private information. If your colleagues in procurement currently conduct assessments independent of your organization's information security and legal functions, you can help them in several ways. For example, you can

- provide education regarding their legal requirements in the privacy area;
- keep them current with privacy-related issues;
- provide questions to help them assess potential vendors and evaluate the responses, and
- supply boilerplate contract clauses to protect customer and employee data (in some cases, you may be required by regulations to include certain clauses).

Privacy-Related Legal Requirements for Third Parties

There are U.S. state and federal laws that have specific requirements in relation to privacy and third parties. For example, when a financial services organization contracts with a third party that will have access to customer data, the federal Gramm-Leach-Bliley Act, Health Insurance Portability and Accountability Act and certain state laws require you to use certain protection clauses in your third-party contracts. In the case of international transactions with offshore vendors, you still have to comply with any laws that require organizations to promptly notify customers of any data breach. Additional complications may arise here, with offshore vendors at times it can prove difficult to uncover the details of a breach. The bottom line here is that you can't outsource liability.

Using a Standard Approach to Assess Third-Party Risk

As you evaluate existing or prospective third parties, use a standardized risk assessment process that includes identifying

- relevant risks and vulnerabilities and assessing their potential risk and impact;
- relevant stakeholders and their concerns;
- key performance indicators (KPIs);
- existing or planned controls or mitigation for each risk, and
- any residual risk based on the reduced impact and likelihood that results from mitigation (inherent risk - controls = residual risk).

You should write up the results of the assessment in a risk report specifying information such as

- location where the data will reside, and
- applicable privacy-related laws or lack of them.

The final contract with the third party should include

- Specific information about the services involved;
- Type of information the provider will process at remote locations, and
- What their role will be in the event of a data breach.

- How your organization and the outsourcing provider will transmit information—and what protections you'll apply, and how and when;
- What happens to the data after termination of contract (for example, will the provider destroy it and, if so, what proof is acceptable to you), and
- Your ability to audit the third party for compliance with the above requirements.

After the contract is effective, someone—most likely your contract-management colleagues in consultation with you—will need to implement an ongoing process to manage the risk throughout the life of the contract. As the number of third parties used by the organization grows, so will the level of effort and resources needed to assess and manage risks on an on-going basis.

Implications of Offshore Outsourcing

Although the legal and practical aspects of third-party assessment apply equally to vendors and suppliers regardless of their location, outsourcing jobs to offshore vendors or simply using offshore data storage (including, for example, via "cloud computing"), can sharply increase your data privacy risks and the complexity of managing them. Understanding that your organization's outsourcing includes the transfer of personally identifiable information is extremely important because international privacy and security laws differ. It's also important for companies to thoroughly understand and deal with privacy issues in their contracts. You should spell out specifically the restrictions on the vendor's use and protection of your organization's data as well as what their role will be in the event of any data breach. Your organization should also stipulate that you have the right to audit overseas vendors for compliance with its privacy policies.

Some of the privacy and security risks associated with both domestic and offshore outsourcing with third parties include

- Unauthorized use or disclosure of personal information;
- Inability to provide legitimate access to personal information upon request (by data owner or data subject, if required by law);
- Inability of the organization to investigate or litigate against offshore offenders;
- Inability to guarantee the protection of personal information in foreign jurisdictions, and
- Foreign laws that conflict with U.S. laws or offer less protection for the privacy of personal information.

There are ways your organization can mitigate risks associated specifically with offshore outsourcing. For example, you can

- conduct a privacy impact assessment of the offshore vendor;
- conduct an onsite review of security and privacy controls in place at the offshore vendor—or hire an independent party to conduct the third-party review;
- consider not sending personal information offshore or not allowing offshore service

providers to collect personal information from customers or employees, if practical

- consider whether information covered by an offshore contract can be restricted to only non-sensitive public information;
- diligently review the outsourcing service provider and understand the technological capabilities of its proposed offshore locations, and
- develop contracts to cover all data protection elements including:
  - ○ Spell out data transfer requirements if you belong to a multinational organization (for example, model contract clauses)
  - ○ Specify forum and choice of law
  - ○ Have it reviewed for enforceability under private international law

For more information about working with third parties on privacy issues, see Chapter 4, "Working with Third Parties," p. 147.

Key Resources for Managing the Risks of Offshore Data Exchange

EU publications

- Standard Clauses for the Transfer of Personal Data to Third Countries
  http://europa.eu/legislation_summaries/information_society/l14012_en.htm

- Formal findings on the adequacy of data protection in "third countries" (i.e. non-EU states) online at Commission Decisions on the Adequacy of the Protection of Personal Data in Third Countries
  http://ec.europa.eu/justice_home/fsj/privacy/thridcountries/index_en.htm

- A framework for binding corporate rules: see the consultation documents and resources section for the Working Documents
  http://ec.europa.eu/justice_home/fsj/privacy/workinggroup/consultations/index_en.htm

- The EU has an arrangement with the U.S. government about personal information transfers called Safe Harbor
  www.export.gov/safeharbor

- Frequently asked questions relating to transfers of personal data from the EU/EEA to third world countries
  http://ec.europa.eu/justice/policies/privacy/thridcountries/index_en.htm

OECD publications

- Recommendation on Consumer Dispute Resolution and Redress (cross-border disputes)
  www.oecd.org/dataoecd/43/50/38960101.pdf

- Recommendation on the Cross-border Enforcement of Laws Protecting Privacy
  www.oecd.org/document/60/0,3746,en_2649_201185_38771516_1_1_1_1,00.html

Electronic Privacy Information Centre (EPIC)

- An annual survey of and guide to the state of privacy laws around the world
  http://epic.org/phr06/

MANAGING THE PRIVACY PROGRAM DAY TO DAY

Your privacy program will typically perform the following main clusters of tasks:

- Responding to incoming items, such as queries and complaints
- Managing aspects of privacy, such as opt-out data and requests for personal information

A central role of your privacy program will be to respond to incoming queries, complaints, policy violations, instances of noncompliance and incident reports (usually describing breaches in data privacy and security).

Making It Easy to Reach You

You will need to design a process so that individuals—including your organization's own employees—can easily lodge complaints about any of the following aspects of your privacy operations:

- Privacy policies, procedures and disclosures
- Compliance with those policies, procedures and disclosures
- Compliance with the applicable privacy laws and regulations

Individuals should be able to contact your office by telephone, in writing, electronically or even (if appropriate to your business) in person. Not only is it a good business practice to have an effective process for handling privacy complaints, but also there are federal laws that may actually require you to respond to certain complaints; it's good to familiarize yourself with these laws while you are charting out the legal framework within which your organization operates.

As part of your education and awareness outreach program, let everyone in your organization know how to alert you to privacy violations and breaches. Also, ask colleagues to give you feedback if the organization is not meeting customer expectations and their satisfaction is being compromised. Make contact as easy as possible for your colleagues. Provide convenient communication alternatives such as

- a dedicated toll-free number;
- a box for regular mail, and
- a dedicated e-mail address.

Be sure to assign staff to monitor these collection points frequently and link these conduits to your incident response program. From an assessment perspective, keep metrics to determine the type of complaint, the initial response, follow-up actions taken and cycle times to resolution. This will aid you in determining where you need to focus additional training or resources in your company. You might even consider running table-top exercises to make sure you have an end-to-end system that functions as intended.

Backgrounder: The Potential Cost of Privacy Breaches

A breach can be costly; in a 2009 report, the Ponemon Institute estimated that the cost of a data breach amounted to $204 per affected record. According to the report, breaches at U.S. companies affected between 5,000 and 100,000 customer records. If a breach compromises, for example, 10,000 of your consumers' records, the result is a hefty cost to you. In a similar study, the Ponemon Institute estimated that a lost laptop costs an organization on average $50,000. Breaches are a serious matter and your organization must have a suitable incident response plan in place.

Managing Privacy Complaints

Even when your privacy program is robust, your organization will receive complaints concerning privacy-related issues. For example, a consumer may complain that she is unable to update her personal information on your website. Or a customer who requested to opt out of e-mail communications is still receiving them. More serious complaints—privacy breaches—are dealt with in the next section.

Best Practice Recommendation: Developing a Complaint-Handling Process

To be prepared for complaints, you'll need to:
- Decide who is responsible for receiving and handling them
- Have one department or individual responsible for receiving all complaints to ensure that they are responded to timely and documented appropriately
- Have a clear process for how complaints are received—if another department receives it, staff should know where to forward it for immediate processing
- Include an escalation process
- Develop, document and implement a complaint procedure that is easily accessible, understandable and simple to use

When you receive a complaint:
- Document it with a privacy complaint form and record date of receipt
- Attach any accompanying documentation to the complaint
- Acknowledge receipt promptly
- Consult with legal counsel if warranted
- Contact the person who complained and discuss the complaint (a swift response can help mollify an irate customer)
- Take appropriate measures to rectify the situation
- Notify individuals of the outcome of investigations clearly and promptly in writing
- Record all decisions and outcomes
- Make changes to policies, procedures or practices if necessary
- Verify later that required changes are effective
- Identify trends in complaints and incidents to help inform later training and PIAs

---

At the heart of a robust complaints process is a fast response and a procedure that demonstrates your commitment to privacy. If done correctly, your process for handling complaints will safeguard the confidence of your consumers and customers and help build your organization's good reputation.

Your privacy program needs a clear process and a central location for receiving and handling privacy complaints. You will need to

- have a set of clear procedures for how complaints are handled;
- track complaints by division, type of complaint, number, frequency (a cluster of complaints may indicate the need for training), whether any notifications are required, actions taken and date of resolution, and
- identify if there are problems with your opt-in/opt-out process.

Handling Serious Privacy Breaches

Some complaints are more serious than others. If, for example, you determine that an actual **privacy breach** took place, your office will need to swing into action with a swift response. The process is governed by the **incident response plan** that you will have prepared and have in place for just such incidents.

If handling complaints well is important, responding efficiently to privacy breaches is absolutely essential. More serious than complaints, privacy breaches occur when an organization handles personal data incorrectly and allows, for example, unauthorized access or disclosure of personally identifiable information. Data breaches aren't always the result of malicious actions by people outside the organization; they are often caused by simple errors. For example, someone sends an unencrypted e-mail containing sensitive information to an unintended recipient, or an employee loses a laptop with unencrypted personal information on its hard drive.

Privacy breaches are serious matters and the consequences are potentially very costly to an organization. For a list of state and federal security breach laws, see appendix, *U.S. Security Breach Laws*, p. 212. For additional information about federal breach laws, see the sections in Chapter 2 that deal with the laws applicable to your organization, such as HIPAA and GLBA regulations.

Developing an Incident Response Plan

When you investigate a complaint—whether a complaint from a customer or a tip from an employee—you can quickly determine if it constitutes a more serious privacy breach. Identifying a breach then triggers a planned response. Your documented plan will cover a series of topics, including initial containment, preliminary assessment, risk assessment, notification requirements, root cause analysis, mitigation and prevention. Your privacy incident response plan should also include clear instructions about the following:

Incident Response Plan Phase	Description
Assigning roles and responsibilities	Document and build a virtual organization with a centralized reporting structure to respond to incidents. If a confirmed privacy incident occurs, employees should already know how to identify it and whom to contact in order to alert the response team. Defining each person's role doesn't mean everyone will be involved in every event. However, there will be a core team that is necessarily involved in the program's day-to-day management.
Composing the response team	Include in the team, at a minimum: the CIO, CFO and key players from various areas of the organization, including public affairs, legal, internal affairs, privacy office, information and physical security and appropriate program and operational business managers.
Identifying details of data loss	Identify the risk caused by the data loss. How sensitive was the data, how was it lost, how was it formatted (which tells you how usable is it) and how many people are affected?
Reporting	Train employees how to identify a possible privacy incident and know whom to report to and how fast they need to do it. For example, an employee may be expected to report a suspected privacy incident within an hour.
Escalating incident	Train employees to report an incident immediately to a central location. The central staff will then review the suspected incident and determine who needs to be involved, based on the quantity and type of breached information. Small breaches may be handled at the staff level; other cases may need to go straight to the highest level.
Investigating	Investigate all confirmed incidents in order to understand what happened, which policy failed and how the organization can learn from its mistakes and avoid future recurrences.
Performing notification	Identify different means of notifying individuals based on the risks posed by the loss of the data, and advise them via ready-to-go templates.
Mitigating	Secure all information Take affected systems offline Block exploited ports Notify affected stakeholders and system owners
Closing incident and analyzing root causes	Close an incident after you have identified the cause and mitigated it. Log this information about the incident with sufficient specificity and consistency so that trends can help improve inadequate training and policies.
Reviewing program annually	Review the program at least annually. Depending on the size and complexity of your organization, reviews may need to be more frequent.

Key Resources for Designing a Complaint and Violation Policy and Process

University of Florida: Information Privacy Policies and Procedures
The complaints and violation policy of the University of Florida provides a good model for organizations instituting their own policies.
http://privacy.health.ufl.edu/policies/hipaamanual/privacymgt/PM-05-investig.pdf

---

Creating a Lean Reporting Structure

In the interest of expediency and efficiency, design the organizational structure for incident handling with the fewest number of reporting tiers possible. Ensure that company officials responsible for safeguarding personally identifiable information are fully informed of the incident. You will discover that your incident response program lends itself well to analytics (metrics) and is a wonderful way to show objectively whether your organization is doing well when it comes to data privacy and security.

Private information may sometimes be severely comprised (for example, someone steals a laptop whose hard drive contains unencrypted data for all employee records, including name, address, payroll information and Social Security number). Or, the unauthorized penetration of the organization's network results in access to a million healthcare records. Incidents like the latter may draw the attention of both regulators and major media. In this case, you should expand the response team to include the following, as appropriate:

- Operational business leaders
- Senior managers and executives, including the COO and CEO
- Data forensics experts
- Law enforcement agents

Handling Breach Notifications

If the laws affecting your organization require you to notify affected parties of a privacy breach, a swift response may help to minimize damage to your organization's reputation and business. You will need to understand your organization's legal responsibilities and have a process in place for dealing promptly with any notification obligations.

Key Resources for Understanding State Security Breach Notification Laws

National Conference of State Legislation (NCSL) website
www.ncsl.org/default.aspx?tabid=13489

This site provides up-to-date information about state legislation that affects security breaches and what kind of notification is mandated. These laws constantly change.

Within your organization, there may be various requirements—based on different laws—for providing notices to affected individuals. Your decision whether to combine these various requirements into a single notice will be driven by

- relevant laws;
- the extent to which you can cast a combined approach in language that will make sense to a lay person, and
- your ability to defend to regulators.

For example, there may be five states in which you operate that require similar notifications for a breach. In this case, you should aim high and satisfy the most rigorous law among the five.

Key Questions for Determining Whether Notification Is Required

- What are the regulatory requirements—international, federal and state?
- If the applicable laws mandate notification, does your organization's notice meet regulatory requirements?
- Are you also required to notify third parties, such as the state attorney general or a regulatory or consumer reporting agency?
- What are the reasonable expectations of the affected individuals (for example, customers or employees)?

Other Tasks of the Privacy Office

In addition to responding to complaints and breaches, your privacy office will typically also manage

- opt-out requirements or processes;
- requests for personal information, and
- third-party seal programs.

Managing Opt-Out Requests

Depending on the number of business divisions, country locations and different data sets your company maintains and how large they are and where the data is located, your company will need a process to maintain and manage customer opt-out requests. If the privacy office has limited resources, managing and tracking these requests may be a time-consuming function. This might be managed more efficiently if done centrally within the business unit/division/country itself. Partnering with the business to provide guidance in setting up a process for managing opt-out requests will foster ownership for the process and responsibility for compliance with these requests. The business will appreciate what this entails and will evaluate risks and repercussions when they are planning a marketing campaign.

Within the United States, the business will need to remember to give consumers and customers the option to opt out of communications sent not only via e-mail, but also through postal mail and telephone. In addition, the business unit will need to understand what it must do regarding the Federal Trade Commission's National Do Not Call Registry (for more information about this registry, please see Chapter 2, p. 50). Unless your organization is exempt, the business will need to subscribe to both the national registry and any state registries within your areas of operation. You can provide guidance and support to the business in drafting a compliant process for them. Note that there is no room for error where these laws are concerned. Liability is strict and the laws are vigorously enforced. For more information, see Chapter 4, "Managing Preferences (Contact-Point Requests and Consent)," p. 154.

Managing Requests for Personal Information

Certain laws—for example, the Health Insurance Portability and Accountability Act, the Fair Credit Reporting Act and some state laws—may require you to provide individuals with a copy of the information you have on them. To minimize the risk of improper disclosure, be sure you have a procedure in place to verify the identity of individuals who request the information you have on file. There are different means of doing this. For example, you can ask individuals who want a copy of their personal information to fill out a request form and have it notarized. Only after receipt of the notarized form will you provide the information. Or you may require the requestor to provide a few unique data elements to verify their identity, such as an account number, the first five digits of their Social Security number, the date of birth and the date of the last transaction with your company before providing the requested information.

Managing Third-Party Seal Programs

Third-party seal programs—such as TRUSTe and VeriSign—can help provide additional verification that your practices do match your online privacy policy. The requirements of these seal programs—which allow you to display their seal on your website providing you abide by a set of fair practice rules and agree to participate in their resolution service—can help you craft your privacy policy and also identify problem areas or noncompliance. The programs provide additional forms of redress and are intended to enhance consumer trust. Review the various types of seal programs available and make your choice based on the specific requirements of your organization's overall privacy program.

TESTING AND IMPROVING THE PRIVACY PROGRAM

Once your privacy program is operating, your office must constantly find ways to improve its performance. Information will flow your way from internal audits, routine monitoring and assessments within the organization, as well as external assessments. On the basis of the feedback you receive and analysis you perform, you will be able to adjust and enhance elements of your program.

Leveraging Internal Audits in Privacy Governance

Internal audits are a mechanism you will want to use regularly to ensure that your organization is in compliance with internal policies and applicable legal requirements. Together, assessment results and audits will help to inform and guide your decisions to create or update policy, design or adapt procedures and ensure compliance with both internal and external (mainly regulatory) requirements. Assessments, analyses and audits will become an essential, never-ending process through which you examine and shape the face of your organization's positions on privacy.

Auditing serves several purposes. For example, routine auditing and monitoring will help to:

- Confirm that the privacy processes are still operating—when the novelty of a project fades, employees may inadvertently revert to old practices.
- Keep compliance issues fresh through formal self-assessment and illustrate actual privacy practices to business leaders.
- Flag scenarios where employees change jobs and institutional memory is in danger of leaving the unit.
- Determine whether a compliance process change is necessary as a result of a new business process. Business is a constantly changing environment. Audits help discover when new privacy processes are necessary to meet these new changes.

Prepare the organization for audits or exams by regulators (regularly conducting internal audits allows business to understand and address privacy risks before a regulator conducts an audit and reduces the risk of regulatory enforcement and fines).

Every manager in your organization whose business activities involve in some way the use of personal information is responsible for privacy compliance. With its focus on compliance, an internal audit ensures that your organization's systems, policies and procedures work as intended. An audit can identify noncompliance gaps and bring to light instances where, for example

- managers are not updating internal e-mail address suppression lists promptly;
- a system is not capturing privacy preferences, or
- a marketing department isn't following privacy policies and procedures during a marketing campaign.

However, even the most thorough audit may not identify all problems and vulnerabilities. If, despite your internal auditors' best efforts, something does go wrong, your organization will still be able to confidently assert that it actively monitors privacy compliance. In such a case, the organization stands a better chance of minimizing the damage and retaining the credibility in the eyes of customers and regulators.

Forging a Relationship with Internal Auditors

There is a natural linkage between your work and that of your organization's internal auditors. It's an excellent idea to cultivate good working relationships and close collaboration with your organization's internal auditors. Take every opportunity to help educate them about privacy issues and keep them current with both internal policies and procedures, as well as with the compliance requirements of the relevant regulatory bodies. In fact, depending on your organization, the internal auditors may have more clout than your privacy office. If that's the case, use it to your advantage and let them become your enforcement arm.

Consider meeting regularly with your counterpart or peer in that area. It's especially helpful to develop a relationship with the person responsible for carrying out audits. During these meetings, you can discuss current and upcoming audits and legal issues that may affect data and its use. Additionally, consider meeting a few times per year with a larger team from internal audit's team. Here you can discuss areas across the organization where you believe an audit may be necessary to compel compliance with a law or policy for which you have oversight. You can also discuss any areas where the number of incidents appear to be higher than elsewhere in the company. You can formalize your roles by using an ARCI (accountable/responsible/consulted/informed) Matrix to make sure that you are part of all audits involving IT or the use of personal data.

Your goal is to ensure that your team is "a player" and is regularly consulted for additional information and clarification of items discovered during an audit. After the audit is complete, you may be able to join the project team created to close any identified control issues.

Here is a sample outline of a process that can help you meet your goal:

Annual audit list: Auditors should consult with you on ideas for areas or topics that should be considered for an audit.

Pre-audit: Auditors consult with you on the scope of the specific audit.

Audit: Auditing team provides updates of the audit.

Audit report: Auditors provide you with a pre-read of the audit report. You review and offer suggestions, revisions and recommendations for remediation.

Audit closing meeting: Auditing staff invite you to the closing meeting, particularly if you are going to be responsible for working with the affected business unit on remediating some activity.

Best Practice Recommendation: A Proactive Process for Third-Party Audits

If your organization works with partners or you are a service provider that holds sensitive data from clients, you should be prepared for the occasional third-party audit. One strategy is to train any staff in your organization who are potentially involved in responding to third-party audits. This training can focus on market conduct and/or federal regulatory exams.

The best thing you can do is to help document all the policies and procedures designed to keep your organization's operations within the parameters of applicable laws and regulations. As Chapter 2 made clear in presenting the legal framework for privacy operations, the nature of your organization's business will determine (especially, in the United States) which laws apply and how you comply.

A best practice is to conduct, wherever possible, a "test once, use many" process for dealing with external or third-party audits of your program. This entails preparing a portfolio of ready-to-go, boilerplate responses and reports to answer typical questions from a regulatory or third-party assessor. You can create this material using templates from sources such as

- the model examiner's handbook, published by the National Association of Insurance Commissioners, or
- the audit handbook for regulators, published by the Federal Financial Institutions Examination Council.

Study whatever general guidelines your industry's examiners might use and create stock answers to the many questions. Although, this activity requires an investment of time upfront, it will prepare you for audits and save you time later. You can scale your efforts and repeat this process as often as you need.

Note: It's important that the privacy office is never accountable for closing a control issue. Business units must be accountable. Privacy can help them close the gap.

Enabling Privacy Self-Assessments

In addition to conducting periodic internal audits (which may only cover certain privacy functions once or twice a year) to identify noncompliance, organizations can voluntarily take the initiative to carry out their own ongoing privacy assessments. A privacy self-assessment is a ready-made process that a privacy office can use for individual business areas—such as sales and marketing—to evaluate their privacy practices for the purpose of benchmarking and improving their own privacy systems and practices over time. The process includes the business owners' assessment of the degree to which the organization performs against a set of expectations. When it measures compliance, an organization may identify gaps and risks that can then guide follow-up and remedial action. By using a self-assessment approach, an organization helps to

- reduce the need to develop its own particular assessment instruments;
- scale itself (in the case of a small privacy office), and
- educate business units about their responsibilities and actions.

Key Resources for Learning about Privacy Self-Assessments

Office of the Privacy Commissioner of Canada
This is a very good example of a Canadian government-provided privacy self-assessment toolkit. This toolkit is a resource for Canadian entities that have to meet the requirements of Canada's Personal Information Protection and Electronic Documents Act.

www.priv.gc.ca/information/pub/ar-vr/pipeda_sa_tool_200807_e.pdf

---

Providing Compliance Checklists for Self-Assessment

Your privacy office can provide a valuable service within the organization by crafting compliance checklists for specific subjects or areas, such as telemarketing. For colleagues who are tasked with evaluating compliance in their part of the organization, the checklist will guide the process by providing key questions. It will become clear whether the appropriate policies and procedures are built into the systems and if employees are following them as intended. By the end of the evaluation, your colleagues will generally know whether their units' systems and processes are in compliance with both internal privacy policy and external regulatory requirements. Using checklists is a great way to implement the "80/20 rule." If you provide them with the answers to all the general questions (80 percent +/-) about certain subjects, your colleagues will have a lot of the information they need. You can then devote your time to working on solutions for the remaining 20 percent most complex queries.

For an example of a detailed compliance checklist, see appendix, *Sample Compliance Checklist*, p. 199.

Conducting Business Unit Privacy Risk Assessments

While you may depend on other, better-scaled areas of your organization to provide the processes and colleagues, you can still adopt best practices and have your privacy team conduct more comprehensive business unit privacy risk assessments. You can find the best set of templates for guiding these assessments in the Generally Accepted Privacy Principles (GAPP), jointly developed by professional accountant associations from the United States and Canada (AICPA and CICA). You can use GAPP to assess an individual business unit's compliance with your organization's internal policies and procedures (which should already be keyed to existing domestic and international standards). Adopt a risk-based approach to conducting these assessments. In other words, you should assess low risk areas—where the organization collects little to no personal information—less frequently than areas of your business that collect, process and transfer large amounts of personally identifiable information. In addition, depending on the nature of the organization's business, some principles may not be applicable or will be less important.

Key Resources for Generally Accepted Privacy Principles

The American Institute of CPAs (AICPA) and the Canadian Institute of Chartered Accountants (CICA)
This professional partnership jointly developed the Generally Accepted Privacy Principles (GAPP). Using GAPP, organizations can design and implement sound privacy practices and policies.
www.aicpa.org/InterestAreas/InformationTechnology/Resources/Privacy/GenerallyAcceptedPrivacyPrinciples/Pages/default.aspx

---

Require business units to conduct self-assessments to determine:

- What personally identifiable information they collect
- How they use the personally identifiable information
- Whether they comply with legal and regulatory requirements as well as organizational processes and procedures
- Whether personally identifiable information is retained as legally required
- Whether personally identifiable information is being disposed of appropriately

Strategic Planning Documents for Each Business Unit

Each business unit needs to understand and constantly be on the lookout for privacy-related issues that, if left unattended, might interfere with or increase the cost of doing business. Make sure that your strategy offices understand these issues and work them into their contingency plans.

For business units that depend on personally identifiable information (for example, consumer sales), privacy has become a strategic factor. If your organization is like this, consider that privacy should be part of the organization's culture. The unit's privacy strategy

- must be part of the organization's broader strategic planning;
- will alert the organization to privacy issues, their implications, corresponding public concerns and risks to the organization, and
- should reflect the nature of that organization and be consistent with its mission statement. There are different approaches to a privacy strategy.

Type of Information Privacy Strategy	Features
Minimalist	<ul><li>Basic approach to meet legal requirements</li><li>A basic understanding of privacy and security protection</li><li>An understanding of the organization's personal data</li><li>Recognition that privacy should be built into processes</li></ul>
Comprehensive	<ul><li>Organizational understanding that privacy is essential to the relationship with employees and customers</li><li>A more comprehensive privacy strategy that:<ul><li>Identifies and protects all data</li><li>Recognizes benefits and inefficiencies in data management (for example, sourcing and storing data)</li><li>Ensures data is unconsolidated data if there are multiple sources</li><li>Retains data no longer than necessary</li></ul></li></ul>
Broad	<ul><li>Understanding and consideration of other privacy concerns (for example, effect of certain marketing such as behavioral advertising or use of social media)</li><li>Encompassing of impact on other types of privacy, such as personal privacy and communications</li></ul>

Using a Privacy Maturity Model

It's important to see privacy compliance as a journey. Not every organization needs to apply maximum measures to achieve an acceptable level of privacy. The progress you make along the way strengthens the organization. The American Institute of Certified Public Accountants and the Canadian Institute of Chartered Accountants have together created a privacy maturity model tool to help organizations assess and maintain their compliance with privacy regulations and policies. The tool enables you to measure progress against benchmarks established by the GAPP criteria and to assess at which level of maturity (there are six) your organization currently operates. To work with the maturity model, AICPA and CICA recommend that you

- appoint a project lead and create a committee (including representatives from legal, human resources, risk management, internal audit, information technology and the privacy function);
- document the findings (an accurate and complete reflection of current privacy initiatives reviewed by the committee), and
- assess maturity (compare the organization's activities to the description of each maturity level and, once classified, examine whether the entity should strive to meet the next level of maturity).

CHAPTER 4

Privacy Program Governance

The last chapter provided a road map to help guide you through the process of developing a privacy program—from penning the initial mission statement to getting the program up and running and, finally, to instituting processes for testing and improving the program over time. This chapter takes a closer look at the key aspects of managing an ongoing program. Accepting that your privacy office is subject to the particular politics of your organization, you'll find that governing your program depends on the effective management of two different areas—the human and technical dimensions.

The human aspect involves:

- Evangelizing the privacy function and ensuring awareness of related policies
- Defining your privacy office's own roles and responsibilities
- Positioning its leadership for maximum visibility and success
- Working with various constituents across your organization—including colleagues in IT, marketing, compliance, finance and procurement—whose work bears directly or indirectly on privacy-related issues

The technical aspect refers to governing the actual personally identifiable information that your privacy office is charged to help protect. Data governance

- involves the process of authorizing decisions in matters related to data, including its use, life cycle and protection, and
- provides the rule book for how to handle privacy-related data during the day-to-day operations of your organization.

EVANGELISM AND THE POLITICS OF BUILDING A PRIVACY OFFICE

Obtaining executive buy-in and communicating privacy throughout the organization will help prevent or preempt turf wars. However, politics is a reality in every kind of organization;

it's the forming of alliances, the daily give and take, the working out of compromises and the exercise of power and influence that makes most organizations function—for better or worse. The success of your organization's privacy function will depend on the collaboration of managers from all business units and departments. If your managers feel threatened, they will likely not cooperate or worse, they may try to covertly undermine the privacy agenda. The most likely potential turf wars are between the privacy office and those colleagues who work in the areas of IT security, marketing, legal and compliance.

This is where your executive sponsors come in and why it is worth getting them on board in the first place. They have the clout to help you clearly communicate the mission and authority of the privacy office throughout the organization. If there is real or potential conflict about individual roles, the lines of accountability and authority must be drawn and then respected by both the privacy office and the other department and business unit managers. In this way, turf wars are confined to being rare exceptions rather than an ongoing challenge or concern that drains your time and energy.

Getting Buy-In from the Top

Privacy is unlikely to be a top priority for your organization for more than a short period of time, and it will also vie for attention with many other initiatives. For this reason, it's your top priority to communicate the privacy message and agenda throughout the organization. The support of senior executives who understand and buy into the privacy agenda will be invaluable to your efforts. Realistically, winning that support may be quite a challenge. So what is the best approach?

Aligning Privacy with Business Objectives

The key is to frame the privacy agenda in the context of the organization's business or institutional objectives. By framing your agenda in this way, you can then demonstrate how privacy supports the objectives of not only the overall organization but also its constituent parts. For example, a company's vice president of sales and marketing—if not formally required to do so—is more likely to support the privacy function and agenda if he or she understands how building customer trust through understandable and concise online privacy statements will help drive higher online sales and revenue.

Facilitating the Integration of Privacy

Be sure to enlist the help of others as you work to persuade the business or other compliance areas to bake privacy-related awareness and action into their day-to-day operations. The bottom line is to look at the time you spend cultivating buy-in through meetings and communications with high-level executives as an investment that will pay dividends later. You want key sponsors to treat privacy as naturally as breathing; then you can be sure that your privacy program has solid support from the top.

Clarifying Accountability

Establishing clear accountability for privacy-related tasks and projects is vital for a well-functioning privacy program. As a rule, if no one is accountable for successfully completing a project, the work doesn't get done. Most of the time, your privacy office itself will not be accountable for implementing new privacy-related initiatives. More likely, your office will be the party to identify and call out a problem; however, accountability for taking action will probably lie within another group, such as marketing or IT. It's important to know where the buck stops, especially in cases where your organization's operations are found to fall short of legal requirements. Some organizations create a "signature table" with sign-offs based on the relative level of risk, providing a useful paper trail in case of an audit.

Targeting Privacy Communications Throughout Organization

Of course, it's not just buy-in from the top that you need. Your privacy program will need to be understood and supported at all levels of your organization. Your own knowledge of your organization's culture, communication style, management structure and internal politics will help you tune your communications at the right pitch and from the best angle. As in any communication effort, you can use your knowledge of each particular audience to craft the right message and deliver it via the right medium. A good first step is to ensure that privacy issues are presented with consistency across the organization. To achieve this, inventory all policies, procedures and statements that relate to privacy and create a standard approach to communicating them.

Evangelizing via communications requires the right choices. For example, you may recognize that some groups or individuals will identify better with visual presentations rather than a recitation of facts and figures. Remember that the more senior the audience, the shorter the time they have to devote to your message. Crisp, concise messaging—both electronic and in print—is vital. For example, e-mails with pithy subject lines, a top-down approach to the most important information and short, punchy bulleted lists will get the message across. Your constituents will appreciate the clarity. Internal social media also offer you a platform to create a blog that comments specifically on privacy and security issues. The use of postcards and strategically placed posters can also quickly convey salient information to further round out your communications.

Here's an overview of some of the different audience groups—and their characteristics—with whom you'll need to communicate.

Board of Directors and Senior Executives

Senior executives usually have limited time and will want to focus on how privacy supports overall business and organizational objectives. If your organization operates in a highly regulated industry—such as healthcare, utilities and finance—many senior executives will already recognize the importance of complying with legal and regulatory requirements. If your organization operates in Europe and has chosen to self-certify under the Safe Harbor framework, it is important that you involve and gain the support of an executive officer. For more information about the European Safe Harbor frameworks, see Chapter 2, "United States–European Union Safe Harbor", p. 69.

The potential cost—tangible and otherwise—of noncompliance is too important to ignore. Your presentations to this group need to be concise, to the point and not steeped in details. The time spent preparing for and presenting to this influential group is well worth the effort, and others in the organization take their cues from the senior executive group. If you make it clear that your efforts support the organization's bottom line, the senior executives are more likely to care about privacy. When their supportive attitude is known, others will naturally follow.

There may be times when you need to call the attention of top executives, or even the board of directors, to a particular privacy issue. As we've already seen, some situations—such as a highly public data breach—can severely harm the hard-won reputation of an enterprise and the good will it has earned. Such events require a fast, decisive response. You may find yourself, in the best interest of the organization, having to escalate a problem to the highest executive level. It's important, however, to consider this option very carefully—you want to avoid going to the well too often. Proactive communication with upper management is always a good idea. Tell them what is happening with privacy initiatives throughout the organization and point out the areas where things are going well as well as areas for improvement. For more information about using metrics to quickly communicate privacy-related key performance indicators, see "Metrics and Key Performance Indicators that Demonstrate Success," p. 158.

Mid-Level Directors

This group of managers will need more detailed information than the senior executives before they understand and support the privacy function. While they will need to understand the strategic importance of privacy to the organization and their particular area of oversight, they will also need to understand more of the tactical or operational details of privacy, their impact and what assistance they need to provide. For example, you might need to ensure that the manager responsible for the corporate website content understands your organization's privacy mandate—not just the importance of providing online privacy and meeting legal requirements, but also the operational implications. The mechanics of privacy will include having a prominent link to the organization's privacy statement on the site's homepage and other relevant pages (especially those where private information is solicited for online transactions). Another example would be your helping the manager of e-mail marketing to understand the difference between a transactional and marketing message—and, if it's a marketing message, the requirements under CAN-SPAM legislation.

Staff

Staff usually focus on their own jobs and the tasks at hand. They want information that is relevant to their job—understandable, tactical and reinforced over time. Staff represent the largest part of the workforce; they handle the most information, have the most interactions with customers and other employees and can have the greatest effect on how privacy policies and procedures are carried out—or not—on a daily basis. They are the troops on the ground and, as such, are perhaps the most important audience for privacy communications and especially training. Privacy-related actions must be easy to perform and integrated into everything they do.

General Public

Typically, an organization communicates its approach to privacy to the general public via its website. The information appears in the form of a privacy policy statement or, in many cases, as a notice that is mandated by regulatory frameworks such as HIPAA or GLBA. These regulatory notices may serve to keep the organization in compliance with legal and regulatory requirements. A clear, concise privacy statement, accurately aligned with your procedures and purged of legalese, will most effectively educate consumers. Make every effort to create a privacy statement that is as readable as possible. If you can reassure consumers and the general public that your organization honors their privacy, you are in a position to maintain or build relationships of trust—an important foundation for both commercial and institutional business.

Access to the Board of Directors

The privacy office will generally not have direct access to the board of directors and committees of the board. This lack of direct access isn't unique to the privacy office but is more a function of how boards work. Board members have limited time to devote to the organization, and there are always full agendas that must be carefully crafted to ensure the board has the necessary information to discharge their responsibilities. Matters raised with the board or associated committees must have an overall high priority and be presented at an appropriate level of detail. However, it is possible for a senior executive who attends board-level meetings to sponsor an agenda item and discussion about privacy. It is also quite possible that the board requests a briefing on the organization's privacy program. From a practical perspective, if you believe there is a privacy matter that warrants the board's attention, then, as a preliminary step, first ensure a review by appropriate senior management, general counsel or the chief audit executive. It's also important that you understand and employ the most appropriate means for communicating the matter to the board.

KEY ROLES AND RESPONSIBILITIES

Chapter 3 provided guidance in assembling the best privacy team to do the job. Once the initial team—real or virtual—is in place, it becomes an ongoing task to maintain the right people with the right skills. Of necessity, the privacy team requires a diverse range of skill sets—including experience with compliance issues, legal expertise, project management and knowledge of IT and technical resources. Because privacy programs are often viewed as the new kid on the block, the team members will to some extent all be working to develop the program's presence and effectiveness. In addition to being well-qualified for the work, staff will also need the skills to effectively integrate themselves (and the privacy program they represent) into the organization. Action-oriented (and courageous!) personalities will likely be an asset to your efforts.

Privacy Office Leadership

By appointing a privacy leader, your organization has signaled its recognition that the privacy realm is important enough to require top-level management. Ultimately, what your organization decides to call the position—chief privacy officer (CPO) or privacy director, for example—is less important than ensuring the "right" person is appointed and empowered to lead the effort. Necessary qualifications will vary depending on the nature of your organization and the goals of your privacy program. For example, a company that operates in a highly regulated industry—such as the utilities, pharmaceutical, healthcare, and financial sectors—is likely to need a lawyer or someone with significant experience working with regulatory compliance issues. Other organizations may not require a leader with the same depth of legal qualification.

Because legal and regulatory requirements are at the core of privacy, many privacy leaders are lawyers. However, non-attorney privacy leaders can come from a wide variety of academic backgrounds and work experiences in areas as diverse as IT, finance, compliance and sales and marketing. Because privacy touches on many areas of an organization's operations, the more varied experience the person has, the better he or she can understand and work with stakeholders from various disciplines. Whether a lawyer heads up your privacy office, your organization should look for certain traits that indicate successful performance. Generally, individuals who are successful privacy leaders

- excel at being an effective change agent and collaborator;
- have a high energy, executive presence;
- demonstrate excellent communication and interpersonal skills, decisiveness and sound judgment;
- as a team player, respect a diversity of opinion, work styles and personalities;
- see the "big picture" from an organizational perspective;
- work effectively under pressure and multi-task effectively, and
- effectively sell ideas and persuade others.

The first two skills—being a high-energy, collaborative change agent— are critical because organizations embarking on a formal privacy program by necessity experience changes to or creation of new policies and business processes. Change is not always quick to be embraced and requires the touch of a skillful leader. Anyone who has worked under a good leader will recognize the requisite skills, including the ability to

- think long-range and keep the team's "eyes on the prize";
- motivate the team, especially under adverse conditions, and
- choose interpersonal styles and strategies appropriate to ever-changing circumstances both within the team and with constituents throughout the organization

Aligning Privacy Staff with Program Strategy

As in any area of your organization, having well-defined job descriptions that support the privacy function mission is critical. Depending on the mission of your privacy office—for example, a focus on legal analysis, compliance and proactive or reactive project consulting to business departments and units or both—the job functions and descriptions for the privacy team will vary. Your organization will need to align job descriptions with the high-level description of the privacy leader's role. The detailed components of each job description outline the specific activities for a particular staff level. For more information see appendix, "Privacy Team Specialists–Roles and Sample Job Descriptions", p. 185.

Reporting Lines for the Privacy Program

Just as the backgrounds of privacy leaders vary, so do reporting lines. For example, the privacy office can report to the office of the general counsel, IT, compliance, or the chief financial officer. The reporting lines in your organization will reflect the focus of your privacy program as well as the infrastructure, culture and politics of your organization. The focus itself can vary. For example, it can

- be aimed primarily at legal and regulatory compliance;
- result from a general privacy mandate, or
- grow out of an initiative to position privacy as a market differentiator.

Ideally, your privacy office will report to a department or function that has a strong leader who actively embraces and supports the privacy agenda and its staff. Obviously, a lack of support or just half-hearted support for the privacy team will likely hinder its effectiveness and detrimentally affect its profile within the organization. In addition to direct reporting, there is almost always dotted-line reporting across departments. Indirect reporting lines help engage various departments in privacy efforts, but they need to be carefully defined and managed so that the privacy team's efforts are not hobbled by too many stakeholders with different agendas.

Working with Your Constituents Across the Organization

Your efforts to implement your privacy program require you to work closely with colleagues in a variety of functions across your organization. During this collaborative work, you will adopt the roles of both advisor and advocate. Your expertise will help staff in other functions meet the privacy requirements of your organizational policy and applicable laws and regulations. Your advocacy and proactive approach will help float privacy as an important, valuable and ongoing consideration in many of the organization's internal groups. These groups include:

- Marketing and customer relations
- Product development
- Human resources
- Legal and compliance groups
- Procurement
- IT and IT security
- Public and media relations
- Internal auditors
- Third parties
- Procurement and vendors
- Supply chain networks
- Outside counsel
- External auditors and consultants
- Organizations with direct access to your data
- Regulators

Working with Sales, Marketing and Customer Relations

First and foremost, the privacy office exists to support the business units—marketing, sales and service—in meeting the organization's privacy policies. Moreover, your relationship with the various business groups is a two-way street. By working in an integrated fashion with your business colleagues, you will not only be able to offer expertise, knowledge and advice about privacy, but also you will learn to see the world from their point of view. This understanding will help you develop a vision for exactly how the privacy program can further the aims of the organization.

As every business colleague will tell you, customer satisfaction is essential to any successful business. However, customer satisfaction is not just about delivering quality goods or services on time at the right price. In the realm of confidential or personal and nonpublic information, it also involves trust. Consumers want to know that their personally identifiable information will be secure and protected from the threats of unauthorized sharing, fraud and identity theft—you must meet their expectations. Every year, more business is transacted online and highly publicized security breaches make consumers feel increasingly vulnerable. If your organization sells products or services to consumers, you will want to focus carefully on this key area of privacy.

Every employee and department in your organization with direct, front-line contact with customers—such as customer sales and service representatives and delivery center staff—needs to understand the privacy policy and practices that apply to the customer information they handle as part of their routine work with customer orders, questions and complaints. Your job is to make sure that staff in the relevant departments can confidently handle any privacy-related customer questions or complaints and, if need be, escalate them promptly to your office. Part of your monitoring and compliance effort should include asking for periodic reports from managers on the front lines of customer relations. These reports should include information about the number, nature and resolution of privacy-related calls and questions.

If your organization addresses and resolves its customers' questions and complaints quickly, it can avoid the often unnecessary escalation into a legal matter or a complaint to a regulatory agency such as a state attorney general's office, the Federal Trade Commission or an overseas data protection commissioner's office. Resolving privacy questions or complaints quickly is always in the company's best interest. To make this a reality, you can propose a process that automatically escalates all privacy-related inquiries to your office and ensures a uniform response. Speedy resolution is always good for customer relations and ultimately in the organization's best interest.

Note: You can also make sure that your organization meets any legal requirements for the complaints process. For example, some jurisdictions may require you to include details of your complaints process in your privacy statement.

Working with Product Development

Product development is a key area for focusing on privacy issues. As already mentioned, the earlier in the product development phase that privacy concerns are addressed, the better the outcome—your organization can preempt regulatory noncompliance and you can bake best practices into your development before products and services ever see the light of day. This integrative approach is sometimes called "Privacy by Design"—a useful way to communicate the concept to others.

Becoming Part of the Business Solution

It's worth repeating that the earlier privacy principles become part of new products and service development, the better. Ideally, the privacy function should have a seat at the table from the start of product or program design so that any privacy considerations can be surfaced and discussed. This kind of early collaboration is always preferable than retroactive catch-ups, which may be too late to work. By dint of your earlier evangelism, winning executive support and communication efforts, you will ideally be in the position where staff from the privacy program are invited to important meetings when new developments are on the agenda. Your goal is to be viewed by the business sponsor and other players as a trusted advisor to enable the business.

The best possible solution is for you to implement an assembly-line approach so that all new products, services or marketing campaigns must automatically come to the privacy office for review. The advice your office provides will enable the development team to incorporate privacy considerations as the innovation life cycle continues. Your informed views will help the team achieve their objectives while meeting the organization's privacy principles. Your knowledge will help them leverage privacy-related information for economic gain without compromising privacy principles.

Not all personally identifiable information has equal value or risk, so it is important to understand the answers to the questions above. This information will help guide the privacy advice you give.

Finally, if you are able to establish your privacy program as a key checkpoint in the development of new programs, your office must be prepared to act and provide value promptly. It's important to avoid becoming a speed bump—or worse, a bottleneck—in the process.

Key Questions for Building Privacy into Product and Program Design

The starting point for helping to build privacy into the design of products and programs is to have a complete understanding of the following:

- What personally identifiable information will be affected?
- What is the source of the personally identifiable information?
- How will it be collected, used and stored?
- Was the personally identifiable information collected with notice and consent (opt-in or opt-out)?
- What business partners or third parties will have access to the personally identifiable information and for what purpose?

Note: Your organization may be among the growing number that operate, often via co-innovation initiatives, in a web of contractually obligated vendors, third parties and business partners. Baking privacy measures into product development is complicated when it extends beyond the organization's boundaries. For more guidance about working with third parties, see the section on the topic later in this chapter.

Working with Human Resources

Your organization's human resource (HR) group collects, uses and stores a great deal of sensitive data about its employees. You cannot expect employees to diligently protect customer information if they don't trust your organization with their own. It's vital, then, that your HR group models best practices as it endeavors to protect the personally identifiable information of employees.

In addition to being one of your privacy program's constituents, HR staff play two important roles as a proxy privacy agent. Firstly, with respect to protecting the organization's own information assets, they are a key component in the interface between employees and the organization. HR plays an active part in formalizing employees' relationships to protected information by way of notices that spell out confidentiality agreements and organizational policies in other areas where sensitive information is at hand. Secondly, HR orchestrates the training that will provide the knowledge and skills employees need for their outward-facing work, such as customer service and sales. For example, employees must be aware of your organization's privacy policy and its impact on their daily activities, and see themselves as participants of and contributors to the organization's privacy initiative.

Important note: The following sections refer to specific documents, such as notices and reports. If your privacy program sits outside the legal department, be sure that legal counsel reviews and approves all notices prior to distribution.

Employee Confidentiality Notices

A clearly written confidentiality notice or statement of policy will help ensure that every individual in the organization understands what is expected of them with regard to handling protected information. Typically, employees are required to sign a confidentiality notice or policy statement and acknowledge that they have received, read and understood it. They agree to comply with the policy and acknowledge that noncompliance is a serious matter and could result in disciplinary action up to and including termination.

Tip: It's also good practice to include information about and expectations for confidentiality, privacy and security in the organization's HR policy guide. You may be able to work with your HR colleagues to achieve this.

"Acceptable Use" Policies

As part of a confidentiality agreement or other policy statement, your organization should also inform employees about acceptable use of the information they handle. Acceptable use agreements should address

- personal use of company resources such as e-mail and Internet connectivity (and, if limited personal use is allowed, a statement that the company accepts no liability); and
- use of information collected, processed, stored or transmitted as part of job responsibilities.

For example, your organization may allow limited personal use of e-mail and Internet connectivity provided the use is incidental to work-related tasks, not for inappropriate or illegal purposes, and does not interfere with the employee's job productivity. Alternatively, an organization may decide to entirely prohibit any personal use of company resources. Either way, a clear communication must spell out to employees acceptable use and its restrictions, as well as the consequences of noncompliance. A formal signoff notice helps ensure enforceability and reduce misunderstandings. At a minimum, HR policy should spell this out.

If your organization plans to conduct workplace monitoring such as tracking employees' use of e-mail and Internet or recording their telephone calls and using video surveillance, you should follow best practice guidelines such as:

- State explicitly that you may conduct monitoring at your discretion on all company-provided assets such as phones, computers and networks.
- Be clear about what types of monitoring you plan to use
- Define the purpose of the monitoring by "business reasons" (there are many reasons: quality control, to maintain an environment free of harassment, protection of confidential corporate information, productivity and to look for violations of law or corporate policy)
- Describe what you are within your rights to do with the information (for example, use it for investigative purposes or provide it to law enforcement)

Background Checks and Credit Reports

For many organizations, carrying out background checks, including credit checks, is a routine part of due diligence during the hiring process. However, checks of this kind should not be performed without notifying and gaining consent from the applicant. Notice and consent are typically obtained via an appropriate standalone form. The notice and consent should be clear and complete and describe the purpose for which the information is sought.

A note of caution here: there are three areas of concern regarding the use of background checks.

Concern	Details
Protect sensitive information (just as you would for customers)	Because background checks can contain very sensitive information about an individual, make sure you have a process to protect data from accidental disclosure or unauthorized access. The process should have a data retention plan and allow for the destruction of the information when it is no longer necessary.

Seek legal counsel if outside scope of your expertise	If you are considering the use of a third-party vendor to perform background checks, use caution. There may be limitations on what kind of information you can ask for. If you are not a lawyer, you may lack the legal expertise needed. In this case, hire an expert and seek the advice of outside legal counsel.
Identify applicable foreign data restrictions	Some countries restrict the type of information an employer can seek from an applicant. Be mindful of the laws of countries in which your company operates—not just the laws that govern privacy, but also restrictions that may apply to background checks on applicants or existing employees.

Disciplinary Action for Privacy Violations

To ensure that employees take your organization's privacy and confidentiality requirements seriously, consequences for noncompliance need to be clear from the outset. The consequences often follow a progressive disciplinary process, and the severity of disciplinary action is proportionate to the seriousness of the violation. The ultimate form of discipline is termination of and potential legal action against an employee for serious violations such as the theft of intellectual property. The range of disciplinary actions should be clearly communicated to employees and at a minimum spelled out in your organization's HR policy guide.

Working with Legal and Compliance Groups

Legal matters—knowing the relevant laws and regulations and how to comply with them—are at the heart of privacy. In fact, privacy offices often reside in an organization's legal department and report to the office of general counsel. In other cases, the privacy office may comprise a hybrid team, part of which is drawn from the organization's existing legal function. When internal resources fall short—for example, when highly specialized legal knowledge is needed—you may need to reach out to other legal experts outside the organization.

Working with Government Relations and Lobbyists

Depending on your organization's structure and where your privacy office is located, there may be additional allies or partners with whom the privacy team needs to establish good relations. Contact with government officials, trade associations and other lobbying groups who are relevant to the interests of your industry or sector of operations can be especially helpful. For example, if a particular aspect of privacy regulation or legislative content impacts your organization and you have an important position on the matter, it behooves your privacy team to have its voice heard where it counts. Lobbying groups can help make your organization's position known and protect your interests. In addition, they can help educate and influence regulators and legislators on the business realities, implications and consequences of regulations or potential legislation. This process not only serves to protect your interests, but it can have the wider benefit of resulting in more realistic and balanced legislation.

Keeping Up with Legal and Compliance Requirements

The nature and geographic locations of your organization will determine which privacy-related regulations, laws and requirements you must satisfy. Legal requirements are constantly evolving both inside and outside of the United States and, for an organization with operations in many countries, the task of staying abreast of all applicable privacy legal requirements is a daunting task.

The job of quickly finding all the information you need is always a challenge. There is no single source for everything you need to know. However, some sources—for example, the Bureau of National Affairs (BNA) and IAPP's Privacy Tracker—will provide much of what you need to stay current. In addition, your team can glean information where it is available; for example, there are news clipping services, law firm newsletters and blogs that contain useful information. In addition, some companies provide tools, logs and services for tracking and analyzing legislation. In dealing with legislation that arises in other countries, there is the additional challenge of obtaining reliable English translations of relevant documents and draft copies of legislative bills. A rule of thumb here is to never work in a foreign market without the help of trusted, local resources.

Given the challenges in this area, it's important that you develop an overall strategy that includes not only sources that can keep you apprised of legislative activities but also staff who can analyze activity and discern its applicability and implications for your organization. The staffing can come from a combination of privacy office team members, paralegals and internal or outside counsel—depending on how your office is organized.

Working with IT and IT Security

Ultimately, your organization's privacy program depends entirely on the ability of your information technology to control the security of and access to personally identifiable information. By promoting an excellent collaborative relationship between the privacy office and your organization's IT experts, you can secure for yourself a seat at the technology table and be in a position to incorporate privacy-related matters into relevant IT initiatives. This collaboration may also provide an opportunity to grow the scope of your office.

There is a natural, mutually beneficial opportunity that exists between the information security and privacy offices. They are complimentary functions—there cannot be privacy without information security and the information security agenda requires input and support from the privacy office. Again, it's a two-way street. On the one hand, your privacy team delivers expertise and advice and makes sure privacy implications are addressed; on the other hand, your team learns how your IT colleagues perceive the organization and understands their mandates and priorities. A close relationship with the chief information security officer (CISO) and the senior IT team is worth the investment of time; the IT managers will come to view the privacy office as part of their team effort and help keep your staff informed about developments in the IT project portfolio.

Information security is part of information technology, and ideally your privacy office will also work closely with IT security colleagues. Depending on the size of your organization, you may have a chief privacy officer (CPO) and a CISO. In this case, it's ideal if the CPO and CISO and their respective staffs interact frequently and work together on shared initiatives for privacy and security. The CISO and staff will have developed their own information security policy to serve the organization's interests. This policy sets forth requirements and establishes the rules of the road for the security-related subjects it addresses. If the CPO is a lawyer, he or she often acts as legal counsel for the IT security group, ensuring an integrated approach.

One example where the privacy and IT teams can collaborate is in the area of access and permissions. It's the IT department that will actually implement the technology to secure data and realize the organization's permissions policy. Your team should identify technology that your organization already uses in the privacy sphere. For example, you can identify if there are rules and roles that define who can access personally identifiable information. If there are, you can think about ways to work on further developing and managing them.

Key Questions for Assessing Your In-House Technology that Supports Privacy

- What happens when employees change positions?
- Do employees automatically lose the access they had when they move on?
- To what extent is access restricted among the staff in your organization?
- What, if any, are the existing permissions policies?

A close working relationship between the privacy and security offices—and the recognition of complementary principles—will enable the formal information security and privacy policies to reinforce one another. Consider using the IT security staff to scale your own operation. IT security typically conducts its own assessments of new products, applications and systems. You can propose that they also include privacy assessments in their work. The ultimate goal of the dialog is to ensure that the IT landscape and its security reflects the organization's privacy policies and enables it to meet its legal requirements.

Working with Public and Media Relations

During the normal course of operations, your privacy team may occasionally need to work closely with colleagues from your organization's corporate communications and public and media groups. You may need to act quickly to contain the potentially damaging effects of a privacy breach of some kind. In this case, it will be of great help if you have already estab-lished contact with these groups, educated them about your role and agenda and cemented collaborative relationships. If you have a formal incident management program, which you should, note everyone's roles and responsibilities, including those of your organization's publicity and media specialists.

It is also worth remembering that if these colleagues, whose efforts are constantly in the public view, understand how privacy adds value to your organization's mission and goals, then they may be able to identify and exploit opportunities for positive press. Given the public's pervasive worries about the potential misuse of private data—fueled especially by well-publicized privacy disasters—positive press that reflects your organization's stewardship of personally identifiable data can help build trust and business. When things do go wrong, your colleagues in corporate communications can leverage their skills and present bad news with clear messaging and without brand drift.

Working with Internal Auditors

The internal audit team is a key group in any organization. They are particularly important to the privacy office, both as a potential source of useful feedback and also as partners who can make good use of your expertise and experience.

Auditing the Privacy Program Itself

An organization's internal audit team has a broad domain that typically includes verifying the existence and adequacy of internal controls and compliance with policies and perform-ing independent reviews of operational programs. The privacy program itself is a candidate for internal audit. Auditors can evaluate the structure and effectiveness of your program, as it would for any other, and check that it complies with company policies, procedures and le-gal requirements across the organization. This independent review can be helpful not only in identifying risks that need to be addressed, but also in making observations and recommen-dations that you can use to build a case for additional staff or budget. While no department or function wants to be under the constant eye of the internal audit team—sometimes there is a natural defensiveness among the observed to any kind of critical comment or feedback—an audit can be an invaluable resource for identifying your program's soft spots.

It's good practice to meet regularly with your internal auditing colleagues, share your obser-vations and help them scope their audits of business units and areas where you've identified weaknesses. The internal audit function often has a direct line of communication to the board of directors.

Helping with Internal Audits in Other Areas

Your organization's internal audit team will typically want to address privacy-related risks and factor them into their audit plans. In the process, they may determine that they need additional subject matter expertise to conduct their audits or reviews. The auditor must of course remain independent, and the privacy office should never lead an audit. However, to the extent that it is not a conflict of interest, your privacy office may be able to provide expertise—for example, in interpreting laws and policies. In this way, you can use internal audits to help scale your own efforts, especially when auditors assess the activities of a line of business not under direct control of the privacy office. A working relationship between privacy and internal auditing can benefit both parties, while respecting the independence of each.

Internal Auditors Can Help Design Risk Assessments

The internal auditors in your organization may conduct risk assessments, help to ensure that appropriate corrective actions are specified and developed and then validate implementation. If the internal auditors are familiar with risk-based assessments, they can be one good resource to help your privacy team design risk assessment approaches and tools—and you can help them.

Working with Third Parties

An organization typically shares personally identifiable information with third parties. For some transactions with partners, vendors and contractors, it's an inevitable part of the business. From the perspective of your privacy program, extending your own policies and procedures outside the boundaries of your organization is often a challenge. However, many of the third parties will themselves be trying to do the same thing. This sets the stage in many cases for cooperation. Some of the third parties you are likely to encounter as you work with various groups in your organization are

- procurement and vendors;
- supply chain networks;
- outside counsel;
- external auditors and consultants, and
- organizations with direct access to your data.

Working with Procurement and Vendors

Collaboration with your colleagues in procurement is vital. Purchase orders for goods and services constantly flow from your organization to outside entities. Frequently, these outside organizations—vendors, contractors (individuals and companies) and outsourcing service providers—become privy to information that you already protect. Remember that your organization is legally responsible for the protection of any personally identifiable information it owns, even when you pass along that information to third parties.

Of course, it's also a two-way street. Your organization may well be a vendor itself, in which case, as the custodian of other organizations' data, you'll be equally responsible for performing the appropriate privacy stewardship.

Working with Supply Chain Networks

It's ever more common for business organizations to operate in ecosystems of partners and vendors with shared interests. When a company collaborates with others in a supply chain network to co-innovate and co-market jointly developed products, close working relationships with partners and vendors—including the sharing of sensitive data—are a daily reality. In addition, the fast growth in business process outsourcing means that organizations now often rely on third-party service providers to carry out functions such as sales, payroll processing, benefits administration, e-commerce, health insurance, restaurant reservations, stock transfers and marketing campaigns. Inevitably, these relationships also involve sharing personally identifiable information about customers and employees. So while these collaborative relationships are vital in executing mutually important business processes and meeting objectives, organizations must apply due diligence before entrusting private information to business partners and third-party service providers.

If your organization is party to such relationships, you will want to be sure that partners and providers can commit to the level of data privacy and security you expect and that you reciprocate—it's often a two-way street. With respect to privacy, it's a good idea to think of your service providers, partners and vendors as an extension of your own organization. You want to be sure that they are hewing to the same level of data security as you. For this reason, ensure that the appropriate privacy-related language is written into the partnership contract, that you are adequately indemnified and that you have the right to audit your partner's practices to confirm compliance.

Working with Organizations that Directly Access Your Data

The nature of business often requires that one organization provide another with access to personally identifiable information. If an outside organization uses, accesses, stores or disseminates your data, then you must structure the relationship carefully. You need to think about the following questions:

- What is the nature of the partnership with the other organization?
- What is the nature of the relationship defined in the contract?
- Can the outside organization use the information for purposes other than fulfilling the contract?
- Have you placed explicit controls on the access to or use of the data?
- Are mitigation measures in place to handle all significant risks?

Studying the contract language will help you determine what level of control your organization should exert over the data. In some cases, you may inherit or be constrained by contract language. In other cases, you'll be able to help craft it from the ground up. In some cases, you may co-own data with other entities. For example, some organizations use independent sales representatives with whom they have contracts. A contract may establish the representative as co-owner of the data, which he or she can then use to sell non-competing products. However, it's important to keep in mind that if the other organization is not a true partner, then end customers will still hold your organization accountable for any misuse or abuse of their information. The bottom line is that you can't contract away liability. Your organization is ultimately responsible for the protection of personally identifiable information that passes through its hands.

The Importance of Contract Language

Underlying your organization's relationships with service providers and business partners are the contracts you sign. If any of these third parties collects, processes, stores or transmits personally identifiable information on behalf of your organization, privacy requirements must be part of the contract. The contractual language must spell out how the third party has to meet your requirements regarding privacy, confidentiality and legal compliance. Working in close collaboration with your colleagues in the legal and procurement departments, you can develop boilerplate language and incorporate it into your standard contracts. Because contract language is often the subject of negotiation with the other party, you can expect changes. If they are not one and the same, your privacy team and legal colleagues should always review and approve proposed changes carefully before a contract is executed. Good collaboration with your colleagues in the procurement area will ensure that this happens.

In dealing with third parties, you have the option to include your organization's own stock privacy provisions—for example, in the form of boilerplate text specific to a particular industry. If you were sharing information about health or finances, the language would of course differ according to the needs of the regulations that apply to each sector.

> **Best Practice Recommendation: Managing Partner and Vendor Accountability**
>
> Your organization's key means for managing the key accountabilities is a comprehensive information security infrastructure. This enabling framework includes:
>
> - Having in place meaningful policies, procedures, training, ongoing communications, risk assessments, remediation of weaknesses and ongoing monitoring of design and operating effectiveness of controls
> - Collaborating with business unit managers to understand the information life cycle that involves third parties
> - Assessing whether service providers are meeting expected security requirements
>
> You may not have the resources to apply the necessary due diligence to all third parties at once. Where should you start? You could launch an initiative, taking into account the following steps:
>
> 1. Create an inventory of all third parties—partners, vendors and service providers and define the nature of the information and the quantity
> 2. Rank the providers in order of privacy magnitude, using data sensitivity (e.g., health records) and volume
> 3. Begin a phased program to initiate discussions with the highest-ranking third parties and find out what controls they have in place
> 4. Set a schedule of target dates to do the same with each successively lower tier of third parties until you have completed the list
>
> Where will the resources come from? You will certainly need the time of internal staff, usually drawn from IT or IT security resources. You may also section off some of the work to outside consultants. If you have to rely on internal staff, be sure to spread the load so that individuals are not buried by the challenging task.

You can consider the following measures to protect data that is accessible by vendors and so on:

- Clearly define personally identifiable information
- Specify reasonable and appropriate security measures to protect data from alteration, destruction, loss, modification and unauthorized access
- Specify the jurisdiction where the data must reside (for example, within the United States, in other specific countries but not in others)
- Possibly prohibit the storage of sensitive information on a laptop or portable storage device
- Insist on compliance with applicable laws or industry standards
- Encrypt the personal information
- Apply all provisions to any subcontractors
- Describe required response to a privacy breach, specifying, for example, that the

vendor:

- Notify you immediately after discovering a breach (you can expect lots of negotiations in agreeing to define the term "immediately"!)
- Cooperate with your organization to identify the root cause and aid in any lawsuit or investigation that results
- Will not contact any of the affected individuals without contacting you first
- Agree that, when the contract expires, the personal information will either be returned or destroyed, based on your instructions (some vendors may reasonably request to retain certain data due to legal obligations—if so, they must agree to protect the data while in their custody)
- Indemnify your organization against liability for a privacy breach (this is likely to be contentious!)

In relation to indemnity, consider two caveats:

1. Agreeing on indemnity is a source of contention because no one can estimate the actual cost of a breach. As a result, your vendor will rightly argue that unlimited liability is too much risk exposure and try to limit the indemnification to a specific number. On the other hand, your organization will argue that a breach might easily surpass the cap on liability.
2. Your contractual agreement might already contain an indemnification or liability provision in the agreement. If so, there is no need to include another provision. Just try to make sure that the indemnification provision is broad enough to include any costs associated with a privacy or data breach. While you can't expect your partners to be your insurers, you can expect them to have enough "skin in the game" to take their responsibilities seriously.

Working with Outside Counsel

Depending on the size and nature of your organization, there may be times when your legal team needs to reach out to external resources. It may be a question of bolstering your own capacity to handle a particular project, or you may need specialized legal expertise to complement the skill set of your own colleagues. Before you go outside the organization, be sure to first gain a good understanding of your own in-house legal resources.

Whether you use outside counsel will depend on the size of your legal group and the depth and breadth of its collective expertise. If your organization is relatively small and has only a couple of lawyers, you may well want to oursource some of the privacy-related legal work. Larger organizations with a sizeable legal staff may find it makes more sense not to use outside counsel at all, but to hire and train a lawyer to fill a specialist niche. If you do need to hire outside counsel, do it sparingly and strive for an effective transfer of knowledge.

Working with Outside Auditors and Consultants

If you work with outside auditors and consultants, aim for clarity in the engagement and plan to bring newly gained knowledge and expertise back into your own organization. It's a good approach to

- ask clear, specific questions;
- scope their activities well;
- set clear goals and timelines;
- use them to gain knowledge, and
- have them teach you so you can repeat the process on your own.

Working with Regulators

It will help your privacy efforts enormously to develop good working relationships with the regulators whose purview includes your organization's sphere of operations. Your organization may need to work with regulators from agencies at different levels of government—state, federal and even international. The best strategy is to reach out to all of them, get to know them and collaborate with them. Participate in forums, provide information and input and help them understand what you are doing in your organization. This proactive attitude shows not only a determination to comply, but also a respect for the regulating body. This can only enhance your organization's professional image and reduce risk.

DATA GOVERNANCE AND PRIVACY

Every individual or group in your organization—especially your privacy office—that is affected by how data is created, collected, processed, manipulated, stored, made available for use and retired has an automatic interest in data governance. Data governance describes the processes for authorizing decisions about an organization's data and its management—including its use, life cycle and protection. Because data governance processes include the management of personally identifiable data, the job of your privacy office is to become a stakeholder. You will need to work to integrate sound privacy procedures into your data governance processes according to the requirements of both applicable laws and your own organization's privacy policy.

The relationship between organizational data governance and privacy is so strong that a trend is emerging whereby some organizations are starting to amalgamate the two groups. In some cases, your privacy office may have a seat on the committee that steers data governance across your organization. For more information about the future of privacy and data governance, see appendix, *Data Governance Resources*, p. 206.

Importance of Privacy Office Involvement

Specifically, a data governance program lays out a system of decision rights and accountabilities for information-related processes. The program is executed according to agreed-upon models that describe who can take what actions with what information, when, under what circumstances and using what methods. Data stakeholders frequently leave decisions to their IT and data management colleagues. However, these data-related activities sometimes require a broader decision-making process that includes groups of stakeholders, including the privacy office. That's where the concept of data governance comes into play; decision-making becomes more coordinated and is facilitated by centralized resources.

It's imperative that your privacy office is involved in this joint effort. In that way, you can advocate practices that will realize your organization's privacy policy and procedures. For example, your organization's various groups—such as finance, marketing and logistics—may make use of a single source of centralized data. In this case, it will be very helpful from the privacy perspective to make sure that customers' personal preferences regarding their protected private data—such as opt-in and opt-out requests—are captured in the applicable master records in the organization's central databases. You can also work to make sure that information about the appropriate legal and business rules—such as the rules for data record retention—is attached to the relevant "data elements" (for example, a customer's master record) and flows wherever the data is used.

Best Practice Recommendation: Privacy's Role in Data Governance
Your privacy office can use the following guidelines to guide your own data governance efforts and those of your constituent groups across the organization:

- Know and understand your data
- Collect only the minimum amount of data necessary to accomplish the business purpose
- Remember you have an obligation to protect any data that you do collect
- Be mindful that data collected may be subject to data destruction or retention requirements
- Ensure there are processes and procedures to guarantee data accuracy
- Manage data in accordance with legal and business rules
- Understand the obligations that are tied to data from different sources
- Ensure that required legal disclosures are appropriately provided for certain sources at certain collection points
- Understand the intended use of data when it's collected and try to anticipate proposed future use
- Consider whether you need to apply meta-tags to indicate the source of data (if you don't know the origin, you won't be able manage whether it is an opt-in or an opt-out process for using the data for different uses or different parts of the organization)
- Consider whether you want the ability to audit and ensure legal and procedural compliance, including breach mitigation and log management to document access to and use of data
- Remember that technology can be a double-edged sword (on the one hand, a useful data governance tool to easily manage the rules of opt-out requests; on the other hand, the vehicle by which a single change in one line of business can quickly replicate itself throughout the organization and affiliates)

For more detailed information about data governance, including a key resource, please see the appendix, *Data Governance Resources*, p. 206.

Managing Preferences (Contact-Point Requests and Consent)

Typically, an organization and its consumers, clients or partners communicate at different points of contact. The contacts may take place via telephone, e-mail, the Web and other electronic media or even face to face. During many of these contacts, personally identifiable information changes hands—sometimes in ways that are not visible to the consumer. These transactions and interactions, and the ability of staff to know how to correctly handle personal information, are a key focus of a privacy program.

Remember that managing preferences is a living process. As you receive various opt-in and opt-out requests from customers and as privacy-related data flows into the organization, you must have effective processes for updating and maintaining your lists. In the context of data governance, your role will be to ensure that your organization's IT architecture supports the needed data processing, maintenance and storage. A good example here is the management of requests from consumers not to receive unsolicited and unwanted marketing calls. Your organization may be required to subscribe to the National Do Not Call Registry, a database of the names and telephone numbers of individual consumers who prefer not to receive calls—as well as any state-specific lists that apply to your operations. Your data governance operation will need to facilitate the synchronization of these regulatory-based lists with your own corporate do-not-call list.

Key Questions for Handling and Managing Do-Not-Call (DNC) Requests

Requests received from individuals

- How will these requests arrive (for example: by phone, e-mail or choices made when someone signs up for a service either online or in person)?
- Who will implement the do-not-call request?

Requests received via the national and state-specific do-not-call registries

- Is your organization required to subscribe to the registries (see below)?
- Do you have an effective process for searching the registry's list, as required, at least once every 31 days?
- Do you have a process for handling do-not-call requests you receive from affiliates or others who have shared information with you?

For more information about the laws with which your preference management will need to comply, see Chapter 2, "Understanding Your Organization's Legal Requirements," p. 25.

Keeping the Privacy Program Current

After you have built your program and it is up and running, you can turn your attention to the business of maintenance. Chapter 3 described the privacy program as a never-ending cycle where analysis and assessment leads to action, action leads to results and further review of effectiveness and compliance leads to new or changed policies and procedures. To maintain your program—keeping it dynamic, proactive, and current—you will need to put in place a procedure for regularly revisiting and reviewing the work you have already accomplished with colleagues.

This work can encompass aspects of your organization's technology and your privacy policy and programs. For example, the review structure should call upon your program managers to check in with you at regular intervals. Depending on the area of operations or the project, the intervals may be frequent or widely spaced. Your own experience with colleagues will be an important factor in determining the frequency of reviews. As a privacy officer, you will develop over time a "gut feeling" for which individual parties will faithfully adhere to privacy policies and procedures and which are less likely to.

Frequency of Program Reviews

Certain programs are clear candidates for frequent review. For example, any policies involving data collected via fast-changing social networking sites will need revisiting often. Projects built around newer technology and which introduce novel privacy issues may also need more frequent attention.

Other programs and entities can be maintained adequately via longer-term reviews. In the case of long-standing contracts, for example, nothing much need be done until the contract comes up for renegotiation. Programs that are more developed and mature will also require less regular attention. Once you have helped contribute to the privacy needs of front-end systems (for example, establishing an online sales channel and managing do-not-call lists), you can wait to perform a review until you hear from stakeholders or state attorneys general regarding specific issues.

Depending on the size of your office and the size of the organization you support, here are some steps to consider:

Step	Description
Prioritize the work	• Identify the high-risk programs, based on factors such as the number of individuals impacted, type of information collected and possible harm if there is misuse, abuse or loss of data
Build a scalable process for reviewing programs	• Build processes that are easy and repeatable but meaningful • Have them tied to other requirements in the company that have regular review, such as budget cycles, data governance, architecture and product development, and IT security

Maintain policies and procedures	• Set specific intervals and come up with a checklist • Make the review checklist simpler than for the initial review • Ask program managers to perform a self-assessment and evaluate whether their programs comply fully with existing documentation
Provide oversight	• Build an oversight process for the privacy officer, conduct desk audits and interviews and speak with key stakeholders • Write up your recommendations
Establish "living procedures"	• Show how the business unit operationalizes privacy and review procedures annually to make sure they are up-to-date

Keeping the Privacy Team and Its Skills Current

With regard to your day-to-day operations, you will also need to continually maintain and develop your team. Create the ideal balance of general and specialized knowledge among team members. Basically, everyone on the team must master every area of expertise at a basic level. With that foundational knowledge under their belts, team members can then specialize a bit. However, it's good practice to conduct cross-training and to build in some redundancy and overlap of knowledge and skills. Then, if someone leaves, your team is less vulnerable to single points of failure.

Some general skills are essential.

General Skill	Description
Good communication	Team members should be capable of delivering high-quality written and verbal communications. For many colleagues in your organization, your team's communications will be all they see of you and will define your image across the enterprise.
Organizational and project management skills	Conducting assessments and overseeing numerous touch points throughout an enterprise requires team members who can organize and manage projects well.
Analytical and tactical thinking	Train and expect team members to take responsibility for proactively spotting privacy issues—actual or potential—throughout the organization. You want your team to be able to analyze issues and offer suggestions for handling them, which is why many privacy teams are staffed by lawyers and paralegals.

As always, the mission of the privacy team is to further the goals and interests of the organization while ensuring that programs and projects comply with the law and adhere to the organization's privacy policies.

MEASURING EFFECTIVENESS

In assessing the effectiveness of your privacy office, you can track whether "bad things" happen. If they don't happen, you've been successful! That said, you will still have to demonstrate value within your organization. You must continually show that you have not only proactively helped prevent the next data spill but also that your program facilitates a well-thought out privacy policy in a consistent manner. Your job in measuring effectiveness is to build a portfolio of metrics around these concepts.

Value via Privacy Risk Assessments

Your team can demonstrate its value by facilitating—in a visible way—the consistent application of the organization's privacy policy and procedures. You develop a set of key questions as the basis for assessing each new program. In the process, you document what the program managers agreed to and, if appropriate, in what ways the technology or program meets the requirements of your privacy policy. This documentation is only for use inside your organization; you use it to assess the privacy risks and mitigation strategies of the program. Later, the program managers can use it to conduct both self-assessments and, if applicable, third-party assessments. During this entire process, you are creating tangible results that document your team's work and can be used to demonstrate its effectiveness. Your value is to

- put in place the organization's privacy policies;
- operationalize policies and ensure business processes and applications meet legal requirements, and
- evaluate whether the policies are actually working.

Promoting Self-Assessments

A good approach is to facilitate self-assessment for your stakeholder groups, making it as easy as possible for them to perform. For example, you can consider using an online system —or governance, risk and compliance tool—to help you scale and manage assessments and the resulting data. Develop enabling, fact-based questions that the program manager knows how and will want to answer (for example, a question about what information is collected rather than a more loaded question about why Social Security numbers are collected). The questions you frame will ultimately enable managers to make privacy-sensitive decisions as they build their program. For example, a question about the length of time data is maintained may prompt your colleagues in the program to think through whether the data should have a limited shelf life. Self-assessments should also note procedural and regulatory issues so that each can be tactfully addressed. The ideal outcome from the privacy point of view is to motivate program and project managers to willingly incorporate policy into their work.

You can also use resources from the American Institute of CPAs (AICPA) and the Generally Accepted Accounting Principles (GAAP). For more information, see "Key Resources for Generally Accepted Privacy Principles," p. 127.

Getting Outside Assessments by Third Parties

Initiating outside assessments of your program by third parties will help you understand not only how you are doing compared to other organizations but also will help you discover pockets in programs where issues have turned out to be not as straightforward as initial discussions implied. You may also find that the more basic questions that were asked during the initial assessment had faulty assumptions and have led you down the wrong path.

Metrics and Key Performance Indicators that Demonstrate Success

A solid approach to metrics can make or break the long-term success of a privacy program. Executives who fund a privacy office are accustomed to having their performance measured. When they're called upon to explain and defend what value the privacy program is adding to the organization during a round of budget cuts, a timely and easily understandable report can save the day.

Because of the relative novelty of the privacy profession, the implementation of privacy metrics is still in its formative stages. The early lessons privacy professionals have learned as they've implemented privacy metrics and key performance indicators (KPIs) in their organizations fall into three categories:

- What to measure
- How to measure
- What mistakes to avoid

What to Measure

Before deploying a privacy-metrics program, you need to revisit some of the questions you examined as you developed your organization's existing privacy office or started one from scratch.

Key Questions to Ask Before Developing a Set of Metrics and KPIs

- What is our privacy program trying to accomplish?
- What does success look like for the program?
- What do our executive sponsors think is the main value we add to the organization?

These are three ways of asking the same basic question: What is the end result, or return-on-investment, of the privacy program? The early experience of privacy professionals suggests that there are five potential, measurable outcomes that cut across sectors:

- Risk reduction
- Compliance
- Business enablement
- Value creation
- Trust enhancement

Risk Reduction

The risk-reduction outcome is a common starting point for privacy programs in unregulated industries, particularly in jurisdictions subject to mandatory or recommended reporting of breaches of personally identifiable information. In these organizations, the top-level executives measure the contribution of the privacy program in terms of its ability to minimize and ultimately avoid data breaches and related regulatory enforcement actions. Examples of risk metrics include:

Metric	Area of Risk Measured

Number of . . .	• Events per 1,000 employees reported to or detected by the incident response team
	• Hours of slow network performance due to malware outbreaks
	• Lost or stolen
	  • Laptops per 10,000 issued
	  • Flash drives or CD ROMs per 10,000 employees
	  • iPhones, BlackBerrys or Droids per 10,000 headquarters employees
	  • iPhones, BlackBerrys or Droids per 10,000 field employees

Average number of . . .	• Days taken to notify individuals affected by a privacy breach • Hours taken to restore affected services following a security incident
Percentage of . . .	• Confirmed privacy and security incidents closed within 30 days per the company's incident-response policy • Privacy incidents that only involved one person's information

Compliance

The compliance outcome is a common starting point for privacy programs in regulated industries and jurisdictions subject to national data protection laws. In these organizations, a state of noncompliance is also seen as a risk ultimately resulting in regulatory enforcement actions. But progress is often measured more positively in terms of organizational status relative to privacy regulatory requirements. Examples of compliance metrics include the percentage of

- employees completing annual privacy training (online or classroom);
- employees properly naming the data classifications;
- unique, company-owned, public-facing websites with company-approved privacy policy displayed;
- consumers sent a privacy policy by mail;
- paper forms collecting PII that also include at least a basic, one-line privacy notice;
- marketing e-mails with functional unsubscribe mechanism;
- unsubscribe requests fulfilled within 10 days;
- departments and business units completing a personal data inventory, and
- data-subject access requests answered within 30 days.

Business Enablement

The business enablement outcome occurs when a sound or compliant approach to privacy creates new opportunities for the organization to complete its mission. This can occur, for example, when a U.S.-based company wants to expand into Europe or an Australia-based company wants to consolidate its EU-based servers in Australia. In both cases, deploying a privacy program that meets EU requirements can enable the business objectives. Examples of business enablement metrics include:

- Number of business clients inquiring about Safe Harbor status
- Average days negotiating new client contract privacy provisions
- Terabytes of data hosted outside the EU
- Percentage of call volume handled outside the EU

Value Creation

The value-creation outcome occurs when a privacy program directly eliminates costs or directly increases revenues. This can occur when implementation of a data-retention policy enables an organization to delete large amounts of data and forego purchasing servers. Examples of value-creation metrics include:

- Number of terabytes of data
- Dollar savings from reduction of data storage
- Percentage of customer profiles without accuracy errors
- Dollar revenues per customer profile with opt-in consent
- Dollar revenues from direct marketing cross-selling to opt-in customers
- Dollar revenues from inbound marketing to opt-in customers
- Dollar revenues from European business clients

Types of Metrics	When these Types of Metrics Are Used
% compliant or % complete	Measuring and comparing status toward a commonly agreed goal or standard, particularly when 100 percent is the end goal
Scale	Tracking ratings along a spectrum of opposite outcomes, particularly when the ratings are subjective
Count	Measuring the absolute value of a situation
Rates per unit	Measuring process effectiveness
Indices	Creating estimates for intangible realities or combining multiple factors into a single number
Monetary value	Expressing bottom-line impact to revenue and cost

How to Measure

Determining what metrics to track is the easy part. Maintaining an ongoing process to keep those metrics current and relevant to executive sponsors is more challenging. What are some proven approaches for meeting those challenges? Consider the following eight steps.

Step	Suggested Activities
Prototype	• Hold an offsite meeting with staff-level people involved in parts of the privacy mission to prototype a first version of your metrics approach • Start with about a dozen KPIs to keep things simple and focused • Use prototyping to work out kinks before presenting to your executive sponsor to seek buy-in
Get stakeholder support	• Present your prototype metrics report to key privacy stakeholders: the CIO, general counsel, HR leader and potentially your CFO • Explain what the report means to their agendas and how often you plan to provide updates • Clarify the amount of time you need from their staff to be successful • Ask them to authorize the collection of these particular metrics
Assign metrics owners	• For each metric you've identified in the prototype, assign a metric owner—a person responsible for gathering data on a regular basis • Educate them on the exact format and criteria of their assigned metrics and discuss the sources they'll draw on to gather information • Be aware of how many different ways different people can interpret and report on the same metric
Get business-unit sign-off on value-creation metrics	• Identify other business units in your organization that have generated privacy-related metrics in conjunction with your own efforts • Be sure to give them credit for the results you are presenting • Sit down together with colleagues in other business units and discuss your common agendas and reporting chains • Work out ahead of time how you will collaborate in achieving those objectives and communicating the results

Plan for trial and error	• Be prepared for your privacy-metrics scorecard to change over time
	• Plan from the start how you will formalize changes
	• Determine how you will:
	  ○ Gather feedback on the scorecard
	  ○ Know a metric is or isn't achieving its objectives
	  ○ Identify who decides to change a metric and how that change will be implemented

Integrate with other executive reports	• Avoid creating a privacy-metrics scorecard that sends a message to executives that conflicts with the message from your head of information security or head of audit • Before you create a standalone privacy-metrics report, identify other reports about information risk that executives are receiving, and see if you can weave your report into those vehicles
Adapt your report for different audiences	• If you don't have access to high-level executives, consider presenting your privacy working group with a more detailed set of metrics (longer than the single-page report you send to the audit committee) • After you've established your prototype one-page report, start planning for the other audiences and consider the level of information they need to support the privacy agenda
Benchmark peers	• After the first few rounds of reporting your privacy-metrics scorecard to your various audiences, be prepared for questions such as "So what?" or "I don't know if this is good or bad?" or "How do we compare to our peers?" • Plan for these questions by exploring local and national alternatives for sharing or pooling privacy metrics (note: an increasingly popular yardstick is a "privacy maturity model"—see example below)

The following diagram shows a sample presentation slide that uses the privacy maturity model to compare performance with peers.

PRIVACY OPERATIONS: BENCHMARKING

Privacy Maturity Model Framework for Benchmarking Peers	0 Nonexistent	1 Initial	2 Repeatable	3 Defined	4 Managed	5 Optimized
Program management			X			
Privacy notice				X		
Privacy choice				X		
Limited data collection			X			
Limited data use and retention		X				
Data-subject access		X				
Data disclosure to third parties				X		
Security of personal data					X	
Personal data quality		X				
Monitoring and enforcement				X		

For more info...   John Smith, Chief Privacy Officer

Mistakes to Avoid

There are a number of different ways to succeed at implementing sustained privacy-metrics programs. There are also a few proven ways to get bogged down and run out of steam. Keep these two lessons in mind:

1. **Don't track too many metrics**

   The privacy profession can attract highly analytical people. The most insightful and creative among these can potentially produce several dozen metrics in one sitting. Tracking too many metrics can be your downfall.

2. **Make sure metrics are tied to decisions**

   Privacy metrics have no value unless they produce decisions or outcomes for the organization. Don't track metrics just for the sake of saying you have a metrics program, or you might have a hard time explaining to your organization's attorney why you've created this discoverable evidence of your organization's less-than-perfect performance.

CHAPTER 5

Building a
Privacy Career

Throughout this book, we've explored the myriad obligations and demands that will be placed on an effective privacy program in today's information economy. This information should be enormously helpful as you build your own privacy program. While the process of building such a program is never complete—it will always be a dynamic, evolutionary task—it is also appropriate to look forward. What should you, as a privacy pro, be thinking about for the future of your role, your privacy program and your organization's use of data?

This chapter will explore some of the considerations that a privacy pro should ponder during those quieter moments when contemplating "what comes next." Much of the content for this chapter is derived from a research project the IAPP conducted in 2010. The project looked at the next decade of privacy program management and resulted in a report entitled "A Call for Agility: The Next-Generation Privacy Professional." Spearheaded by former IAPP Board President and IBM Corporation Chief Privacy Officer Harriet Pearson and authored by Minnesota Privacy Consultants President Jay Cline, the report consists of quantitative and qualitative research conducted by the IAPP and involved interviews with many leading chief privacy officers.

Of course, any prediction of what will happen in the future is fraught with peril. Forecasting specific outcomes, even near-term outcomes, with any level of accuracy is difficult, if not impossible. However, it is possible to look at the significant drivers that have shaped privacy over the past decade and the current state of transition and derive some possible scenarios for the profession of privacy and privacy program management in the future. These trajectories will certainly evolve over time. And, it is perhaps most important for privacy professionals to recognize the need for ongoing engagement, knowledge and flexibility in order to respond to this dynamic field.

To read the report "A Call For Agility: The Next-Generation Privacy Professional," go to the IAPP Knowledge Center at www.privacyassociation.org/knowledge_center.

So let us then examine some of the significant drivers in the information economy today and how they may trend forward in the future. We will look at the current state of privacy law and the momentum behind privacy issues in popular society. We will also explore the changing role of the privacy pro and how the field has migrated from a strictly compliance-driven focus to a much broader—and perhaps more compelling—role responsible for data governance. We'll also look at some of the "hot" areas in privacy that will surely see continued discussion and debate over appropriate data protection standards.

PRIVACY MOMENTUM CONTINUES

Surely, the first issue we must recognize is the issue of privacy itself. Make no mistake; privacy is growing as a consumer, legal and societal concern.

Nary a day goes by when the media does not report on some aspect of privacy. Data breaches make headlines, and consumers voice concerns about how their personally identifiable information is being used and how vulnerable they are to serious problems such as identify fraud. New technologies give marketers ever more precise tools with which to identify consumer behavior and pinpoint their advertising dollars. Consumers want transparency and the option to opt in or out. Legislators try to walk the line between the legitimate demands of both consumers and business. As a privacy professional, you can expect this growth trend to continue into the future. Put simply, privacy has momentum.

MOVING FROM COMPLIANCE TO ROI

The first generation of privacy professionals has witnessed phenomenal and rapid growth in the volume and scope of the regulations that govern privacy issues. A quick look back at Chapter 2 will remind you of the amount of knowledge needed and effort expended to comply with the laws and apply the high standards that regulatory bodies and consumers demand today. Compliance has been the primary driver. But this is evolving. Industry leaders now recognize that privacy is also a key component in providing high-quality service to customers and consumers; privacy, in other words, has business value. In fact, an astute team of privacy professionals can now add real value to a corporation's marketing efforts. Well-developed privacy policies and procedures and the inclusion of privacy considerations in upstream program development can contribute to the bottom line. Handling privacy strategically can help a company differentiate itself from competitors. The next generation of privacy pros will benefit from a focus beyond compliance. Those among us who embrace data as a core asset of the organization and build programs that generate trust and competitive differentiation will invariably be more valuable to their employers.

THE CHANGING ROLE OF THE PRIVACY PRO

The profession of privacy is still relatively new. Within organizations, privacy pros are beginning to find their footing and build the programs and procedures described in this book. Inevitably, this means that privacy professionals and the programs they manage will evolve as the field evolves. Put another way, the skills and knowledge necessary for a successful privacy pro today will not be the skills and knowledge necessary for a successful privacy pro in the future.

So what is changing for privacy pros? How is the profession maturing? And how are the programs we manage evolving?

Organizational Diversification

In the first years of the privacy profession, large organizations—those ranking in the equivalent of the top 2,000 companies worldwide—employed the lion's share of privacy professionals. In the 2010 IAPP salary survey, three quarters of respondents worked for organizations with more than 5,000 employees. But even this is starting to change. As the risk of noncompliance rises for organizations of all sizes, small- and medium-sized organizations are starting to adjust their cost-benefit analysis on hiring data protection and privacy experts, and there is a trend toward greater reliance on privacy professionals within these organizations.

This trend seems likely to continue and grow further. According to credit card issuer VISA, most credit card breaches occur at the smallest-level merchants. Each breach carries with it the potential for fines originating from the payment card brands, as well as more costly compliance obligations. Smaller companies that provide services to larger corporations are also falling within the purview of the larger corporations' vendor-assurance programs, which are dictating privacy requirements to them. The IAPP is seeing more individuals from small- to mid-size organizations at its events and certification testing venues.

This shift could significantly change not only how the privacy profession meets and learns but also shape what issues become its top priorities. The complex organizational challenges of large multinationals may be joined by the more tactical and sector-specific realities of the small business.

But this does not just represent a change for small- and medium-sized business. Today's information economy exists as an enormously complicated matrix of data relationships. Small organizations process data for large organizations. Large organizations handle data on behalf of medium-sized organizations. Consumers interact with multiple organizations—both small and large—in a single transaction. As a result, the marketplace will continue to exert pressure on small- and medium-sized organizations to embrace privacy as a business imperative.

Regional Diversification

IAPP research has demonstrated that there appears to be more privacy professionals employed in the field of privacy in North American organizations. This may seem counterintuitive given that EU member states were the first to enact national data protection laws. Why wouldn't Europe dominate the profession? Some observers have noted that North American businesses, particularly those in the United States, have a commercial custom of collecting more information about people than their European counterparts and therefore have more information risk to be managed. Indeed, Ponemon Institute research shows that European companies collect less personal information about customers and are less likely to use it for secondary purposes.

So, the North American appetite for data may have led to a high concentration of privacy professionals on the continent. But some suggest the numbers could be deceiving.

Bojana Bellamy, 2011 IAPP board chairman and director of data privacy at Accenture, says that while European companies employ privacy professionals and have done so for 10 years, the role is not at the level of the U.S.-based CPO; it is more legally- and compliance-focused, often sitting in the legal department or mid-level management. However, Bellamy notes that following some high-profile data breaches in Europe, the role has become higher level and more strategic.

Deirdre Mulligan, a former privacy advocate and current professor at the University of California-Berkeley, agrees. "To a greater extent than in other geographies," says Mulligan, "the most strategic and high-level privacy officers tend to work for U.S.-based organizations where they are tasked with creating and deploying sophisticated information-governance strategies for highly visible brands."

Nonetheless, the profession continues to evolve. The number of non-U.S. members of the IAPP has increased over the past several years. Moreover, the respondents to the 2010 IAPP salary survey showed an even greater diversification outside the U.S. The adoption of breach notification requirements across Europe and Asia could accelerate the diversification of the profession, as organizations become compelled to make their data practices more transparent to the public. If the center of gravity of the privacy profession shifts from Washington and Ottawa toward Brussels, Buenos Aries and Beijing, the profession will likely get an injection of fresh new ideas on how to conduct privacy assessments, how to document and communicate privacy policies, how to hold vendors accountable and even how to define what privacy is.

Just as the information economy sends data around the world in mere seconds and globalization demands greater understanding and flexibility for participants in a worldwide marketplace, the privacy profession will increasingly become international, multilingual and multicultural.

Migration Across the Organization

When companies appointed chief privacy officers in the late 1990s and early 2000s, typically they placed these leaders within senior positions but with limited budgets and staffs. A lot has changed since then. While large multinationals and government agencies still employ high-ranking CPOs, IAPP data suggest that a majority of privacy professionals are positioned below the director level in their organizations, suggesting that there is no longer a single model for privacy professionals' placement within an organization. It could also be indicative of a growth in privacy departments across multiple levels.

> "
> It takes a team to develop and then to
> support an organization's implementation
> of information privacy policies.
> "

"It takes a team to develop and then to support an organization's implementation of information privacy policies," adds IBM's Pearson. "Our team members come from a wide range of disciplines and levels, but we're united by our common strategy."

Today's privacy professionals also find themselves in a variety of departments. Three reporting structures are emerging as dominant

- reporting up through the general counsel;
- reporting up through a business executive, and
- reporting up through the chief information officer.

The heightened risk of privacy noncompliance—of data breaches in particular—has probably contributed to the focus on the legal and compliance areas.

Many corporate privacy professionals find themselves within a structure similar to that depicted below, where privacy reports in through legal or compliance and information security reports in through the CIO.

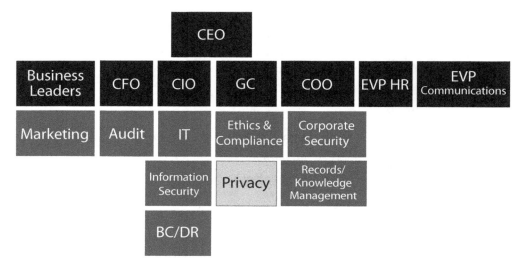

But the information governance organizational structure is in flux, and as a result, today's privacy professional is at a crossroads. Indeed, most expect their job responsibilities will change in the coming months. In addition, most believe that promotion possibilities depend upon the creation of a new role in the organization. Short of creating a new role, privacy professionals responding to the IAPP salary survey indicated a desire to assume responsibility for data security as well.

STABILIZATION OF DAILY PRIVACY TASKS

Historically, many privacy professionals have been focused on developing policies and procedures and responding to incidents. As a result, many of the privacy programs led by privacy veterans may be reaching maturity. A full 34 percent of the respondents to the IAPP's 2010 Privacy Professional's Role, Function and Salary Survey say their privacy programs are in the mature stage, and 49 percent say they are in the middle or late-middle stages.

When asked where they currently spend their time versus where they wish they could spend their time, respondents to the survey said they had found the right balance between foundational, process and strategic tasks. This is an indicator that the privacy professional's daily tasks may be arriving at some predictability. It may also suggest that privacy professionals are self-directed and have a good amount of control over establishing and prioritizing work items.

That said, the daily tasks of the privacy professional are not on the verge of becoming stale. Most organizations today are in constant flux, with changing products, business and employees. Governing this will continue to necessitate the updating of policies and procedures and the monitoring of legacy programs.

"There will always be work in the program-build area as programs seek to improve and as underlying laws and risks change," says Zoe Strickland, vice president and chief privacy officer at Walmart. "However, privacy programs will indeed mature. That will allow the privacy leader to work strategically, beyond compliance, regarding the management of personal or business data."

The former chief privacy officer at Microsoft and founder of the Corporate Privacy Group sees much more work to be done. Richard Purcell says, "An important question before us as we look forward is this: 'How can we establish accountability and self-discipline while maintaining localized autonomy?'" He says one answer may lie in "how well we separate ourselves from the bad actors and free riders through stronger and more harmonized policy frameworks, compliance practices and accountability standards."

Anecdotal evidence from privacy consultants operating across multiple sectors and geographies suggests that corporate privacy programs have been maturing over time but at different paces in different regions. Canada has been a noteworthy leader.

"I look to Canada frequently to see the future of where we're going," notes Michelle Dennedy, founder and CEO of iDennedy Project.

A lack of enforcement and resources at other organizations has left them in the earliest stages of privacy maturity. Maturity levels may also be varying geographically, potentially causing the agendas of privacy professionals to vary by region.

Perhaps the greatest indicator of a growing stability in the operational demands on privacy pros is the existence of this book. It is certainly easy to predict that resources such as Building a Privacy Program: A Practitioner's Guide will continue to emerge as the roles, responsibilities and daily activities of the privacy professional become more established and understood.

THE FUTURE OF PRIVACY

Change is constant in the field of privacy. Technological advances, new business models and shifting societal expectations all result in a complex—and some would say unstable— environment. Perhaps more than any other skill, privacy professionals today and in the future will require agility. Understanding emerging trends, digging into the latest gadgets and technologies and closely watching the legislative environment are critical functions of any privacy professional's job.

So let's look at what some leaders in the field of privacy predict will be some of the hotter issues that will be confronting privacy pros going forward.

Employee Privacy

The blending of our professional and personal lives continues to place pressure on historical boundaries of privacy. What we do at home is frequently professional in nature and vice versa; e.g., how many of us use social networks or personal e-mail while at work? This dynamic will continue to create friction and challenges for privacy professionals.

But what may flare up as a subset of this issue? "Corporate video monitoring in the U.S.," says Brian O'Connor, chief security and privacy officer at Eastman Kodak Company. "This is already hard to do in Canada and Europe."

RFID / Smart Grid / Smart Meters

The "Internet of things" may continue to come under regulatory scrutiny as smart devices that communicate with humans and one another continue to be developed.

Information Security Law

"Compliance-driven information security requirements will very likely increase in the coming decade," says IBM's Pearson. Certainly, the introduction of major data security laws in Massachusetts and Nevada portends greater activity in this area.

Breach Notification

The popularity of security breach notification has already gained traction in Canada, the United Kingdom, Germany, France, Australia, New Zealand and Japan, and could well expand to all OECD countries. If breach notifications expose underlying weaknesses in corporate data practices, the laws could trigger a second wave of information security regulation. Similarly, the success of the PCI Security Standards Council in enforcing the PCI DSS in North America could result in enforcement of the standard in Europe, Asia and beyond.

Emerging Markets and Data Protection Law

The prominence of the European market and the requirements of the EU Data Protection Directive may well continue to persuade new countries to adopt national data protection laws. South Africa, India, Mexico and Malaysia are already poised to do so, and other APEC and Latin American countries might then find it more difficult to remain unregulated. "Legislation will continue to increase," notes O'Connor. "This will be a significant compliance issue, requiring privacy professionals to drive corporate programs."

Global Harmonization…Or Not?

As more countries regulate privacy, and if privacy is regulated across more sectors and technologies, will world privacy regulations begin to converge? Opinions vary. Some see the convergence of rules and, as a result, the rules will be more principle-driven and technology-neutral. Others note that while a single, enforceable global standard won't materialize overnight—if ever—there is a determined push on a global level toward a more consistent and collaborative approach to the protection of personal information and global corporations. Understanding that common and well-understood regulations could offer a degree of legal certainty, they have embraced this.

Others see further Balkanization of privacy laws into conflicting local and regional variances. And others still see a middle ground, where perhaps perfectly harmonized global regulations do not exist, but a convergence of key requirements found in the patchwork of laws and regulations already out there begins to take place.

What does this mean for the privacy professional of the future? More laws in more places mean an extended role for legal experts both inside and outside of corporations, governments, nonprofits and universities. It also means new positions within government agencies to enforce the new laws. A landscape of conflicting privacy laws could leave the privacy profession mired in a protracted period of untangling the conflicts and adding less value to organizations and society. A Balkanized regulatory landscape could leave organizations viewing their privacy professionals as necessary tacticians but not strategists invited to the planning table. To avoid this perception, "today's CPO needs to think broadly beyond legal terms and more about information risk and social impact," says Microsoft Corporation Chief Privacy Strategist Peter Cullen. It is incumbent on privacy officers to become more strategic and less reactionary.

Privacy by Design and Accountability

The increasing importance of a proactive approach to privacy is a message frequently delivered by Ontario Information and Privacy Commissioner Ann Cavoukian, who has argued that the future of privacy cannot be assured solely by compliance with regulatory frameworks. Rather, Cavoukian says, "privacy assurance must come from making privacy the default within technology, business practices and networked infrastructure."

Corporate Privacy Group's Purcell thinks corporations can forestall more regulation through more comprehensive approaches to information governance. "At the end of a decade of growth in the professionalization of privacy and data protection," he explains, "there have been a number of leading companies such as Microsoft, HP, IBM, GE, Intel, Oracle and Schering-Plough that have established enterprise-wide programs to manage personal information in strategically smart and responsible ways." He adds that these approaches "have helped to diminish the appetite and perceived need for legislative and regulatory interventions."

If organizations continue on a more fragmented approach toward information governance, however, Purcell sees more regulation in the future. "That tolerance for independent judgment and decision (within autonomous operating units) may have the unintended consequences of data breaches and regulatory noncompliance that invite external control."

Nonetheless, ongoing regulation could have the indirect positive effect of propelling the upward maturity of privacy programs across all regions. Law firms, consultancies and technology vendors serving privacy professionals in this scenario would face a market of increasing but still varied levels of privacy maturity. In order to remain competitive, they would need to offer high-end products and services to the North American, European and some Asian markets and foundational products and services to emerging markets.

At the same time, a rising awareness among small- and medium-sized businesses of the need for privacy compliance would generate new markets for delivering privacy products and services in a mass-produced, low-cost manner. As privacy compliance needs spread to new geographies and the vast market of small- and medium-sized businesses, today's privacy professionals will be best poised to compete for these new career opportunities.

THE AGILE PRIVACY PROFESSIONAL

If regulation, information technology and government data collection continue to shape the profession, how can today's privacy professional take full advantage of the emerging opportunities?

According to the experts, more agility is a must. The agile privacy professional, amid a period of ongoing transformation, will be able to clearly identify new opportunities, move to these and manage them responsibly.

What defines the agile privacy professional? And what can today's privacy professional start doing now in order to successfully achieve agility in the future? Here are five strategies for action:

1. Redefine the privacy role
2. Rotate through departments/business units
3. Develop multicultural literacy
4. Understand legal and technical disciplines
5. Instill direction and leadership

Any one, if not all, of these strategies will enable today's privacy professional with greater agility in confronting the privacy challenges of the future.

Redefine the Privacy Role

As organizations struggle to determine where to place privacy in the organization and with what responsibility to endow it, opportunities will emerge for agile professionals to provide answers. Experts interviewed for IAPP research believe that the role of the privacy professional will grow beyond regulatory compliance into the information risk arena and, finally, into information governance and information optimization. In this scenario, the privacy discipline becomes a subset of the broader practice of minimizing the cost of information and maximizing its value. Above the chief privacy officer, chief information security officer and records-management director will be an information optimization officer. Agile privacy professionals will socialize these concepts and seek sponsors and advocates.

"The percent of usable information among all of the noise that we're collecting is going down," says Dennedy. "Tomorrow's privacy professional will need to help articulate the value of information and then what would be a reasonable cost to protect it."

Many feel that privacy programs and enforcements will evolve to focus more on data usage versus data protection.

Jim Koenig, leader of the privacy and identity theft practice at PricewaterhouseCoopers, sees integrated frameworks emerging versus the more siloed, law-by-law regulatory approaches often seen today. The health information industry offers an example.

"Healthcare companies, given the change in information uses and investments from ARRA/ HITECH (the American Recovery and Reinvestment Act of 2009 and the HITECH Act of 2009), will help to set best practices versus financial institutions and retailers who are historically known for this," says Koenig.

Commissioner Cavoukian believes that there is a real opportunity for privacy professionals to adopt a new role of "privacy ambassador," within their organizations. "…Privacy professionals can advance the goal of proactively embedding privacy into their organizations' programs. And if privacy is proactively designed into technology, business practices and infrastructure right from the outset, then the maximum degree of privacy protection can be ensured."

Rotate Through Departments/Business Units

Today's privacy professional is adept at meeting compliance requirements and crafting policy, but the agile privacy professional of the next decade will rotate through business units and field operations where higher level decisions about information management are being made and implemented. Privacy professionals who embed themselves where value is created in an organization will expand their network and influence the role their organizations play in building trust in the global information ecosystem and with stakeholders. Those who don't will risk being among the last to know about critical changes to business strategy and information uses.

"Business experience is probably the most important success factor for tomorrow's privacy professional," says Sandy Hughes, information governance and global privacy executive at The Procter & Gamble Company. "You can always learn the privacy requirements afterward. The best way to obtain this business experience as a privacy professional is to conduct an inventory of where and when and how personal data is collected and used."

"It's important to signal your willingness to take on broadening experiences," says IBM's Pearson. "The fact that I've had assignments in legal, human resources and public affairs has enhanced the perspective that I bring to my responsibilities."

"Anti-money laundering and healthcare expertise" will be increasingly valuable skill sets for privacy professionals to obtain, adds TD Bank Group Global Chief Privacy Officer Agnes Bundy Scanlan.

Develop Multicultural Literacy

As privacy regulations take root in a greater number of jurisdictions around the world, and as the value chains of organizations further internationalize, privacy professionals—particularly those based in the more culturally homogenous North America—may face a crossroads. The privacy professional of today may be inclined to completely delegate questions of local concern to local subject matter experts and local privacy champions. Western leadership training often teaches the value of delegation, after all. But an agile privacy professional will see opportunity in understanding how variances in culture create variances in information risk and optimization. After acquiring this understanding, the agile professional will be able to communicate strategy, policies and solutions across cultural boundaries.

"I see four success factors for tomorrow's privacy professionals," notes Nuala O'Connor Kelly, chief privacy leader at General Electric Company. "One, making the case for privacy in positive, measurable terms. Two, obtaining cross-functional talent beyond privacy. Three, obtaining enough knowledge about technology and data systems to ask probing questions. Four, gaining international experience and cross-cultural literacy. This will only grow over time."

Understand Legal and Technical Disciplines

While there is little debate as to whether privacy professionals ought to have a basic grasp of legal and technical concepts around data privacy and security, experts' opinions diverge on whether tomorrow's privacy professional would, by necessity, need a legal or technical degree. The central role of regulatory and IT drivers shaping the privacy profession almost ensures an ongoing need for privacy professionals to be conversant in not one but both of these disciplines. Some may indeed become mid-career attorneys or mid-career masters of information systems. The most agile privacy professionals may also recognize the need to pursue literacy in finance and economics in order to quantify the value of information.

"One of the interesting things about the privacy profession is how many disciplines can provide useful background," says Walmart's Strickland.

"Legal or IT experience is common. Other desirable backgrounds, depending on the goals of the organization, are marketing, customer service, compliance and communications."

Dennedy says, "We need two types of privacy professionals—the great lawyer who is a tactical, focused specialist, and the broad-thinking, strategic person who integrates technology, law, marketing and sociology."

But others feel the true privacy professional does both the strategic and tactical work. Accenture's Bellamy says it's someone with a legal degree or background who has transcended a pure legal-advisory role and has become a trusted business advisor, as well as a complaints ombudsman, technologist, strategist and government-relations person—a diplomat.

Instill Direction and Leadership

Many things change, but some remain the same. Amidst continuing change, organizations will need charismatic strategists who can lead, persuade, persevere and provide stability. And, with a forecast of ongoing regulation, the effective privacy leader will be a public speaker who works a vast personal network of legislators, industry groups and standards bodies to articulate a vision and position.

"Strong leadership abilities will be the biggest success factor for privacy professionals in the future," notes Royal Bank of Canada Chief Privacy Officer Jeff Green. "To be successful, they must be able to influence across all lines of business—and the operational and functional areas that support them—to drive a consistent approach to information governance."

Additional Resources
for the Privacy Professional

The appendix includes a variety of resources to help you create or further develop a privacy office in your organization. The resources include templates, checklists, sample job descriptions and links to in-depth sources of information.

PCI COMPLIANCE REQUIREMENTS BY LEVEL OF TRANSACTION VOLUME

The Payment Card Industry Data Security Standard (PCI DSS) specifies compliance requirements based on a company's transaction volume. The size of an organization determines the requirements for compliance. For detailed information, see the PCI Security Standards Council's site at: www.pcisecuritystandards.org/security_standards/index.php. The following table provides an overview of requirements by transaction volume level.

Level/ Tier	Merchant Criteria	Validation Requirements
1	Merchants processing over 6 million Visa transactions annually (all channels) or Global merchants identified as Level 1 by any Visa region	Annual Report on Compliance (ROC) by Qualified Security Assessor (QSA) Quarterly network scan by Approved Scan Vendor (ASV) Attestation of Compliance Form
2	Merchants processing 1 million to 6 million Visa transactions annually (all channels)	Annual Self-Assessment Questionnaire (SAQ) Quarterly network scan by ASV Attestation of Compliance Form
3	Merchants processing 20,000 to 1 million Visa e-commerce transactions annually	Annual SAQ Quarterly network scan by ASV Attestation of Compliance Form
4	Merchants processing less than 20,000 Visa e-commerce transactions annually and all other merchants processing up to 1 million Visa transactions annually	Annual SAQ recommended Quarterly network scan by ASV if applicable Compliance validation requirements set by acquirer

Each SAQ includes a series of yes-or-no questions about your security posture and practices. The SAQ allows for flexibility based on the complexity of a particular merchant's or service provider's business situation, as shown in the table below—this determines validation type. The SAQ validation type is not correlated with a merchant's classification or risk level.

SAQ Validation Type	SAQ Form	Description	Scan Required?
1	A	Card-not-present (e-commerce or mail/telephone-order) merchants, all cardholder data functions outsourced. This would never apply to face-to-face merchants.	No
2	B	Imprint-only merchants with no cardholder data storage	No
3	B	Stand-alone dial-up terminal merchants, no cardholder data storage	No
4	C	Merchants with payment application systems connected to the Internet, no cardholder data storage	Yes
5	D	All other merchants (not included in descriptions for SAQs A-C above) and all service providers defined by a payment brand as eligible to complete an SAQ.	Yes

RESOURCES FOR UNDERSTANDING PRIVACY INITIATIVES IN OTHER COUNTRIES

Australia's Policies and Legislation for Privacy Protection
www.privacy.gov.au/

This site is run by the Office of the Privacy Commissioner for the Australian government. It provides a comprehensive body of resources about every aspect of the country's efforts in the area of privacy protection.

Jones Day's Summary of Japan's Personal Information Protection Act
www.jonesday.com/newsknowledge/publicationdetail.aspx?publication=2920

The site provides a summary of Japan's major piece of privacy protection legislation, enacted in 2005.

Information Shield's List of International Privacy Initiatives by Country
www.informationshield.com/intprivacylaws.html

The site is an excellent resource for finding international privacy laws by country. The list cites the major piece of privacy-related legislation that a country has so far enacted.

The Morrison Foerster Privacy Library
www.mofo.com/privacylibrary

In addition to providing free, domestic privacy-related information, this foundation provides a fine overview of privacy considerations in the international arena.

PRIVACY PROGRAM CHARTER

The privacy program charter documents the program's objectives, scope and outputs. It also documents the value of the program, its *raison d'être*, by describing the problem/opportunity statement and quantifying the program's benefits in the business case. It also lays out the parameters for its execution in terms of time and resource commitment, as well as organizational alignment and sponsoring. The program charter should be documented at various levels of detail to cater to various audiences: from a one-pager for the steering committee— as shown below—to a multiple page document for the program team, including a detailed activity schedule and resource plan, benefits realization metrics, program governance and communications plan.

Problem/Opportunity Statement Describe the current privacy-related pain points in the organization. Think broadly in terms of organizational and process impact (HR, business, legal, IT).	**Business Case** Describe the drivers for change in terms of regulatory mandate, cost-savings and simplification, and quantify the benefits as much as possible.
Goal Statement and Deliverables What is the goal of your privacy program? Describe at a high level the new processes that will be enhanced or established and the main deliverables or program output.	**Project Scope** List the processes, organizational functions and products and services that will be impacted by the privacy program. In addition, list what is left out of scope.
Time and Resource Expectations Describe the internal FTE and external cost of your program. Indicate the expected return on investment by providing a benefits realization timeline.	**Sponsor/Leader** Name the organizational champion and any cosponsors. Also name the process and/or functional program owners and the program manager.

STAKEHOLDER MAP FOR CHANGE MANAGEMENT AND COMMUNICATIONS

You can use a list of internal and possibly external privacy stakeholders to create a map of key players, the impact they have on change and their likely reaction to change. You should also document the stakeholders' position on the company's privacy program to better plan and prioritize communications based on this information and determine the critical partnerships to build or improve upon. In addition, the stakeholder list takes into account the stakeholders' roles in the organization, their business priorities, their potential impact on privacy-related matters and any access or communications challenges that apply.

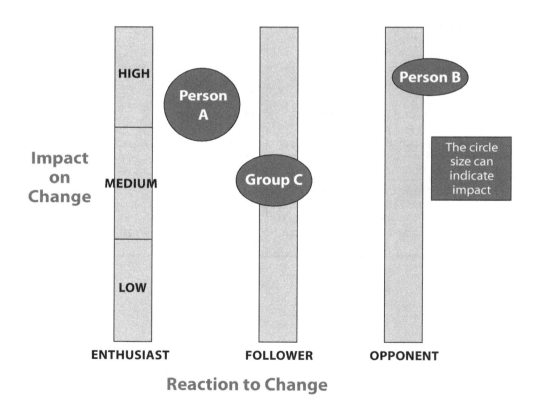

PRIVACY TEAM SPECIALISTS—ROLES AND SAMPLE JOB DESCRIPTIONS

The following section provides sample job descriptions for key players in the establishment and execution of an organization's privacy program. The key roles include those of chief privacy officer (CPO); chief privacy, security and data strategy officer; and the role of supporting the CPO.

Chief Privacy Officer
Below is a detailed job description for a traditional CPO. You can use it as a template for your own organization.

Function Description
This position is a leadership and compliance role. The chief privacy officer (CPO) oversees and champions all activities of [Company] (the Company) related to the development, implementation, oversight, maintenance of and adherence to the Company's policies and procedures covering the privacy of, and access to and use of, personally identifiable information (PII) of the company's customers and personal information of employees in compliance with applicable U.S. federal and state laws and regulations, relevant international laws and regulations and the company's own information privacy practices. The CPO will lead a cross-organizational privacy team and will be responsible for management reporting, budgetary control of privacy activities, regulatory filings, maintenance of acceptable third-party audit documentation and project management of ongoing privacy activities and support of ongoing key initiatives that impact privacy. The CPO may hold simultaneously another position with the company provided that such individual is able to dedicate sufficient time and attention to his/her responsibilities as CPO.

Responsibilities	
Compliance	**Notices** Ensuring that the Company and each location of operation has and maintains appropriate privacy compliance and information notices and materials complying with current regulatory and legal practices and requirements. **Policies and Procedures** Developing, implementing and maintaining applicable policies and procedures for privacy compliance, information risk management and identity theft prevention as it relates to the operations of the Company, including as it relates to operations, customer service, technical and physical security, human resources, procurement, treasury and finance, auditing, legal, sales and marketing and other functions.

Information security	Oversee the development, implementation, maintenance and coordination of a privacy project management office and a comprehensive written information security program that includes administrative, technical and physical safeguards appropriate to the size and complexity of the company and the nature and scope of its activities information security program designed to • ensure the security and confidentiality of customer transactions, records and information; • protect against any anticipated threats or hazards to the security or integrity of such transactions, records and information, and • protect against unauthorized access to or use of such records or information that would result in substantial harm or inconvenience to any customer, employee or business partner.
Governance	***Privacy Oversight Committee*** Working with the board, management and key other stakeholders to establish and implement an organization-wide privacy oversight committee. ***Involve the Board of Directors*** ***Reporting*** Facilitating the reporting to the board or an appropriate committee of the board at least annually addressing issues such as risk assessment; risk management and control decisions; service provider arrangements; results of testing; security breaches or violations and management's responses and recommendations for changes in the information security program.
Manage and control risk	***Assess Risk*** Conduct, oversee and/or coordinate the conducting of risk assessment designed to • identify reasonably foreseeable internal and external threats that could result in unauthorized disclosure, misuse, alteration or destruction of customer information or customer information systems; • assess the likelihood and potential damage of these threats, taking into consideration the sensitivity of customer information, and • assess the sufficiency of policies, procedures, customer information systems, and other arrangements in place to control risks. ***Design*** Oversee and/or coordinate the design of the information security program to control the identified risks, commensurate with the sensitivity of the information as well as the complexity and scope of the company's activities.

Train and communicate	*Training* Developing and implementing organization-wide privacy training and testing for all staff, with additional specialized training for individuals who handle customer data or interface with the public. **Communication Program** Developing and implementing an organization-wide communications program on privacy and information-security issues, including related emerging and new laws and regulations, industry practices, regulatory concerns and risk-management protocols.
Privacy risk assessment	Ensuring that the company develop, implement, maintain and regularly independently test the key controls, systems and procedures of the information security program protecting PII.
Oversee contract arrangements	Participating in the development, implementation and ongoing compliance monitoring of all agreements and relationships with affiliates and non-affiliated third-party vendors handling PII on behalf of the company to ensure that privacy concerns, requirements and responsibilities are addressed and appropriate information security safeguards and controls are maintained and, where appropriate, vendors are assessed prior to and/or during the term of any arrangement with the company.
Privacy and identity theft incident response	Formulating and managing the company's response to privacy incidents and investigation of data mishandling, privacy complaints, data security breaches and other security-related issues.
Cross-functional coordination and planning	• Collaborating with senior management, leaders of the company's compliance and IT functions, as well as, when necessary, with legal counsel, on responding to regulatory inquiries that may involve or affect privacy and/or data security issues or practices. • Interfacing with senior management as necessary, providing reports, presentations and recommendations covering the operational aspects of security and privacy, as well as producing executive management reports on current practices that may expose the company to privacy or security risks.
Experience	• Five to 10 years of experience in privacy, data protection/security and/or information risk management and compliance, preferably in the company's industry • Five to 10 years of management experience, preferably including significant interactions with executive management • Ten years industry experience gained in working in the pharmaceutical industry and/or at international consulting firms • Experience working in a heavily regulated and/or audited environment

Skills	• Subject matter expertise in privacy, knowledge and understanding of current and emerging international, U.S. federal and state and other government privacy laws and regulations, compliance issues and leading practices within the financial services industry • Strong analytical skills and organizational, planning and administrative abilities. Knowledge of and the ability to apply the principles of project management and change management • Excellent oral and written communication skills • Energetic self-starter and confident with strong interpersonal skills • Good judgment, a sense of urgency and demonstrated commitment to high standards of ethics, regulatory compliance, customer service and business integrity • Promotes team building, excels at conflict resolution • Must have an understanding of the company's industry, operations, technologies and practices used to collect, store, access, transmit and retain PII in an international environment • Overall knowledge of mainframe and distributed Software Development Lifecycles (SDLCs) • Detailed knowledge of one or more project management methodologies and experience applying them in diverse organizational environments • Strong PC skills including but not limited to Microsoft Office, Lotus Notes and Microsoft Project
Qualifications	Bachelor's degree in business administration, law, finance, accounting, computer science or a related discipline. MBA, JD and CIPP preferred.

Chief Privacy, Security and Data Strategy Officer

Aside from the traditional role of CPO, there is a new related role emerging—the chief data strategist who is responsible for data management and new uses of data for marketing and other purposes across the company in accordance with laws and regulations as well as policies. Importantly, this emerging role also manages use of such information with new technologies and channels (for example, social media and direct and interactive marketing) as well as in new business ventures, products and services. The chief data strategist has oversight over data handling practices and policy making as it relates to use of the data of the company and the related compliance and protection of the sensitive data handled by the company including personal information, IP, trade secrets and financial reporting.

Function description	The chief privacy, security and data strategy officer is a senior position responsible for managing data compliance and protection as well as championing data as a strategic business asset and driver of revenue. Key privacy, data protection/security and data usage/strategy responsibilities include but are not limited to the following areas:
Privacy	Responsible for managing the risks and business impacts of privacy laws and policies and employee, customers and other stakeholder expectations. Key privacy-related responsibilities include but are not limited to: • Oversees ongoing activities related to the development, implementation, maintenance of and adherence to the organization's policies and procedures covering the privacy and security of personal information in compliance with U.S. federal, state and global laws. • Working with the chief compliance officer, general counsel, chief regulatory counsel, outside counsel and others in interacting with regulators and complying with regulatory orders and agreements. • Responding to incidents, including both technical investigation/remediation and breach notification procedures.
Security and data protection	Responsible for establishing and maintaining the enterprise vision, strategy and program to ensure information assets are adequately protected. Key security-related responsibilities include, but are not limited to: • Evaluating, shaping/reshaping and leading the information security organization. • Identifying, developing, implementing and maintaining processes across the organization to reduce information and information technology risks. • Establishing appropriate standards and controls and directing the consolidation and simplification of related policies and procedures to drive understanding, compliance, efficiencies and cost-savings and to satisfy regulatory review.
Data use and strategy	Responsible for guiding, supporting and/or implementing data strategies, standards and procedures as well as accountability for key initiatives involving the use of sensitive, valuable and/or regulated data. Key data use/strategy-related responsibilities include but are not limited to: • Supporting the business in identifying and pursuing new business opportunities pertaining to new uses of data, new interactive and direct channels and new markets—while balancing respect for customer privacy and loyalty. • Leading a data governance council charged with defining and coordinating strategic priorities in the area of new data uses/channels, data analytics, data compliance and other strategic opportunities. • Championing data as a strategic business asset and driver of revenue by communicating to executives, employees and customers the strategic value and sensitivity of the company's data.

CPO Support

The CPO support job description can apply to an international CPO reporting to the global CPO or to a deputy CPO who focuses on more operational matters, assessments and collaboration on IT matters to allow the CPO to focus on policy and legal matters. This role reports to the senior vice-president and chief privacy officer.

International responsibilities	This position is responsible for corporate oversight of privacy policies, practices and procedures in [company]'s non-U.S. operations.
	Formulate and disseminate enterprise-wide policies for non-U.S. operations, in partnership with corporate ethics and compliance (CEC), IT and other relevant departments and in consultation with country managers and local [company] associates responsible for data protection.
	Ensure that each [company] operation has fully documented policies and practices in place that give reasonable assurance that • individual data is collected, used and disclosed only for legitimate business purposes and in a manner that satisfies all applicable laws and regulations and [company] enterprise-wide policies; • no individual data is transferred or made accessible outside the country of origin except in compliance with that country's laws and regulations; • each operation complies with all other privacy and related laws; • compliance with privacy policies and practices is monitored on an ongoing basis; • statements of policy and privacy notices will be developed and distributed as needed, and • communications and training with regard to privacy policy and compliance requirements are delivered on a regular basis to all associates and utilized effectively.
Data governance and compliance responsibilities	Manages the personal data governance team and oversees privacy and data compliance in the collection, use, disclosure and transfers of personal information throughout all applicable company business processes.
	In collaboration with key stakeholders, establishes enterprise-wide processes for privacy and data protection compliance verification and oversees the coordination of compliance verification activities with divisional and functional privacy compliance leaders and regional privacy leaders, including annual Safe Harbor certification, local registration with DPA and HIPAA privacy compliance verification.

Integration with business processes and IT	In partnership with IT, collaborates with process councils and information governance councils to ensure that privacy and data protection requirements are effectively integrated into applicable business processes and supported by associated information systems and external service providers.
Risk assessments	Oversees the evaluation of enterprise privacy risk assessments, privacy compliance and privacy performance metrics.
Privacy laws and regulations monitoring	Responsible for developing and augmenting internal enterprise in integrated personal data governance by monitoring the relevant legal, regulatory and policy developments, collaborating with external stakeholders and attending appropriate privacy and data protection meetings, conferences and symposia.

THE PRIVACY PROGRAM'S ORGANIZATIONAL STRUCTURE

The table below describes an organizational structure based on functional collaboration. The risk and security committee brings together all functions to discuss cross-functional privacy, security and risk matters monthly.

Stakeholder	Role	Responsibilities
Privacy compliance coordinator and team	Coordinate privacy efforts centrally	• Define overarching privacy policy suite • Be the first line of response for employee questions • Sponsor privacy communications campaign and privacy general awareness training • Provide consulting advice to business units on privacy matters
Legal counsel and legal team	Provide privacy legal advice	• Keep updated with emerging global privacy laws and regulations • Provide regulatory advice to the privacy compliance designee, business units and special projects on privacy matters • Meet with privacy compliance coordinator
Internal audit	Perform privacy audits	• Work with privacy officer to define a privacy audit plan according to the policy suite and privacy risks
Learning and development and communications teams	Support privacy learning solutions and communications efforts	• Develop and implement general awareness privacy training • Support development of specialty privacy training (level-2 training) • Update and implement employee and contractor on-boarding training with the latest privacy learning • Develop a communications strategy with the privacy coordinator, execute communications and events and monitor feedback loop

Risk and security committee (comprises members from physical and information security, compliance, internal audit, legal, procurement, HR and the business)	Filter and determine resolution strategy for privacy issues/incidents	• Review security reports (laptop loss/ theft report and physical security) • Determine severity of incident and determine course of action • Assign incident resolution • In the event of a privacy breach, start application of the incident response and notification plan
Divisions compliance (sales and marketing, operations, R & D, HR, finance, and IS/IT)	Ensure privacy compli- ance at the division level	• Translate the privacy policy suite into divisional SOPs, guidance documents and/or FAQs • Monitor employees' completion of general awareness privacy training • Ensure employees' compliance with privacy compliance requirements • Identify and escalate inquiries, issues and grievances related to privacy and security as required • Respond to inquiries, issues and grievances related to privacy and security, as needed • Communicate with corporate senior management as appropriate • Coordinate privacy assessments/audits
Privacy champions (employees responsible for risk management, compliance or unit information security)	Privacy ambassadors in the business units	• Complete privacy risk assessment in their divisions in collaboration with key personnel • Identify activities with privacy impact in the business unit and recommend consultation with legal or compliance

Privacy-Related Organizational Chart—Example

The organizational structure below is projectized. Functional representatives have been appointed to participate in working groups to plan and execute several global privacy—related projects.

When determining a privacy program organizational structure, several parameters need to be considered, for example: permanence; accountability; funding; functional and regional coverage; agenda; company culture and existing committees or roles to be leveraged.

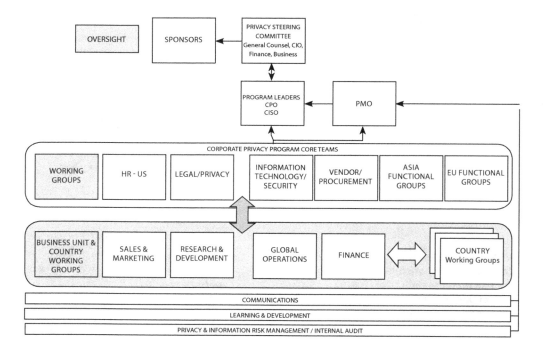

COMMUNICATIONS PLAN

A communications plan is a schedule of tactical communications and events that aim at impacting specific stakeholders or stakeholder groups to change their behaviors and encourage them to think and act differently. The plan is developed after the privacy team has completed its stakeholder list, mapped the stakeholders based on their approach to change and level of influence and ascertained to whom to target communications.

The plan also follows the prior development of a communications strategy document aligned with the privacy program objectives. The strategy document lays out guidance such as communication objectives, key communication themes and messages, risks and challenges, communications governance, success measures and the core program stakeholders identified in the stakeholders list.

Communications Plan

Completed by: _____

Date: _____

Audience	Message	Medium	Author	Timing/ frequency/ effort	Responsibilities	Performance measure
Describe the intended audience (leverage stakeholder list)	*Key messages/ content for the communications (reconcile with communications strategy)*	*Means to create, store and deliver the communications*	*Tasks/roles of the different authors of the content*	*Frequency, timing and amount of effort required to perform each role*	*Describe the responsibilities for the creation, review, approval and delivery of the communications*	*How communication is tracked and measured to determine whether the communications have made the appropriate impact*
All employees	Announcement of the general privacy awareness training rollout	Article on the Intranet site	Training manager (name) and HR manager (name)	January 3rd to January 10th	• Message drafted by (name) • Message reviewed and approved by (name) • Message launched by (name)	• Web page/ training link accessed • Training started • Training completed
All employees	Identity theft awareness campus presentation by guest speaker	On-campus event	Privacy manager (name)	February 1	• Schedule sessions (name) • Create communications (name) • Develop posters/plasma screens (name) • Introductions (name) • External speaker (name)	• Preregistration • Attendance sign-in sheet • Session evaluation forms completed
HR and benefits employees	What is PII/ PHI? What is the HIPAA program?	Materials (PII posters, cheat sheet on the 18 elements of PII/PHI and HIPAA security and privacy controls framework)	Privacy compliance (name)	March 1	• Develop posters (name) • Develop cheat sheets (name) • Publish to HR and benefits intranet (name) • Inform the ISO network (name)	• Display of posters in HR and benefits working area • Distribution to on-boarding training of cheat sheet and at HR meetings in March • Materials orders

ASSESSING THE CURRENT PRIVACY-RELATED ENVIRONMENT

The goal of this step is to evaluate current processes, procedures, uses of data and so on. The evaluation will depend on an extensive series of individual assessments that include:

Subject of Analysis	Typical Questions You Can Ask
Analysis of legal requirements	• Which existing federal and state privacy laws affect the organization? • What are the specific requirements of each privacy law? • How are the various parts of the organization complying with the patchwork of regulations?
Evaluation of existing privacy standards, practices, and philosophies	• Does your organization have existing standards, practices and philosophies regarding privacy? ◦ If any of these elements exist, where are they documented and who is responsible for their creation and maintenance?
Evaluation of information security practices	• Does your organization have an information security policy? ◦ Does the policy meet the standards of the Safeguard Rule (the companion information security regulation within GLBA)?
Collection of personal information	• Which areas of the organization are collecting personal information? • What type of information is being collected? • What is the purpose of collecting this type of information? • Where is the collected information stored? • Is your organization collecting only the personal information necessary to complete the customer's request?
Use of personal information	• How is the information being used? • What organization goals does the information help fulfill? • Is there a legal or rational basis for each use of personal information?
Access to personal information	• Who has access to the personal information? • Is access given to individuals on a business need-to-know basis? • Is access monitored? • Does available technology allow users to access off-limits personal information?

Disclosure of personal information	• How is personal information shared within the organization? • Are the principles of need-to-know enforced? • Do these disclosures have a legal basis?
Disclosure of personal information with third parties	• Does a contract exist with all third parties that receive your organization's information? • Have you conducted an information security audit to determine whether third parties are capable of adhering to information-protection laws? • Do you have an end-of-service data disposal policy? • Are service providers and vendors obligated to pass down privacy requirements to their subcontractors?
Data integrity	• Is data accurate and up-to-date? • Is there a way for customers to access their data and correct errors?
Management	• What documentation or privacy procedures exist? • Is documentation up-to-date, accurate and sufficient for each organizational unit? • Do management processes need to change to satisfy new laws? • Can it be extrapolated to the rest of the organization as a best practice? • Is there an individual responsible for ensuring organization compliance with laws and regulations?

SAMPLE COMPLIANCE CHECKLIST

Checklist Item	Typical Questions You Can Ask

Analysis of data	• What types of personal data are you collecting and using, and why?
	• Is any data sensitive (i.e. Social Security numbers, health-related data)? If so:
	  ○ Why is your organization collecting sensitive data?
	  ○ Have you identified different categories of sensitive personal data?
	  ○ Are there procedures for the handling, storage and use of sensitive data?
	  ○ Do you receive information about individuals from third parties?

Notices and consent	• Do individuals receive appropriate notice before their information is collected or used? • Can individuals opt out of data collection and use? If so, how do you register, maintain and honor the opt-out choice? • Are you relying on explicit consent to collect and use data? • When and how will that explicit consent be obtained? • When and how will that explicit consent be tracked?

Data maintenance	• Are there procedures to
	  ○ maintain a full and up-to-date record of use of personal data?
	  ○ ensure data collection and use complies with the disclosed purpose?
	  ○ determine when and how often personal data requires updating?

Data retention	• What are the criteria for determining retention periods of personal data?
	• How often are these criteria reviewed?
	• When data is no longer needed for a stated purpose, is there a process to specify
	  ○ whether the data should be deleted?
	  ○ how often the review should be conducted?
	  ○ who is responsible for determining the review?
	  ○ what guidance exists for data deletion and in-place policies?

Data use in marketing

- Does your organization intend to use personal data to send direct marketing such as telephone, fax, e-mail, text message, pictures including video, automated calling systems or other technologies?
- Will direct marketing communications be aimed at consumers or businesses or both?
- Are marketing communications unsolicited?
- Do you use an automated calling system for marketing communications? If so:
  - Do you have the prior consent of the subscriber?
  - If you have the prior consent of the subscriber, how do you assess and verify the accuracy of your subscriber records?
  - How will you address withdrawal of consent?
- If you use faxes for marketing communications do you have prior subscriber consent? If so:
  - How do you audit and verify the accuracy of your subscriber records?
  - How will you address withdrawal of consent?
- If you use live voice telephone for marketing communications, have you been previously notified not to call certain subscriber numbers?
- Do you scrub your lists according to names on the National Do Not Call Registry?
- If you use e-mail or text messages for marketing communications, do you ask for opt-in consent from subscribers? If so, how do you collect, audit and verify the accuracy of your opt-in subscriber records?

SAMPLE RISK ASSESSMENT TOOLKIT
FROM THE UNIVERSITY OF ARIZONA

The following section is part of a toolkit used by the University of Arizona to assess risk in its IT and information security operations. The FAQ format is a practical approach and may be useful as a model for your own communications regarding risk assessment.

Why Does My Unit Need to Complete a Risk Assessment?

A risk assessment is a prerequisite to the formation of strategies for developing, implementing and maintaining an information security posture.

Who Should Be Part of Conducting the Risk Assessment in My Unit?

The team will need to consist of at least the following people in your unit:

1. Information Security Liaison
2. Senior Financial Administrator
3. Senior IT Administrator

In some units, all three of these roles may be filled by the same person.

In addition to these individuals, you may choose to have additional members who can help assist in conducting the inventory portion and can help answer the questionnaires. The team members will need to be familiar with four areas of analysis: infrastructure, applications, operations and people.

How Should Our Unit Perform the Risk Assessment? Is There a Specific Format or Process?

Follow the Risk Assessment Procedure (IS-P1200) and the Overview Handout for full instructions. You will find the documents you need at http://security.arizona.edu/risk. Scroll down to the section titled "2009 Information Security Risk Assessment Documents."

While other methods may work well, this approach ensures consistency across the university.

When Referring to "the Network," Does This Refer to the Network Our Unit Provides or the Entire Network Provided by UITS?

We are referring to your unit's network. This is a particularly important distinction because the scope of the assessment is your unit. It also can make answering the questionnaires challenging.

Does the Term "Third Parties" Include Other University Units?

Yes. Third parties include non-employee students, vendors, business partners, customers or other third parties in other units or organizations.

Which Applications Should Be Listed in the Unit Application and Data Inventory (Part 3 of the Excel Workbook)?

Include all types of applications. You will find it useful to approach this as a business continuity and disaster recovery exercise. For example, although MS Office is mundane, it also is very necessary or useful to continued operations. If you do not already use an automated tool to collect this type of information, check out some of the inventory tools listed at the bottom of http://security.arizona.edu/risk. The script is a very usable and relatively simple tool for Microsoft Windows domains.

How Long Will the Risk Assessment Take to Perform?

The questionnaires (Parts 5 and 6 of the Excel workbook) will typically take approximately two hours for your team to perform. Some teams may require more time than this.
The amount of time needed for the inventory will depend on how recently your unit has performed an inventory and the size and complexity of your unit's IT infrastructure. Parts 2, 3 and 4 of the Excel workbook collect a basic inventory of hardware and software commonly used in your unit. Free tools for the inventory are listed at http://security.arizona.edu/risk. Scroll down to the section titled "Inventory Resources (optional freeware).

Doesn't Risk Assessment Just Lead to More and More Security Requirements, Most of Which Aren't Necessary?

No. When done properly, it should identify the measures that are needed to effectively reduce risk that is unacceptable and no further. It is important to remember that risk assessment can demonstrate that your unit's information assets are adequately secured with the measures you already have in place and that no further measures need to be put into place.

How Do We Answer a Question that Is Not Applicable to Our Unit?

(For example, question C3c asks, "Has encryption software been installed on unit systems storing Social Security, credit card and driver's license numbers?" and some units may not store this information.)

If a question is not applicable to your unit and "not applicable" is not a possible answer, leave the question unanswered and indicate in your transmittal of the completed questionnaire why the question is not applicable.

Integral to any Information Security Management System is the process of "assessing" the control environment to understand where control gaps may be leaving the organization at unacceptable risk. Information Security Assessment activities generally fall into three categories:

- Design Assessment activities which evaluate the appropriateness of controls by comparing the control design against the client's control objectives, industry good practice, laws/regulations and/or the auditor's professional judgment (e.g., an Application Architecture review).

- Compliance Assessment activities that validate that the control measures established are working as designed, consistently and continuously (e.g., a Password Audit).

- Substantive Assessment activities that provide the auditee with assurance that the "net" control objectives are being achieved and, where they are not, provides a measure of probability and business impact (e.g., a penetration test).

Resource for risk assessment: http://www.gao.gov/special.pubs/ai00033.pdf (United States General Accounting Office: Accounting and Information Management Division 1999)

http://www.census.gov/cspi/pdf/Security_Controls_Assessment_Kevin_Stine.pdf (National Institute of Standards and Technology 2008)

Source for the above risk-assessment information: http://security.arizona.edu/risk.

CERTIFICATIONS OFFERED BY THE IAPP

The International Association of Privacy Professionals (IAPP) offers the following five certifications:

Certified Information Privacy Professional (CIPP)
This CIPP certification debuted in 2004 and has since become the industry-standard certification in compliance with U.S. private-sector privacy laws and regulations as well as European requirements for transfers of personal data.

Certified Information Privacy Professional/Government (CIPP/G)
This specialized certification is designed exclusively for employees of U.S. federal and state government agencies as well as vendors and consultants who serve U.S. government clients.

Certified Information Privacy Professional/Canada (CIPP/C)
CIPP/C is the first national certification to be offered in privacy and data protection. It is targeted to the specific needs of Canadian privacy professionals as well as any practitioner who manages information that is subject to Canadian jurisdiction.

Certified Information Privacy Professional/Information Technology (CIPP/IT)
This certification assesses understanding of privacy and data protection practices in the development, engineering, deployment and auditing of IT products and services.

Certified Information Privacy Professional/Europe (CIPP/E)
The CIPP/E is currently under development and is designed to cover the essential pan-European and national data protection laws as well as industry-standard best practices for corporate compliance with these laws.

For current information about certification by the International Association of Privacy Professionals, see the organization's website at www.privacyassociation.org.

PRIVACY LEGISLATION WORLDWIDE

Comprehensive data protection laws in 44 countries, coupled with a growing body of targeted state and federal privacy laws in the U.S., are forcing organizations to create, implement and sustain data privacy compliance programs that are extremely difficult to manage. Meeting the requirements of European privacy laws, with their strong restrictions on transborder data transfers, may make daily business more difficult. International compliance to consider:

European Union
Austria, Belgium, Bulgaria, Cyprus, Czech Republic, Denmark, Estonia, Finland, Lithuania, Luxembourg, Malta, Netherlands, Poland, Portugal, Romania, Slovakia, Slovenia, Spain, Sweden and the United Kingdom

Other Countries
Argentina, Australia, Bahamas, Canada, Chile, Dubai, Guernsey, Hong Kong, Iceland, Isle of Man, Israel, Japan, Jersey, New Zealand, Norway, Russia and Switzerland

While there is no universal definition for information privacy, the most common concept is the right of an individual to control how one's personal information is used. That right covers the collection, use, retention and disclosure of personal information.

One of the key principles of the European rights-based approach is that an organization must have a reason for processing personal data, and it can not be used for additional purposes. Another key EU principle is the prohibition to transporting personal data of EU individuals to a country with inadequate data privacy laws (see above).

Compliance Options for Importing European HR Data

Safe Harbor:
voluntary adherence to seven privacy principles in a program with FTC oversight

Model Contracts:
implementation of privacy protections specified in a set of standard contractual clauses

Binding Corporate Rules:
a worldwide corporate privacy code approved by European data protection authorities

Employee Consent:
a limited option, useful only in contexts where consent is freely-given, specific and informed

DATA GOVERNANCE RESOURCES

The function of data governance is closely related to privacy. The following section describes the role of this important area.

The Scope of Data Governance Programs

If your privacy program is involved in data governance, be aware that the term can refer to any or various combinations of the following

- organizational bodies;
- rules;
- decision rights (how to "decide how to decide");
- accountabilities, and
- monitoring, controls and other enforcement methods.

Data governance programs themselves can differ significantly depending on their focus. For example, a particular program might focus on compliance, data integration or master data management. Regardless of the "flavor" of governances however, every program will essentially have the same three-part mission, and that is to

- make, collect and align rules;
- resolve issues, and
- monitor and enforce compliance while providing ongoing support to data stakeholders.

When Do Organizations Need Formal Data Governance?

An organization can tell when it's time to move from information governance to formal data governance. The move to formalize governance should take place under any of the following circumstances, when

- the organization gets so large that traditional management isn't able to address data-related, cross-functional activities;
- the organization's data systems get so complicated that traditional management isn't able to address data-related, cross-functional activities;
- the organization's data architects, service-oriented architecture (SOA) teams or other horizontally focused groups need the support of a cross-functional program that takes an enterprise (rather than siloed) view of data concerns and choices, and
- the complexity of regulation, compliance or contractual requirements calls for a more formal approach.

Who Manages the Data Governance Program?

The location of the data governance program can vary in different organizations. For example, a program may be centered in business operations, the IT department, the compliance or privacy offices or the data management or analytics group. Wherever the location, the key to success is the appropriate level of enterprise-wide leadership support and involvement of data stakeholder groups.

Tip: It's worth noting here that data governance programs rarely succeed if they are located as part of the application development group. Application development teams are often expected to make compromises to satisfy the needs of other stakeholders. Likewise, data governance programs that report to a project management office may also be compromised; project managers who are charged with finishing projects on time and within budget may not want to surface types of data-related issues that require governance attention. The ideal group to run data governance is the one responsible for a central data storage and management system, one that acts as a data repository for all front-end applications that involve customers.

Using a Formal Data Governance Framework

A framework helps a data governance program organize how its stakeholders think and communicate about complicated or ambiguous concepts. By using a formal framework, your organization can help data stakeholders from diverse areas such as business, IT, data management, legal and compliance to come together and achieve clarity of thought and purpose. The use of a framework can help management and staff make good decisions—decisions that stick and endure over time. It can help them reach consensus on how to "decide how to decide." That way, they can more efficiently create rules, ensure that the rules are being followed and deal with noncompliance, ambiguities and other related issues. Ultimately, the key to governance is managing access to data and the visibility into its use.

Implementing Data Governance

To implement a data governance program, an organization typically uses the following steps:

Step	Involves
1	Deciding what is important to them and what the program will focus on
2	Agreeing on a value statement for their efforts
3	Establishing scope and specific, measurable, attainable, realistic and timely (SMART) goals, as well as defining success measures and metrics
4	Developing a road map for their efforts
5	Acquiring the support of stakeholders

6	Designing a program (with the expectation that the "devil is in the details")
7	Deploying the program
8	Using the new processes involved in governing data, and evolving and improving existing processes
9	Performing the processes involved in monitoring, measuring and reporting status of the data, program and projects

Data governance programs tend to start by focusing their attention on finite issues, then expanding their scope to address additional concerns or sets of information. As a result, establishing data governance tends to be an iterative process. A new area of focus may go through all of the steps described above at the same time that other governance-led efforts are well-established in the "govern the data" phase. The implementation of data governance presents a great opportunity to integrate right into data attributes all privacy and security controls.

Deciding How Much Data Governance to Use

Your organization should aim to use as little data governance as will meet your goals. For example, the data governance framework recommended by the Data Governance Institute can be applied to pervasive, "big-bang" programs, but it was specifically designed for organizations that intend to apply governance in a limited fashion, then scale as needed. All the 10 components of data governance described in the framework will be present in the smallest of programs and projects; the level of complexity will grow as the number of participants or complexity of data systems increases.

Key Resource for Data Governance

The Data Governance Institute—an organization that offers consulting and training and a community of practice and information resources—has extensive material on the subject. You can find comprehensive information about topics such as governance frameworks, creating a data governance office, roles and responsibilities and data stewards—at its website:

www.datagovernance.com/index.html

By familiarizing the various teams with the framework's terminology and concepts, you're actually training staff from the business, IT and compliance groups to communicate with each other in a way that will lead to realizing value from your data assets, managing cost and complexity and ensuring compliance. An "act locally but think globally" approach to data governance means your teams will be ready when it's time to tackle large or complex data-related issues.

Reality Check: Assessing Readiness for Data Governance

If your organization is preparing to move from the current state to a more formal approach to governance and stewardship, it's important to assess readiness for data governance beforehand. After all, there may be valid reasons why the current model is in place. Likewise, there may be a good reason why change could be detrimental to the enterprise, a particular program or project or even an individual's career. Red flags include

- Refusal of business groups to get involved
- Refusal of leadership to sponsor a centralized data governance effort
- Deciding to implement a "bottom-up" program when decisions and rules to be implemented must clearly come from the top of the organization
- Deciding to empower a group (an outsourcer, partner or team) to make decisions for a data-related effort where they would benefit from **not**
  - considering an enterprise view;
  - involving data stakeholders;
  - correcting data issues, or
  - acknowledging data issues.

Communication Skills: Often Overlooked

A key success factor in data governance is good communication. The staff who work on the front lines of data-related concerns and decision-making will need excellent communication skills in order to articulate the needs and concerns of diverse stakeholders and describe them in various ways using different media. As a result, it's important that your organization assesses skill levels and provides training as necessary. The staff in question will need help learning data-specific communication skills, creating communication plans and developing e-mail templates that ensure all stakeholders get the right level of information at the right time—and in the right sequence to avoid political issues.

United States Information Security Laws

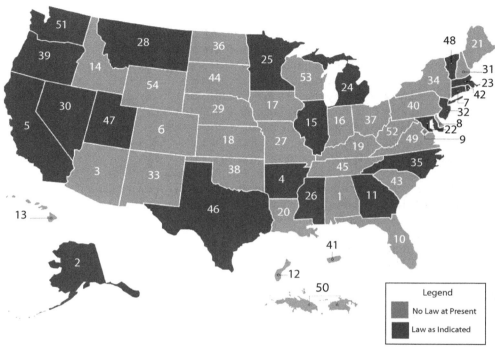

Legend
No Law at Present
Law as Indicated

1. Alabama - No Law
2. Alaska - Alaska Stat. §45.48.010 et seq.
3. Arizona - No Law
4. Arkansas - Ark. Code Ann. §4-110-101 et seq.
5. California - Cal. Civ. Code §1798.80 et seq.
6. Colorado - No Law
7. Connecticut - Conn. Gen. Stat. §42-471
8. Delaware - No Law
9. District of Columbia - No Law
10. Florida - No Law
11. Georgia - GA Code Ann. §10-15-1 et seq.
12. Guam - No Law
13. Hawaii - No Law
14. Idaho - No Law
15. Illinois - 740 Ill. Comp. Stat. Ann. 14/1
16. Indiana - No Law
17. Iowa - No Law
18. Kansas - No Law
19. Kentucky - No Law

20. Louisiana - No Law
21. Maine - No Law
22. Maryland - MD Code Comm. Law §14-3501 et seq.
23. Massachusetts - Mass. Gen. Laws M.G.L. Ch.93H §1 et seq. and 201 CMR 17.00
24. Michigan - M.C.L.A. §445.61 et seq.
25. Minnesota - Minn. Stat. §325E.64
26. Mississippi - Senate Bill 2651
27. Missouri - No Law
28. Montana - Mont. Code Ann. §30-14-1701 et seq.
29. Nebraska - No Law
30. Nevada - Nev. Rev. Stat. §603A.010 et seq.
31. New Hampshire - No Law
32. New Jersey - N.J. Stat. Ann. §56:8-161 et seq.
33. New Mexico - No Law
34. New York - No Law
35. North Carolina - N.C. Gen. Stat. §75-60 et seq.
36. North Dakota - No Law
37. Ohio - No Law

38. Oklahoma - No Law
39. Oregon - O.R.S. §646A.600 et seq.
40. Pennsylvania - No Law
41. Puerto Rico - No Law
42. Rhode Island - R.I. Gen. Laws §11-49.2-1 et seq.
43. South Carolina - No Law
44. South Dakota - No Law
45. Tennessee - No Law
46. Texas - Tex. Bus. & Comm. Code Ann. §521.001 et seq.
47. Utah - Utah Code Ann. §13-44-101 et seq.
48. Vermont - VT Stat. Ann. Tit. 9 §2430 et seq.
49. Virginia - No Law
50. Virgin Islands - No Law
51. Washington - Wash. Rev. Code §19.255.020
52. West Virginia - No Law
53. Wisconsin - No Law
54. Wyoming - No Law

United States Data Destruction Laws

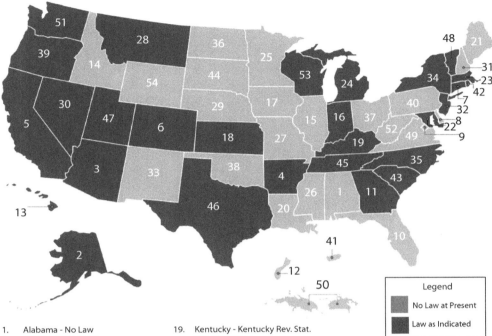

Legend

No Law at Present

Law as Indicated

1. Alabama - No Law
2. Alaska - Alaska Stat. §45.48.500 et seq.
3. Arizona - Ariz. Rev. Stat. Ann. §44-7601
4. Arkansas - Ark. Code Ann. §4-110-101 et seq.
5. California - Cal. Civ. Code §1798.80 et seq.
6. Colorado - Colo. Rev. Stat. Ann. §6-1-713
7. Connecticut - Conn. Gen. Stat. §42-471
8. Delaware - No Law
9. District of Columbia - No Law
10. Florida - No Law
11. Georgia - GA Code Ann. §10-1-911 et seq.
12. Guam - No Law
13. Hawaii - Hawaii Rev. Stat. §487R-1 et seq.
14. Idaho - No Law
15. Illinois - No Law
16. Indiana - Ind. Code §24-4-14 et seq.
17. Iowa - No Law
18. Kansas - Kan. Stat. Ann. §50-7a01 et seq.

19. Kentucky - Kentucky Rev. Stat. 365.720 et seq.
20. Louisiana - No Law
21. Maine - No Law
22. Maryland - MD Code Comm. Law §14-3501 et seq.
23. Massachusetts - Mass. Gen. Laws Ch.93I
24. Michigan - M.C.L.A. §445.61 et seq.
25. Minnesota - No Law
26. Mississippi - No Law
27. Missouri - No Law
28. Montana - Mont. Code Ann. §30-14-1701 et seq.
29. Nebraska - No Law
30. Nevada - Nev. Rev. Stat. §603A.010 et seq.
31. New Hampshire - No Law
32. New Jersey - N.J. Stat. Ann. §56:8-161 et seq.
33. New Mexico - No Law
34. New York - N.Y. Gen. Bus. Law §399-h
35. North Carolina - N.C. Gen. Stat. §75-60 et seq.
36. North Dakota - No Law
37. Ohio - No Law
38. Oklahoma - No Law

39. Oregon - O.R.S. §646A.600 et seq.
40. Pennsylvania - No Law
41. Puerto Rico - No Law
42. Rhode Island - R.I. Gen. Laws §11-49.2-1 et seq., R.I. Gen. Laws §6-52-1 et seq.
43. South Carolina - S.C. Code Ann. §37-20-190
44. South Dakota - No Law
45. Tennessee - Tenn. Code Ann. §39-14-150(g)
46. Texas - Tex. Bus. & Comm. Code Ann. §521.001 et seq.
47. Utah - Utah Code Ann. §13-44-101 et seq.
48. Vermont - VT Stat. Ann. Tit. 9 §2445 et seq.
49. Virginia - No Law
50. Virgin Islands - No Law
51. Washington - Wash. Rev. Code §19.215.005
52. West Virginia - No Law
53. Wisconsin - W.S.A. §134.97
54. Wyoming - No Law

U.S. Security Breach Laws

State	Law Name	Comment	Web Address
Alaska	Alaska Personal Information Protection Act – Alaska Stat. §45.48.010 et seq.	This security law addresses breach notification, data destruction, security freezes, and protection of Social Security numbers	http://www.legis.state.ak.us/PDF/25/Bills/HB0065Z.PDF
Arizona	Ariz. Rev. Stat. Ann. §44-7501, Notification of breach of security system	This law deals strictly with notification of security breaches	http://www.azleg.state.az.us/FormatDocument.asp?inDoc=/ars/44/07501.htm&Title=44
Arkansas	Arkansas Personal Information Protection Act – Ark. Code Ann. §4-110-101 et seq.	This security law addresses breach notification and data destruction	http://www.dis.arkansas.gov/security/Documents/Act1526.pdf
California	Cal. Health & Safety Code §1280.15	This law deals with notification of breaches of medical information	http://www.leginfo.ca.gov/cgi-bin/displaycode?section=hsc&group=01001-02000&file=1275-1289.5
California	Cal. Civ. Code §1798.80 et seq.	This security law addresses breach notification and data destruction	http://www.leginfo.ca.gov/cgi-bin/displaycode?section=civ&group=01001-02000&file=1798.80-1798.84
Colorado	Colorado Consumer Protection Act – Colo. Rev. Stat. Ann. §6-1-716 – Notification of security breach	This law deals strictly with notification of security breaches	http://www.michie.com/colorado/lpext.dll/cocode/1/9a3a/9a5e/9a60/9e0c/9f29?f=templates&fn=document-frame.htm&2.0#JD_6-1-716
Connecticut	Conn. Gen. Stat. §36a-701b - Breach of Security re Computerized Data Containing Personal Information	This law deals strictly with notification of security breaches	http://www.cga.ct.gov/2009/pub/chap669.htm#Sec36a-701b.htm
Delaware	Del. Code Ann. Tit. 6, §12B-101 et seq. - Computer Security Breaches	This law deals strictly with notification of security breaches	http://delcode.delaware.gov/title6/c012b/index.shtml

State	Law Name	Comment	Web Address
District of Columbia	Consumer Personal Information Security Breach Notification Act of 2006 – D.C. Code §28-3851 et seq.	This law deals strictly with notification of security breaches	http://www.dccouncil.washington.dc.us/images/00001/20061218135855.pdf
Florida	Fla. Stat. §817.5681 et seq. - Breach of security concerning confidential personal information in third-party possession	This law deals strictly with notification of security breaches	http://www.leg.state.fl.us/Statutes/index.cfm?App_mode=Display_Statute&Search_String=&URL=0800-0899/0817/Sections/0817.5681.html
Georgia	GA Code Ann. §10-1-911 et seq.	This law deals strictly with notification of security breaches	http://law.justia.com/georgia/codes/10/10-1-911.html
Hawaii	Hawaii Rev. Stat. §487N-1 et seq. - Security Breach of Personal Information	This law deals strictly with notification of security breaches	http://www.capitol.hawaii.gov/hrscurrent/Vol11_Ch0476-0490/HRS0487N/HRS_0487N-.htm
Idaho	Idaho Code §28-51-104 et seq.	This law deals strictly with notification of security breaches	http://www.legislature.idaho.gov/idstat/Title28/T28CH51.htm
Illinois	Personal Information Protection Act – 815 Ill. Comp. Stat. Ann. 530/1 et seq.	This law deals strictly with notification of security breaches	http://www.ilga.gov/legislation/ilcs/ilcs3.asp?ActID=2702&ChapAct=815&ChapID=67&ChapterName=BUSINESS+TRANSACTIONS&ActName=Personal+Information+Protection+Act.
Indiana	Ind. Code §24-4.9-1-1 – et seq. – Disclosure and notification requirements	This law deals strictly with notification of security breaches	http://www.in.gov/legislative/ic/code/title24/ar4.9/
Iowa	An Act Relating to Identity Theft by Providing for the Notification of a Breach in the Security of Personal Information – Iowa Code §715C.1 et seq.	This law deals strictly with notification of security breaches	http://coolice.legis.state.ia.us/Cool-ICE/default.asp?category=billinfo&service=billbook&GA=828hbill=SF2308

Provided by NYMITY

State	Law Name	Comment	Web Address
Kansas	Kan. Stat. Ann. §50-7a01 et seq. - Protection of Consumer Information	This law addresses breach notification and data destruction	http://www.kslegislature.org/legsrv-statutes/getStatute.do?number=21181
Louisiana	Database Security Breach Notification Law – LA Rev. Stat. Ann. §51:3071 et seq.	This law deals strictly with notification of security breaches	http://www.legis.state.la.us/lss/lss.asp?doc=322027
Maine	Notice of Risk to Personal Data Act – ME Rev. Stat. Ann. Tit. 10, §210-B-1346 et seq.	This law deals strictly with notification of security breaches	http://www.mainelegislature.org/legis/statutes/10/title10ch210-Bsec0.html
Maryland	Personal Information Protection Act – MD Code Comm. Law §14-3501 et seq.	This security law addresses breach notification and data destruction	http://www.michie.com/maryland/lpext.dll?f=templates&fn=tools-contents.htm&cp=mdcode/4563/59bc/5e d8&2.0
Massachusetts	Mass. Gen. Laws M.G.L. Ch. 93H §1 et seq.	This security law addresses breach notification and grants the Department of Consumer Affairs and Business Regulation power to adopt regulations concerning safeguarding data	http://www.mass.gov/legis/laws/seslaw07/sl070082.htm
Michigan	Identity Theft Protection Act - M.C.L.A. §445.61 et seq.	This security law addresses breach notification, data destruction, and procurement of telephone records through deceptive means	http://www.legislature.mi.gov/(S(gtorho55odxw0ueoew0yam55))/mileg.aspx?page=getobject&objectname=mcl-Act-452-of-2004-&query=on&highlight=445.61
Minnesota	Minn. Stat. §325E.61 - Notice Required for Certain Disclosures	This law deals strictly with notification of security breaches	https://www.revisor.mn.gov/bin/getpub.php?pubtype=STAT_CHAP&year=2007&section=325E
Mississippi	An Act to Require Notice of a Breach of Security	This law deals strictly with notification of security breaches	http://billstatus.ls.state.ms.us/documents/2010/pdf/HB/0500-0599/HB0583SG.pdf

Provided by **NYMITY**

State	Law Name	Comment	Web Address
Missouri	Mo. Rev. Stat. §407.1500	This law deals strictly with notification of security breaches	http://www.moga.mo.gov/statutes/c400-499/4070001500.htm
Montana	Mont. Code Ann. §30-14-1701 et seq. - Impediment of Identity Theft	This security law addresses breach notification, data destruction, and security freezes	http://data.opi.mt.gov/bills/mca_toc/30_14_17.htm
Nebraska	Financial Data Protection and Consumer Notification of Data Security Breach Act of 2006 – Neb. Rev. Stat. §87-801 et seq.	This law deals strictly with notification of security breaches	http://nebraskalegislature.gov/laws/browse-chapters.php?chapter=87
Nevada	Nev. Rev. Stat. §603A.010 et seq.	This security law also addresses breach notification and data destruction	http://www.leg.state.nv.us/NRS/NRS-603A.html
New Hampshire	New Hampshire Right to Privacy Act – N.H. Rev. Stat. Ann. §359-C:1 et seq.	This law addresses breach notification and disclosure of financial records	http://www.gencourt.state.nh.us/rsa/html/NHTOC/NHTOC-XXXI-359-C.htm
New Hampshire	N.H. Rev. Stat. Ann. §332-I:1 et seq.	This law addresses the use and disclosure of patient identifiable medical information	http://www.gencourt.state.nh.us/legislation/2009/HB0619.html http://www.gencourt.state.nh.us/legislation/2009/HB0542.html
New Jersey	N.J. Stat. Ann. §56:8-161 et seq.	This security law addresses breach notification, data destruction, and protection of Social Security numbers	http://lis.njleg.state.nj.us/cgi-bin/om_isapi.dll?clientID=260902868&Depth=2&depth=2&expandheadings=on&headingswithhits=on&hitsperheading=on&infobase=statutes.nfo&record={17FC2}&softpage=Doc_Frame_PG42

State	Law Name	Comment	Web Address
New York	New York Information Security Breach and Notification Act – N.Y. Gen. Bus. Law §899-aa	This law deals strictly with notification of security breaches	http://www.cscic.state.ny.us/security/securitybreach/NYS-General-Business-Law-899-AA-4-08-10.pdf
New York City	New York City Administrative Code §20-117 - Licensee Disclosure of Security Breach; Notification Requirements	This law addresses breach notification and data destruction	http://law.justia.com/newyork/codes/new-york-city-administrative-code-new/adc020-117_20-117.html
North Carolina	Top of Form North Carolina Identity Theft Protection Act – N.C. Gen. Stat. §75-60 et seq.	This security law addresses breach notification, data destruction, security freezes, and protection of social security numbers	http://www.ncga.state.nc.us/EnactedLegislation/Statutes/HTML/ByArticle/Chapter_75/Article_2A.html
North Dakota	N.D. Cent. Code §51-30-01 et seq. - Notice of Security Breach for Personal Information	This law deals strictly with notification of security breaches	http://www.legis.nd.gov/cencode/t51c30.pdf
Ohio	Ohio Rev. Code Ann. §1349.19 - Private disclosure of security breach of computerized personal information data	This law deals strictly with notification of security breaches	http://codes.ohio.gov/orc/1349.19
Oklahoma	Security Breach Notification Act – OK Stat. §24-161 et seq.	This law deals strictly with notification of security breaches	http://webserver1.lsb.state.ok.us/OK_Statutes/CompleteTitles/os24.rtf
Oregon	Consumer Identity Theft Protection Act – O.R.S. §646A.600 et seq.	This security law addresses breach notification, data destruction, security freezes, and protection of social security numbers	http://www.leg.state.or.us/07orlaws/sess0700.dir/0759.htm
Pennsylvania	Breach of Personal Information Notification Act – 73 PA Stat. Ann. §2301 et seq.	This law deals strictly with notification of security breaches	http://www.legis.state.pa.us/CFDOCS/Legis/PN/Public/btCheck.cfm?txtType=HTM&sessYr=2005&sessInd=0&billBody=S&billTyp=B&billNbr=0712&pn=1410

Provided by NYMITY

State	Law Name	Comment	Web Address
Puerto Rico	Citizen Information on Data Banks Security Act – 10 L.P.R.A. §4051 et seq.	This law deals strictly with notification of security breaches	http://www.michie.com/puertorico/lpext.dll/prcode/8bc0/9d2e/a1a2?fn=document-frame.htm&f=templates&2.0#
Rhode Island	Identity Theft Protection Act of 2005 – R.I. Gen. Laws §11-49.2-1 et seq.	This security law addresses breach notification and data destruction	http://www.rilin.state.ri.us/Statutes/TITLE11/11-49.2/INDEX.HTM
South Carolina	S.C. Code Ann. §39-1-90 - Breach of security of business data	This law deals strictly with notification of security breaches	http://www.scstatehouse.net/sess117_2007-2008/bills/453.htm
Tennessee	Identity Theft Deterrence Act of 1999 – Tenn. Code Ann. §47-18-2101 et seq.	This security law addresses breach notification, security freezes and protection of Social Security numbers	http://www.michie.com/tennessee/lpext.dll/tncode/17d7e/18e94/192b9?fn=document-frame.htm&f=templates&2.0#
Texas	Texas Identity Theft Enforcement and Protection Act – Tex. Bus. & Comm. Code Ann. §521.001 et seq.	This security law addresses breach notification, data destruction, and rights of identity theft victims	http://www.statutes.legis.state.tx.us/Docs/BC/htm/BC.521.htm
Utah	Protection of Personal Information Act – Utah Code Ann. §13-44-101 et seq.	This security law addresses breach notification and data destruction	http://www.michie.com/utah/lpext.dll?f=templates&fn=tools-contents.htm&cp=utcode/3288/3b12&2.0
Vermont	VT Stat. Ann. Tit. 9 §2430 et seq. - Protection of Personal Information	This security law addresses breach notification and protection of Social Security numbers	http://www.leg.state.vt.us/statutes/sections.cfm?Title=09&Chapter=062
Virgin Islands	Identity Theft Prevention Act – V.I. Code Tit. 14 §2200 et seq.	This law deals with the offense of identity theft and breach notification	http://www.michie.com/virginislands/lpext.dll/vicode/5548/5d78/5d7a?fn=document-frame.htm&f=templates&2.0#

State	Law Name	Comment	Web Address
Virginia	Va. Code Ann. §32.1-127.1:05 – Breach of medical information notification	This law addresses notification of breaches involving patient identifiable medical information	http://leg6.state.va.us/cgi-bin/legp604.exe?101+ful+HB1039
Virginia	Va. Code Ann. §18.2-186.6 - Breach of personal information notification	This law deals strictly with notification of security breaches	http://leg1.state.va.us/cgi-bin/legp504.exe?000+cod+18.2-186.6
Washington	Wash. Rev. Code §19.255.010 – Disclosure, notice	This law deals strictly with notification of security breaches	http://apps.leg.wa.gov/RCW/default.aspx?cite=19.255.010
West Virginia	W.Va. Code §46A-2A-101 et seq. - Breach of Security of Consumer Information	This law deals strictly with notification of security breaches	http://www.legis.state.wv.us/Bill_Text_HTML/2008_SESSIONS/RS/BILLS/SB340%20SUB1%20enr.htm
Wisconsin	W.S.A. §134.98 - Notice of Unauthorized Acquisition of Personal Information	This law deals strictly with notification of security breaches	http://www.legis.state.wi.us/statutes/Stat0134.pdf Section 134.98
Wyoming	Wyo. Stat. Ann. §40-12-501 et seq. - Consumer Protection	This security law addresses breach notification and security freezes	http://legisweb.state.wy.us/statutes/compress/title40.doc Section 12-501

Jurisdiction	Law Name	Comment	Web Address
Federal	HIPAA Security and Privacy Rules – 45 CFR Part 164 - Subpart D - Notification in the Case of Breach of Unsecured Protected Health Information	This subpart deals strictly with notification of security breaches of protected health information for HIPAA covered entities and their business associates	http://ecfr.gpoaccess.gov/cgi/t/text/text-idx?c=ecfr&tpl=/ecfrbrowse/Title45/45cfr164_main_02.tpl
Federal	HITECH Act §13402 and §13407	These sections deal with notification of security breaches of protected health information and personal health record identifiable health information	http://frwebgate.access.gpo.gov/cgi-bin/getdoc.cgi?dbname=111_cong_bills&docid=f:h1enr.txt.pdf
Federal	FTC Health Breach Notification Rule - 16 CFR Part 318	This rule deals strictly with notification of security breaches of personal health record identifiable health information	http://ecfr.gpoaccess.gov/cgi/t/text/text-idx?c=ecfr&tpl=/ecfrbrowse/Title16/16cfr318_main_02.tpl

Provided by **NYMITY**

U.S. Social Security Number Usage Laws

State	Law Name	Comment	Web Address
Alaska	Alaska Personal Information Protection Act – Alaska Stat. §45.48.010 et seq.	This security law also addresses breach notification, data destruction, security freezes, and protection of Social Security numbers	http://www.legis.state.ak.us/PDF/25/Bills/HB0065Z.PDF
Arizona	Ariz. Rev. Stat. Ann. §44-1373, Restricted use of personally identifying information	This law deals strictly with the protection of Social Security numbers	http://www.azleg.state.az.us/FormatDocument.asp?inDoc=/ars/44/01373.htm&Title=44&DocType=ARS
Arkansas	Ark. Code Ann. §4-86-107 - Prohibiting the misappropriate of social security numbers	This law deals strictly with the protection of Social Security numbers	http://www.biometricsdirect.com/Biometrics/laws/StateandFederal/ARSB335.pdf
California	Cal. Civ. Code §1798.85 et seq.	This law deals strictly with the protection of Social Security numbers	http://www.leginfo.ca.gov/cgi-bin/displaycode?section=civ&group=01001-02000&file=1798.85-1798.89
California	Cal. Lab. Code §226	This law deals strictly with the protection of employee's Social Security numbers	http://www.leginfo.ca.gov/cgi-bin/displaycode?section=lab&group=00001-01000&file=200-243
Colorado	Colorado Consumer Protection Act - Colo. Rev. Stat. Ann. §6-1-715 – Confidentiality of social security numbers	This law deals strictly with the protection of Social Security numbers	http://www.michie.com/colorado/lpext.dll/cocode/1/9a3a/9a5e/9a60/9e0c/9f16?f=templates&fn=document-frame.htm&2.0#JD_6-1-715
Connecticut	Conn. Gen. Stat. §42-471	This security law also addresses data destruction and protection of Social Security numbers	http://www.cga.ct.gov/2009/pub/chap743dd.htm#Sec42-471.htm
Connecticut	Conn. Gen. Stat. §42-470 -Restriction on display and use of social security number	This law deals strictly with the protection of Social Security numbers	http://www.cga.ct.gov/2009/pub/chap743dd.htm#Sec42-470.htm

State	Law Name	Comment	Web Address
Delaware	An Act to Amend Title 18 of the Delaware Code Relating to the Use of SSNs on Insurance Cards	law deals strictly with the protection of Social Security numbers on insurance cards	http://delcode.delaware.gov/session-laws/ga143/chp179.shtml
Georgia	GA Code Ann. §10-1-393.8 - Protection from disclosure of an individual's social security number	This law deals strictly with the protection of Social Security numbers	http://law.justia.com/georgia/codes/10/10-1-393.8.html
Hawaii	Hawaii Rev. Stat. §487J-1 et seq. - Social Security Number Protection	This law deals strictly with the protection of Social Security numbers	http://www.capitol.hawaii.gov/hrscurrent/Vol11_Ch0476-0490/HRS0487J/HRS_0487J-.htm
Idaho	Idaho Code §28-52-108 - Protection of personal information	This law deals strictly with the protection of Social Security numbers	http://legislature.idaho.gov/idstat/Title28/T28CH52SECT28-52-108.htm
Illinois	815 Ill. Comp. Stat. Ann. §505/2RR – Use of Social Security Numbers	This law deals strictly with the protection of Social Security numbers	http://www.ilga.gov/legislation/ilcs/fulltext.asp?DocName=081505050K2RR
Illinois	815 Ill. Comp. Stat. Ann. 505/2QQ - Insurance cards; social security number	This law deals strictly with the protection of Social Security numbers on insurance cards	http://www.ilga.gov/legislation/ilcs/fulltext.asp?DocName=081505050K2QQ
Illinois	815 Ill. Comp. Stat. Ann. 530/35	This law protects SSNs from public display and certain uses	http://www.ilga.gov/legislation/97/HB/09700HB3513.htm
Illinois	Senate Bill 1282 – An Act Concerning State Government	This law protects SSNs from inclusion in patient claims and encounter data	http://www.ilga.gov/legislation/publicacts/97/PDF/097-0180.pdf
Kansas	Kan. Stat. Ann. - §75-3520 - Social security numbers	This law deals strictly with the protection of Social Security numbers	http://www.kslegislature.org/legsrv-statutes/getStatute.do?number=35199
Maine	ME Rev. Stat. Ann. Tit. 10, §208-A-1271 et seq.- Protection of Social Security Numbers	This law deals strictly with the protection of Social Security numbers	http://www.mainelegislature.org/legis/statutes/10/title10ch208-Asec0.html

Provided by **NYMITY**

State	Law Name	Comment	Web Address
Maryland	Social Security Number Privacy Act – Md. Code Ann. Com. Law §14-3401 et seq.	This law deals strictly with the protection of Social Security numbers	http://www.michie.com/maryland/lpext.dll?f=templates&fn=tools-contents.htm&cp=mdcode/4563/59bc/5eca&2.0
Maryland	Md. Code Ann. Labor and Employment §3-502(d)	This law addresses the protection of employee's Social Security numbers	http://www.michie.com/maryland/lpext.dll/mdcode/1a4b4/1a4f7/1a612/1a618?f=templates&fn=document-frame.htm&2.0#JD_le3-502
Michigan	Social Security Number Protection Act – M.C.L.A. §445.81 et seq.	This law deals strictly with the protection of Social Security numbers	http://www.legislature.mi.gov/(S(idrhfvryhli15sqnorj1s255))/mileg.aspx?page=getObject&objectName=mcl-Act-454-of-2004
Minnesota	Minn. Stat. §325E.59 – Use Of Social Security Numbers	This law deals strictly with the protection of Social Security numbers	https://www.revisor.mn.gov/statutes/?id=325E.59
Missouri	Mo. Rev. Stat. §407.1355 – Social Security numbers, prohibited actions involving	This law deals strictly with the protection of Social Security numbers	http://law.justia.com/missouri/codes/t26/4070001355.html
Nebraska	Neb. Rev. Stat. §48-237	This law deals strictly with the protection of Social Security numbers	http://uniweb.legislature.ne.gov/laws/statutes.php?statute=48-237
Nevada	Nev. Rev. Stat. §239B.030	This law deals with the protection of personal information, including Social Security numbers	http://www.leg.state.nv.us/NRS/NRS-239B.html
Nevada	Senate Bill 282 – An Act relating to crimes	This law protects SSNs from wilful and intentional posting	http://www.leg.state.nv.us/Session/76th2011/Bills/SB/SB282_EN.pdf
New Jersey	N.J. Stat. Ann. §56:8-161 et seq.	This security law addresses breach notification, data destruction, and protection of Social Security numbers	http://lis.njleg.state.nj.us/cgi-bin/om_isapi.dll?clientID=26090286&Depth=2&depth=2&expandheadings=on&headingswithhits=on&hitsperheading=on&infobase=statutes.nfo&record={17FC2}&softpage=Doc_Frame_PG42

Provided by NYMITY

State	Law Name	Comment	Web Address
New Mexico	Privacy Protection Act – N.M. Stat. Ann. §57-12B-1 et seq.	This law deals strictly with the protection of Social Security numbers	http://law.justia.com/newmexico/codes/nmrc/jd_ch57art12b-12e51.html
New York	N.Y. Gen. Bus. Law §399-dd - Confidentiality of Social Security Account Number	This law deals strictly with the protection of Social Security numbers	http://public.leginfo.state.ny.us/LAWS-SEAF.cgi?QUERYTYPE=LAWS+&QUERYDA TA=$$GBS399-DD*4$$@TXGBS0399-DD* 4+&LIST=LAW+&BROWSER=3117 3853+& TOKEN=5860 6425+&TARGET=VIEW
New York	N.Y. Labor Law §203-d - Employee Personal Identifying Information	This law deals strictly with the protection of employees' Social Security numbers	http://public.leginfo.state.ny.us/LAWS-SEAF.cgi?QUERYTYPE=LAWS+&QUERYDA TA=$$LAB203-D$$@TXLAB0203-D+&LIS T=LAW+&BROWSER=20189890+&TOKEN =0423693+&TARGET=VIEW
North Carolina	Top of Form North Carolina Identity Theft Protection Act – N.C. Gen. Stat. §75-60 et seq.	This security law addresses breach notification, data destruction, security freezes, and protection of social security numbers	http://www.ncga.state.nc.us/Enact edLegislation/Statutes/HTML/ByArticle/ Chapter_75/Article_2A.html
Oklahoma	OK Stat. §40-173.1 - Employers' Use of Social Security Numbers	This law deals strictly with the protection of Social Security numbers	http://webserver1.lsb.state.ok.us/os/ os_40-173.1.rtf
Oregon	Consumer Identity Theft Protection Act – O.R.S. §646A.600 et seq.	This security law addresses breach notification, data destruction, security freezes, and protection of social security numbers	http://www.leg.state.or.us/07orlaws/ sess0700.dir/0759.htm
Pennsylvania	An Act relating to the Confidentiality of Social Security Numbers - 74 PA Stat. Ann. § 201 et seq.	This law deals strictly with the protection of Social Security numbers	http://www.legis.state.pa.us/CFDOCS/ Legis/PN/Public/btCheck.cfm?txtType=P DF&sessYr=2005&sessInd=0&billBody=S &billTyp=B&billNbr=0601&pn=1791
Rhode Island	Consumer Empowerment and Identity Theft Prevention Act of 2006 – R.I. Gen. Laws §6-48-8	This law deals strictly with the protection of Social Security numbers	http://www.rilin.state.ri.us/Statutes/ TITLE6/6-48/6-48-8.HTM

Provided by NYMITY

State	Law Name	Comment	Web Address
Rhode Island	Unfair Sales Practices – R.I. Gen. Laws §6-13-15, §6-13-17 and §9-13-19	This law protects SSNs in the course of consumer transactions	http://www.rilin.state.ri.us//BillText11/SenateText11/S0179.pdf
South Carolina	S.C. Code Ann. §37-20-180 - Consumer Protection Code - Restrictions on publication and use of social security numbers; exceptions	This law deals strictly with the protection of Social Security numbers	http://www.scstatehouse.gov/CODE/t37c020.htm
Tennessee	Identity Theft Deterrence Act of 1999 – Tenn. Code Ann. §47-18-2101 et seq.	This security law addresses breach notification, security freezes and protection of Social Security numbers	http://www.michie.com/tennessee/lpext.dll/tncode/17d7e/18e94/192b9?fn=document-frame.htm&f=templates&2.0#
Texas	Tex. Bus. & Comm. Code Ann. §501.001 et seq. - Protection of Driver's Licence and Social Security Numbers	This law deals with the protection of Social Security numbers and driver's license information	http://www.statutes.legis.state.tx.us/Docs/BC/htm/BC.501.htm
Vermont	VT Stat. Ann. Tit. 9 §2430 et seq. - Protection of Personal Information	This security law addresses breach notification and protection of Social Security numbers	http://www.leg.state.vt.us/statutes/sections.cfm?Title=09&Chapter=062
Virginia	Va. Code Ann. §59.1-443.2 - Restricted use of social security numbers	This law deals strictly with the protection of Social Security numbers	http://leg1.state.va.us/cgi-bin/legp504.exe?000+cod+TOC59010000035000000000000

Jurisdiction	Law Name	Comment	Web Address
Federal	Public Law 111-318 - Social Security Number Protection Act of 2010	This rule deals with the display of SSNs on government-issued checks and restricting prisoner access to SSNs.	http://www.govtrack.us/congress/billtext.xpd?bill=s111-3789

U.S. Data Destruction Laws

State	Law Name	Comment	Web Address
Alaska	Alaska Personal Information Protection Act – Disposal of Records – Alask. Stat. §45.48.500 et seq.	This security law also addresses breach notification, data destruction, security freezes, and protection of Social Security numbers	http://www.legis.state. ak.us/basis/get_bill_text. asp?hsid=HB0065Z&session=25
Arizona	Ariz. Rev. Stat. Ann. §44-7601, Discard and disposal of personal identifying information records	This law deals strictly with disposal or destruction of data	http://www.azleg.state.az.us/Format-Document.asp?inDoc=/ars/44/07601.htm&Title=44&DocType=ARS
Arkansas	Arkansas Personal Information Protection Act – Ark. Code Ann. §4-110-101 et seq.	This security law also addresses breach notification and data destruction	http://www.dis.arkansas.gov/security/Documents/Act1526.pdf
California	Cal. Civ. Code §1798.80 et seq.	This security law also addresses breach notification and data destruction	http://www.leginfo.ca.gov/cgi-bin/displaycode?section=civ&group=01001-02000&file=1798.80-1798.84
California	Cal. Civ. Code §56.101	This law deals with the disposal of medical information	http://www.leginfo.ca.gov/pub/11-12/bill/sen/sb_0801-0850/sb_850_bill_20111009_chaptered.pdf
Colorado	Colorado Consumer Protection Act - Colo. Rev. Stat. Ann. §6-1-713 – Disposal of personal identifying documents	This law deals strictly with disposal or destruction of data	http://www.michie.com/colorado/lpext.dll?f=FifLink&t=document-frame.htm&l=jump&iid=115d17d4.210a391e.0.0&nid=2409#JD_6-1-713
Connecticut	Conn. Gen. Stat. §42-471	This security law also addresses data destruction and protection of Social Security numbers	http://www.cga.ct.gov/2009/pub/chap743dd.htm#Sec42-471.htm
Georgia	GA Code Ann. §10-1-911 et seq.	This security law addresses handling of payment cards and data destruction	http://law.justia.com/georgia/codes/10/10-15.html

Provided by NYMITY

State	Law Name	Comment	Web Address
Hawaii	Hawaii Rev. Stat. §487R-1 et seq. - Destruction of Personal Information Records	This law deals strictly with disposal or destruction of data	http://www.capitol.hawaii.gov/hrscurrent/Vol11_Ch0476-0490/HRS0487R/HRS_0487R-.htm
Illinois	Data Security on State Computers Act – 20 ILCS 450/20	This law deals with the disposal of sensitive data on State computers	http://www.ilga.gov/legislation/publicacts/97/PDF/097-0390.pdf
Indiana	Ind. Code §24-4-14 et seq.- Persons Holding a Customer's Personal Information	This law deals strictly with disposal or destruction of data	http://www.in.gov/legislative/ic/code/title24/ar4/ch14.html
Kansas	Kan. Stat. Ann. §50-7a01 et seq. - Protection of Consumer Information	This law addresses breach notification and data destruction	http://www.kslegislature.org/legsrv-statutes/getStatute.do?number=21181
Kentucky	Kentucky Rev. Stat. 365.720 et seq. - Destruction of Records Containing Personally Identifiable Information	This law deals strictly with disposal or destruction of data	1. http://www.lrc.ky.gov/KRS/365-00/720.PDF Section 720 2. http://www.lrc.ky.gov/KRS/365-00/725.PDF Section 725 3. http://www.lrc.ky.gov/KRS/365-00/730.PDF Section 730
Maryland	Personal Information Protection Act – MD Code Comm. Law §14-3501 et seq.	This security law also addresses breach notification and data destruction	http://www.michie.com/maryland/lpext.dll?f=templates&fn=tools-contents.htm&cp=mdcode/4563/59b c/5ed8&2.0
Massachusetts	Mass. Gen. Laws Ch. 93I - Dispositions And Destruction Of Records	This law deals strictly with disposal or destruction of data	http://www.mass.gov/legis/laws/mgl/gl-93i-toc.htm
Michigan	Identity Theft Protection Act - M.C.L.A. §445.61 et seq.	This security law addresses breach notification, data destruction, and procurement of telephone records through deceptive means	http://www.legislature.mi.gov/(S(gtorho55odxw0ueoew0yam55))/mileg.aspx?page=getobject&objectname=mcl-Act-452-of-2004-&query=on&highlight=445.61

Provided by NYMITY

International Association of Privacy Professionals

State	Law Name	Comment	Web Address
Montana	Mont. Code Ann. §30-14-1701 et seq. - Impediment of Identity Theft	This security law addresses breach notification, data destruction, and security freezes	http://data.opi.mt.gov/bills/mca_toc/30_14_17.htm
Nevada	Nev. Rev. Stat. §603A.010 et seq.	This security law also addresses breach notification and data destruction	http://www.leg.state.nv.us/NRS/NRS-603A.html
New Jersey	N.J. Stat. Ann. §56:8-161 et seq.	This security law addresses breach notification, data destruction, and protection of Social Security numbers	http://lis.njleg.state.nj.us/cgi-bin/om_isapi.dll?clientID=26090286&Depth=2&depth=2&expandheadings=on&headingswithhits=on&hitsp erheading=on&infobase=statutes.nfo&record={17FC2}&softpage=Doc_Frame_PG42
New York	N.Y. Gen. Bus. Law §399-h - Disposal of Records Containing Personal Identifying Information	This law deals strictly with disposal or destruction of data	http://public.leginfo.state.ny.us/LAWS-SEAF.cgi?QUERYTYPE=LAWS+&QUERY DATA=$$GBS399-H$$@TXGBS0399-H +&LIST=LAW+&BROWSER=20173670 +&TOKEN=58606425+&TARGET=VIEW
New York City	New York City Administrative Code §20-117 - Licensee Disclosure of Security Breach; Notification Requirements	This law addresses breach notification and data destruction	http://law.justia.com/newyork/codes/new-york-city-administrative-code-new/adc020-117_20-117.html
North Carolina	North Carolina Identity Theft Protection Act – N.C. Gen. Stat. §75-60 et seq.	This security law addresses breach notification, data destruction, security freezes, and protection of social security numbers	http://www.ncga.state.nc.us/EnactedLegislation/Statutes/HTML/ByArticle/Chapter_75/Article_2A.html
Oregon	Consumer Identity Theft Protection Act – O.R.S. §646A.600 et seq.	This security law addresses breach notification, data destruction, security freezes, and protection of social security numbers	http://www.leg.state.or.us/07orlaws/sess0700.dir/0759.htm

Provided by NYMITY

State	Law Name	Comment	Web Address
Rhode Island	Identity Theft Protection Act of 2005 – R.I. Gen. Laws §11-49.2-1 et seq.	This security law addresses breach notification and data destruction	http://www.rilin.state.ri.us/Statutes/TITLE11/11-49.2/INDEX.HTM
Rhode Island	R.I. Gen. Laws §6-52-1 et seq. - Safe Destruction of Documents Containing Personal Information	This law deals strictly with disposal or destruction of data	http://www.rilin.state.ri.us/Statutes/TITLE6/6-52/INDEX.HTM
South Carolina	S.C. Code Ann. §37-20-190 Consumer Protection Code - Requirements For Disposition Of Business Records; Exceptions	This law deals strictly with disposal or destruction of data	http://www.scstatehouse.gov/CODE/t37c020.htm
Tennessee	Identity Theft Victims' Rights Act of 2004 – Tenn. Code Ann. §39-14-150(g)	This law deals with the offense of identity theft and the disposal or destruction of data	http://www.michie.com/tennessee/lpext.dll/tncode/1203e/125b7/125c1/126c7?fn=document-frame.htm&f=templates&2.0#
Texas	Texas Identity Theft Enforcement and Protection Act – Tex. Bus. & Comm. Code Ann. §521.001 et seq.	This security law addresses breach notification, data destruction, and rights of identity theft victims	http://www.statutes.legis.state.tx.us/Docs/BC/htm/BC.521.htm
Utah	Protection of Personal Information Act – Utah Code Ann. §13-44-101 et seq.	This security law addresses breach notification and data destruction	http://www.michie.com/utah/lpext.dll?f=templates&fn=tools-contents.htm&cp=utcode/3288/3b12&2.0
Vermont	VT Stat. Ann. Tit. 9 §2445 - Safe destruction of documents containing personal information	This law deals strictly with disposal or destruction of data	http://www.leg.state.vt.us/statutes/fullsection.cfm?Title=09&Chapter=062&Section=02445
Washington	Wash. Rev. Code Top of Form §19.215.005 – Disposal of personal information	This law deals strictly with disposal or destruction of data	http://apps.leg.wa.gov/RCW/default.aspx?cite=19.215
Wisconsin	W.S.A. §134.97 - Disposal Of Records Containing Personal Information	This law deals strictly with disposal or destruction of data	http://www.legis.state.wi.us/statutes/Stat0134.pdf Section 134.97

Provided by NYMITY

Jurisdiction	Law Name	Comment	Web Address
Federal	16 CFR 682 - Disposal of Consumer Report Information and Records	This federal rule deals strictly with the disposal of consumer information	http://ecfr.gpoaccess.gov/cgi/t/text/text-idx?c=ecfr&tpl=/ecfrbrowse/Title16/16cfr682_main_02.tpl
Federal	45 CFR § 164.310 - Security and Privacy	This federal rule requires policies and procedures to address disposition of electronic protected health information	http://ecfr.gpoaccess.gov/cgi/t/text/text-idx?c=ecfr&tpl=/ecfrbrowse/Title45/45cfr164_main_02.tpl

Provided by NYMITY

U.S. Information Security Laws

State	Law Name	Comment	Web Address
Alaska	Alaska Personal Information Protection Act – Alaska Stat. §45.48.010 et seq.	This security law also addresses breach notification, data destruction, security freezes, and protection of Social Security numbers	http://www.legis.state.ak.us/PDF/25/Bills/HB0065Z.PDF
Arkansas	Arkansas Personal Information Protection Act – Ark. Code Ann. §4-110-101 et seq.	This security law also addresses breach notification and data destruction	http://www.dis.arkansas.gov/security/Documents/Act1526.pdf
California	Cal. Civ. Code §1798.80 et seq.	This security law also addresses breach notification and data destruction	http://www.leginfo.ca.gov/cgi-bin/displaycode?section=civ&group=0100 1-02000&file=1798.80-1798.84
Connecticut	Conn. Gen. Stat. §42-471	This security law also addresses data destruction and protection of Social Security numbers	
Georgia	GA Code Ann. §10-1-911 et seq. GA Code Ann. §10-1-911 et seq. Top of Form GA Code Ann. §10-15-1 et seq.	This security law addresses handling of payment cards and data destruction	http://law.justia.com/georgia/codes/10/10-15.html
Illinois	Biometric Information Privacy Act, 740 Ill. Comp. Stat. Ann. 14/1	This law deals strictly with the collection and processing of biometric information	http://www.ilga.gov/LEGISLATION/ILCS/ilcs3.asp?ActID=3004&ChapAct=740%26nbsp%3BILCS%26nbsp%3B1 4%2F8&ChapterID=57&ChapterName=CIVIL+LIABILITIES&ActName=Biometric+Information+Privacy+Act

State	Law Name	Comment	Web Address
Maryland	Personal Information Protection Act – MD Code Comm. Law §14-3501 et seq.	This security law also addresses breach notification and data destruction	http://www.michie.com/maryland/lpext.dll?f=templates&fn=tools-contents.htm&cp=mdcode/4563/59bc/5ed8&2.0
Massachusetts	Mass. Gen. Laws M.G.L. Ch. 93H §1 et seq.	This security law addresses breach notification and grants the Department of Consumer Affairs and Business Regulation power to adopt regulations concerning safeguarding data	http://www.mass.gov/legis/laws/seslaw07/sl070082.htm
Massachusetts	201 CMR 17.00 - Standards for The Protection of Personal Information of Residents of the Commonwealth	This security law sets out the requirements for a comprehensive information security program	http://www.mass.gov/Eoca/docs/idtheft/201CMR1700reg.pdf
Michigan	Identity Theft Protection Act - M.C.L.A. §445.61 et seq.	This security law addresses breach notification, data destruction, and procurement of telephone records through deceptive means	http://www.legislature.mi.gov/(S(gtorho55odxw0ueoew0yam55))/mileg.aspx?page=getobject&objectname=mcl-Act-452-of-2004-&query=on&highlight=445.61
Minnesota	Minn. Stat. § 325E.64 Access Devices, Breach of Security	This law addresses the handling of payment card data and assigns liability in the event that payment card data stored in violation of this law was breached	https://www.revisor.mn.gov/statutes/?id=325E.64
Mississippi	An Act to Require Business Entities Providing Credit Card Processing Hardware or Software to Retail Merchants to Provide Such Hardware or Software that Meets the Requirements of Federal Law	This law addresses the payment card processing hardware and software requirements of retail merchants	http://billstatus.ls.state.ms.us/documents/2010/pdf/SB/2600-2699/SB2651SG.pdf

Provided by NYMITY

State	Law Name	Comment	Web Address
Montana	Mont. Code Ann. §30-14-1701 et seq. - Impediment of Identity Theft	This security law addresses breach notification, data destruction, and security freezes	http://data.opi.mt.gov/bills/mca_toc/30_14_17.htm
Nevada	Nev. Rev. Stat. §603A.010 et seq.	This security law also addresses breach notification and data destruction	http://www.leg.state.nv.us/NRS/NRS-603A.html
Nevada	An Act relating to security of personal information - Nev. Rev. Stat. §603A.215	This security law contains encryption and PCI DSS-compliance requirements	http://www.leg.state.nv.us/NRS/NRS-603A.html#NRS603ASec215
New Jersey	N.J. Stat. Ann. §56:8-161 et seq.	This security law addresses breach notification, data destruction, and protection of Social Security numbers	http://lis.njleg.state.nj.us/cgi-bin/om_isapi.dll?clientID=260902868&Depth=2&depth=2&expandheadings=on&headingswithhits=on&hitsperheading=on&infobase=statutes.nfo&record={17FC2}&softpage=Doc_Frame_PG42
New York City	New York City Administrative Code §20-117 - Licensee Disclosure of Security Breach; Notification Requirements	This law addresses breach notification and data destruction	http://law.justia.com/newyork/codes/new-york-city-administrative-code-new/adc020-117_20-117.html
North Carolina	North Carolina Identity Theft Protection Act – N.C. Gen. Stat. §75-60 et seq.	This security law addresses breach notification, data destruction, security freezes, and protection of social security numbers	http://www.ncga.state.nc.us/EnactedLegislation/Statutes/HTML/ByArticle/Chapter_75/Article_2A.html
Oregon	Consumer Identity Theft Protection Act – O.R.S. §646.600 et seq.	This security law addresses breach notification, data destruction, security freezes, and protection of social security numbers	http://www.leg.state.or.us/07orlaws/sess0700.dir/0759.htm

State	Law Name	Comment	Web Address
Rhode Island	Identity Theft Protection Act of 2005 – R.I. Gen. Laws §11-49.2-1 et seq.	This security law addresses breach notification and data destruction	http://www.rilin.state.ri.us/Statutes/TITLE11/11-49.2/INDEX.HTM
Texas	Texas Identity Theft Enforcement and Protection Act – Tex. Bus. & Comm. Code Ann. §521.001 et seq.	This security law addresses breach notification, data destruction, and rights of identity theft victims	http://www.statutes.legis.state.tx.us/Docs/BC/htm/BC.521.htm
Utah	Protection of Personal Information Act – Utah Code Ann. §13-44-101 et seq.	This security law addresses breach notification and data destruction	http://www.michie.com/utah/lpext.dll?f=templates&fn=tools-contents.htm&cp=utcode/3288/3b12&2.0
Vermont	VT Stat. Ann. Tit. 9 §2430 et seq. - Protection of Personal Information	This security law addresses breach notification and protection of Social Security numbers	http://www.leg.state.vt.us/statutes/sections.cfm?Title=09&Chapter=062
Washington	Wash. Rev. Code §19.255.020 – Liability of processors, businesses and vendors	This law addresses the handling of account information and assigns liability in the event that account information was breached	http://apps.leg.wa.gov/documents/billdocs/2009-10/Pdf/Bills/Session%20Law%202010/1149-S2.SL.pdf

Provided by NYMITY

Jurisdiction	Law Name	Comment	Web Address
Federal	16 CFR Part 314 Standards for Safeguarding Customer Information	This federal rule requires financial institutions to develop, implement and maintain information security programs	http://ecfr.gpoaccess. gov/cgi/t/text/text-idx?c=ecfr&tpl=/ecfrbrowse/Title16/16cfr313_main_02.tpl
Federal	16 CFR 641 - Duties of Users of Consumer Reports Regarding Address Discrepancies	This federal rule requires financial institutions and creditors to develop an Identity Theft Prevention Program if they hold an account for which there is a reasonably foreseeable risk of identity theft	http://ecfr.gpoaccess.gov/cgi/t/text/text-idx?c=ecfr&sid=0e981c9d877475d18c12cd6208d4ae1d&tpl=/ecfrbrowse/Title16/16cfr641_main_02.tpl
Federal	The Health Information Portability and Accountability Act – 42 U.S.C. 1320d	This federal law provided the Department of Health and Human Services with the power to adopt standards regarding data transactions/transfers and security standards for health information	http://www.gpo.gov/fdsys/pkg/PLAW-104publ191/pdf/PLAW-104publ191.pdf
Federal	45 CFR Part 162 - Administrative Requirements	This federal rule set out the standards for unique identifiers, code sets, health plans, health care claims and general provisions for transactions	http://ecfr.gpoaccess. gov/cgi/t/text/text-idx?c=ecfr&tpl=/ecfrbrowse/Title45/45cfr162_main_02.tpl
Federal	45 CFR Part 160 - General Administrative Requirements	This federal rule set out definitions generally applicable in HIPAA rules, the pre-emption of state law and compliance and investigations by the Secretary of the Department of Health and Human Services	http://ecfr.gpoaccess. gov/cgi/t/text/text-idx?c=ecfr&tpl=/ecfrbrowse/Title45/45cfr160_main_02.tpl

Provided by **NYMITY**

Jurisdiction	Law Name	Comment	Web Address
US Federal	45 CFR Part 164 - Security and Privacy	This federal rule sets out the security standards for protected health information, notification in the case of security breaches, and the privacy of individually identifiable health information	http://ecfr.gpoaccess. gov/cgi/t/text/text-idx?c=ecfr&tpl=/ecfrbrowse/ Title45/45cfr164_main_02.tpl
US Federal	HITECH Act – subtitle D – privacy - §13400 et seq.	This federal law amended HIPAA regarding marketing practices, disclosures of health information, and obligations of business associates, and created a federal breach notification obligation in the health care field.	http://frwebgate.access. gpo.gov/cgi-bin/getdoc. cgi?dbname=111_cong_ bills&docid=f:h1enr.txt.pdf Subtitle D - Privacy
Federal	45 CFR Part 164 - Security and Privacy	This federal rule sets out the security standards for protected health information, notification in the case of security breaches, and the privacy of individually identifiable health information	http://ecfr.gpoaccess. gov/cgi/t/text/text-idx?c=ecfr&tpl=/ecfrbrowse/ Title45/45cfr164_main_02.tpl
Federal	HITECH Act – subtitle D – privacy - §13400 et seq.	This federal law amended HIPAA regarding marketing practices, disclosures of health information, and obligations of business associates, and created a federal breach notification obligation in the health care field.	http://frwebgate.access. gpo.gov/cgi-bin/getdoc. cgi?dbname=111_cong_ bills&docid=f:h1enr.txt.pdf Subtitle D - Privacy

Provided by NYMITY